INTRODUCTION
TO EXPERT SYSTEMS

INTERNATIONAL COMPUTER SCIENCE SERIES

Consulting editors   **A D McGettrick**   University of Strathclyde
                         J van Leeuwen   University of Utrecht

OTHER TITLES IN THE SERIES:

Programming in Ada (2nd Edn.)   *J G P Barnes*

Computer Science Applied to Business Systems   *M J R Shave and K N Bhaskar*

Software Engineering (2nd Edn.)   *I Sommerville*

A Structured Approach to FORTRAN 77 Programming   *T M R Ellis*

The Cambridge Distributed Computing System   *R M Needham and A J Herbert*

An Introduction to Numerical Methods with Pascal   *L V Atkinson and P J Harley*

The UNIX System   *S R Bourne*

Handbook of Algorithms and Data Structures   *G H Gonnet*

Office Automation: Concepts, Technologies and Issues   *R A Hirschheim*

Microcomputers in Engineering and Science   *J F Craine and G R Martin*

UNIX for Super-Users   *E Foxley*

Software Specification Techniques   *N Gehani and A D McGettrick* (eds.)

The UNIX System V Environment   *S R Bourne*

Data Communications for Programmers   *M Purser*

Prolog Programming for Artificial Intelligence   *I Bratko*

Modula-2: Discipline & Design   *A H J Sale*

Local Area Network Design   *A Hopper, S Temple and R C Williamson*

UNIX™ is a trademark of AT & T Bell Laboratories.

INTRODUCTION
TO
EXPERT SYSTEMS

Peter Jackson
University of Edinburgh

ADDISON-WESLEY
PUBLISHING
COMPANY

Wokingham, England · Reading, Massachusetts · Menlo Park
Don Mills, Ontario · Amsterdam · Sydney · Singapore
Madrid · Bogota · Santiago · San Juan

Cover illustration courtesy of Laurence M. Gartel.
Typeset by Quorum Technical Services Ltd.
Printed in Great Britain by Commercial Colour Press.

Library of Congress Cataloging in Publication Data

Jackson, Peter, 1948–
   Introduction to expert systems.

   (International computer science series)
   1. Expert systems (Computer science)   I. Title.
II. Series.
QA76.76.E95J33 1986   006.3'3   86–1050
ISBN 0–201–14223–6 (pbk.)

British Library Cataloguing in Publication Data

Jackson, Peter, 1948–
   Introduction to expert systems. — (International
   computer science series)
   1. Expert systems (Computer science)
   I. Title   II. Series
   006.3'3   QA76.9.E96

   ISBN 0–201–14223–6

ABCDE 89876

Preface

This book began life as a series of notes to accompany my Expert Systems lectures to the undergraduate course 'Artificial Intelligence 2' given by the Department of Artificial Intelligence at the University of Edinburgh. Students taking this course come from a wide variety of other departments in both the science and the arts faculties, although there is usually a majority of computer science students. I have tried to retain both the introductory character of the original lectures and their intelligibility to readers of differing backgrounds. Thus no previous study of artificial intelligence is assumed. The book is aimed mainly at final-year undergraduates who are doing a course in knowledge-based systems and first-year postgraduate students in information technology disciplines. However, many chapters may be of interest to a wider audience of information scientists and persons interested in industrial applications of expert systems technology. It should be stressed that the book is not intended either as an exhaustive catalogue of existing systems or as a course in how to construct knowledge-based systems.

The original course had a programming component in which students learned to program in PROLOG. After some serious thought, it was decided not to wed the book to any particular programming language, nor to delve too deeply into issues of implementation. Such an orientation would have been at odds with the introductory nature of the text, and the level of description employed. Exercises are included at the ends of chapters where the content is sufficiently technical to merit practical involvement on the part of the student. For introductory texts to the more common artificial intelligence programming languages, the reader is referred to Winston and Horn (1984) for LISP, and Clocksin and Mellish (1981) for PROLOG.

I would like to thank colleagues at Edinburgh who commented on earlier drafts of some of the chapters. The comments of the reviewers were also invaluable in helping to redresss many errors of judgement and emphasis; those that remain are entirely my own responsibility. Finally I would like to thank the AI2 class of '84 for helping me to debug my initial set of lecture notes.

Peter Jackson
Edinburgh, December 1985

Contents

Subj matter complicated
has high performance
must give
explanation

Chapter 1 Expert Systems and Artificial Intelligence

An expert system is a computing system capable of representing and reasoning about some knowledge-rich domain, such as internal medicine or geology, with a view to solving problems and giving advice.

It can be distinguished from other kinds of artificial intelligence program in that:

- it deals with subject matter of realistic complexity that normally requires a considerable amount of human expertise;

- it must exhibit high performance in terms of speed and reliability in order to be a useful tool;

- it must be capable of explaining and justifying solutions and recommendations in order to convince the user that its reasoning is, in fact, correct.

The process of constructing an expert system is often called knowledge engineering, and is considered to be 'applied artificial intelligence' (Feigenbaum, 1977). Recent reviews of expert systems research can be found in Buchanan (1982), Barr and Feigenbaum (1982), Hayes-Roth *et al.* (1983), Buchanan and Shortliffe (1984) and Waterman (1985).

The purpose of this book is to give an introduction to the fundamental concepts and basic issues in expert systems research. It is not intended as a survey of the current state of the art; neither is it an advanced text intended for researchers already in the field. Rather it aims to give the new student of artificial intelligence, or the more than casually interested lay person, a grounding in the elements of 'knowledge-based systems', that is, systems which solve problems by applying a symbolic representation of human expertise, instead of employing more algorithmic or statistical methods. In other words, knowledge-based systems attempt to encode the domain-specific knowledge of everyday practitioners in some field, rather than using complex and comparatively domain-free methods derived from computer science or mathematics. We shall develop this important distinction later in this chapter.

This book begins with a brief survey of those developments in artificial intelligence which created the intellectual climate in which expert systems research has been conceived and conducted. Chapter 2 is also introductory in nature, in that it describes a particular expert system in some detail, and tries to explain why and how it works. Chapters 3, 4 and 5 are devoted to knowledge representation formalisms, covering the main techniques for encoding domain-specific knowledge in such a way that it can be applied to complex problems.

Then I consider exemplars of the three main formalisms – production rules, structured objects, and predicate logic – in Chapters 6–11. These exemplars were chosen for pedagogical reasons, rather than because they were necessarily the 'best' in the field. However, they do include what I consider to be two success stories of expert systems research, and I suggest that certain lessons can be learned from the way in which these systems were designed and implemented.

Chapter 12 takes a critical look at the kinds of programming tool and programming environment typically provided for building expert systems. This is followed by two chapters in which the more advanced topics of knowledge acquisition and the generation of explanations are discussed at a somewhat higher level of abstraction. Finally, Chapter 15 contains a survey of the field, some practical guidelines as to what knowledge representation formalism might be best suited to which kind of problem, and the discussion of some outstanding theoretical problems.

The rest of this chapter has the following plan. First, there is a quick look at some aspects of artificial intelligence research over the last 20 years which have fed into the theory and practice of expert systems development. Then five research topics are identified which are still intimately related to the theoretical side of expert systems development.

1.1 An overview of related research in artificial intelligence

What is artificial intelligence? The following definition from Barr and Feigenbaum (1981) is representative of opinion in the field:

> 'Artificial Intelligence (AI) is the part of computer science concerned with designing intelligent computer systems, that is, systems that exhibit the characteristics we associate with intelligence in human behavior – understanding language, learning, reasoning, solving problems, and so on.'

In other words, AI is concerned with programming computers to perform tasks that are presently done better by humans, because they involve such higher mental processes as perceptual learning, memory organization and judgemental reasoning. Thus, writing a program to perform complicated statistical calculations would not be seen as an artificial intelligence activity, while writing a program to design experiments to test hypotheses would.

There are differences of outlook and emphasis among researchers, however. Some incline towards the view that AI is a branch of engineering, since it is ultimately about building intelligent artefacts. Others stress the link with cognitive science: a discipline which concerns itself with the study of human information processing. Still other writers are interested in the overlap with problems of philosophy associated with knowledge and consciousness.

At bottom, AI is about the simulation of human behaviour: the discovery of techniques that will allow us to design and program machines which both emulate and extend our mental capabilities. It is therefore hardly surprising that the discipline should be closely related to a wide range of other academic subject areas such as computer science, psychology, philosophy, linguistics and engineering. The fact that AI crosses a number of traditional inter-disciplinary boundaries sometimes causes friction, but more often is a source of inspiration and new ideas.

As an aid to the general reader, I attempt to give a very brief overview of artificial intelligence research, insofar as it relates to the design and construction of expert systems. I will also try to explain in what way knowledge-based programming differs from both more conventional programming techniques and the general-purpose problem solving methods devised by the pioneers of AI research. For a more general introduction to AI, the reader is referred to Rich (1983), Winston (1984), and Charniak and McDermott (1985).

1.1.1   The Classical Period: game playing and theorem proving

Artificial intelligence is scarcely younger than conventional computer science; the beginnings of AI can be seen in the first game-playing and puzzle-solving programs written shortly after World War II. Game playing and puzzle solving may seem somewhat remote from expert systems, and insufficiently serious to provide a theoretical basis for 'real world' applications. However, it is true to say that a rather basic notion about computer-based problem solving can be traced back to those early attempts to program computers to perform such tasks.

This idea is called 'state space search', and it is essentially very simple. Many kinds of problem can be formulated in terms of three important ingredients:

- a starting state, e.g. the initial state of the chess board;
- a test for detecting final states or solutions to the problem, e.g. the simple rule for detecting checkmate in chess;
- a set of operations that can be applied to change the current state of the problem, e.g. the legal moves of chess.

One way of thinking of this conceptual space of states is as a graph in which the states are nodes and the operations are arcs. Such spaces can be generated as you go. For example, you could begin with the starting state of the chess board and make it the first node in the graph. Each of White's possible first moves would then be an arc connecting this node to a new state of the board. Each of Black's legal replies to each of these first moves could then be considered as operations which connect each of these new nodes to a changed state of the board, and so on.

The simplest form of state space search is called 'generate and test', and the algorithm is easy to specify:

1. Generate a possible solution, in the form of a state in the search space, e.g. a new board position as the result of a move.
2. Test to see if this state actually is a solution by seeing if it satisfies the conditions for success, e.g. checkmate.
3. If the current state really is a solution, then quit, else go back to step (1).

There are two variants on generate and test: depth-first search and breadth-first search. The difference between them lies in the order in which possible solutions are generated in step (1). At any given node, N, depth-first search considers the 'successors' of N, i.e. those states which result from applying operators to N, before considering 'siblings' of N (those states which were generated along with N, when applying operators to N's 'ancestor'). In breadth-first search, it is the other way round: N's siblings are checked out before going on to N's successors. Thus, in breadth-first search, one searches layer by layer through successive levels of the search space, whereas in depth-first search one pursues a single path at a time, returning to N to pick another path only if the current path fails.

Breadth-first search finds the shortest solution path, if there is one, but depth-first search gets there faster as long as it is guided in some way, i.e. if it makes good decisions when choosing which path to pursue next. On the other hand, depth-first search may never terminate if the search space is infinite, even if a solution exists along some as yet unexplored path. Guided depth-first search is therefore preferred; this is sometimes called 'best-first search', since at each choice point, one is trying to make the best decision as to where to look next.

It is not hard to see how the number of nodes may grow exponentially at each stage, regardless of the order in which nodes are generated. This phenomenon is usually referred to as the 'combinatorial explosion', and it poses intractable problems to programs which attempt to play games like chess by 'brute force' enumeration of all the alternatives. Since human beings are slower than computers at such enumeration tasks, and much less reliable, one can safely assume that chess grand masters do not function in this way. Rather they apply their experience, imagination and analytic skills to the selection of both overall strategies and winning moves. We are all inclined to call such behaviour 'intelligent'.

Given that exhaustive search is infeasible for anything other than the smallest search spaces, some means of guiding the search is required. A search which uses one or more items of domain-specific knowledge to traverse a state space graph is called a 'heuristic search'. A heuristic is best thought of as a rule of thumb: it is not guaranteed to succeed, in the way that an algorithm or decision procedure is, but it is useful in the majority of cases.

A common form of heuristic search is referred to as 'hill-climbing'. This involves giving the program an evaluation function which it can apply to the current state of the problem in order to obtain a rough estimate of how well things are going. For example, a simple evaluation function for a chess-playing program might involve a straightforward comparison of material between the two players. The program then seeks to maximize this function when it applies operators, such as the moves of chess. The algorithm for hill-climbing is given below.

1. Generate a possible solution as with step (1) of 'generate and test'.

2. From this point in the state space, apply rules that generate a new set of possible solutions, e.g. the legal moves of chess, that can be made from the current state.

3. If any state in the newly-derived set is a solution, then quit with success, else take the 'best' state from the set, make it the current state, and go back to step (2).

There are well-known problems with this approach, however. To begin with, your evaluation function may not be a faithful estimate of the 'goodness' of the current state of the problem. To pursue the chess example, I may have more pieces than you, but you may be in a better position. Simple estimates based on material advantage will not capture all the subtleties of the game. Furthermore, even if the evaluation function gives a good estimate, there are various states of play that can cause problems. For example, there may be no obvious next move, because they all appear to be equally good or bad. This is like being on a plateau, with no clear path towards the heights. Another problem is that of 'local maxima', whereby your evaluation function leads you to a peak position, from which the only way is down, while your goal is on some other, higher peak. Thus, I can take your queen, but in so doing lose the game.

The point is, that using the power of a computer to search for solutions, either exhaustively or guided by an evaluation function, is not always sufficient to solve problems of realistic complexity. As we shall see, expert systems attempt to tackle the difficulties of search by explicitly representing both the knowledge that an expert has about some domain and the strategies that she uses to reason about what she knows. One can contrast this knowledge-based approach with the internal workings of state of the art chess machines. These devices know almost nothing about chess over and above a few 'book' openings, the legal moves, the rough value of the pieces, and the rule for checkmate. The chess machine I have at home beats me most of the time because (a) I am a poor player, and (b) its hardware incorporates a very clever algorithm called 'minimax' which is continually looking to maximize the machine's opportunities to take pieces and minimize mine. Occasionally, I manage to trade material for a superior position, in which case I usually go on to win.

In addition to game playing, another principal concern of artificial intelligence in the 1950s was theorem proving. Roughly speaking, theorem proving involves showing that some statement in which we are interested follows logically from a set of special statements called 'axioms' (which are known or assumed to be true), and is therefore a 'theorem'. As is the case with chess, some of the concepts and techniques developed in the field of automatic theorem proving provided a starting point for students of general problem solving. Thus, knowledge relevant to the problem solution can be represented as a set of axioms, called a 'theory', and problem solving can be viewed as the process of showing that the desired solution is a theorem, i.e. that it follows from the axioms.

Unfortunately, the process of generating all the theorems that follow from some set of axioms is also combinatorially explosive, since one can add theorems to the axioms and use the new set of statements to derive still more theorems. In other words, searching for a solution among the theorems generated is analogous to traversing a state space graph, and can be considered as such. Nevertheless, at the present time there is a resurgence of interest in the application of theorem proving techniques to both general problem solving and expert systems. This is due to both an improved understanding of how to mechanize those techniques and a disillusionment with methods based on less firm foundations. This renewal of interest in formal methods is reflected to some extent in the contents of this book: Chapter 5 gives the reader an introduction to techniques of automatic theorem proving relevant to expert systems research, Chapter 11 examines in detail the workings of a logic-based problem solver, Chapter 12 includes a survey of logic-based expert systems tools, and Chapter 14 includes an account of logic-based explanations of system behaviour.

Early attempts at game playing and theorem proving are well represented by the collection of papers in Feigenbaum and Feldman (1963). The metaphysical speculation in Alan Turing's paper 'Computational Machinery and Intelligence' still makes interesting reading. A comparison between the content of these papers and those in more recent collections should be enough to refute the assertion made by some philosophers that AI has made no progress over the last 20 years.

I tend to think of the period that begins with the publication of Shannon's (1950) paper on chess and ends with the publication of Feigenbaum and Feldman as the 'Classical Period' of AI research. Among the most important discoveries of this period were the twin realizations that (a) problems of whatever kind could, in principle, be reduced to search problems so long as they were formalizable in terms of a start state, an end state, and a set of operations for traversing a state space, but (b) the search had to be guided by some representation of knowledge about the domain of the problem. In a minority of cases, it proved possible to restrict the application of knowledge to the use of an evaluation function which was able to use features of the problem local to the current state to give the program some idea of how well it was doing. However, in the majority of cases it was felt that something more was required, either in terms of a global problem-solving strategy, or in terms of an explicit encoding of knowledge about the objects, properties and actions associated with the domain.

1.1.2 The Romantic Period: computer understanding

The mid-1960s to the mid-1970s, on the other hand, represents what I call the 'Romantic Period' in artificial intelligence research. At this time, people were very concerned with making machines 'understand', by which they usually meant the understanding of natural language, especially stories and dialogue. Winograd's (1972) SHRDLU system was arguably the climax of this epoch: a program which was capable of understanding a non-trivial subset of English by representing and reasoning about a very restricted domain (a world consisting of toy blocks).

Given that complex problem solving required the representation of knowledge, it was natural for many researchers to explore the range of possibilities for encoding both particular facts and general principles about the world in such a way that they could be applied by a computer program in the course of its goal-directed reasoning. Needless to say, this proved to be a non-trivial exercise, and experience has led many people to conclude that the knowledge representation problem is one of the hardest that AI researchers have to face. The difficulties, dangers and dogmas surrounding this field are all too apparent in the SIGART Special Issue on Knowledge Representation, edited by Brachman and Smith (1980).

Minsky (1968) contains a representative sample of papers from the first half of this period; all of them are interesting, but not all are convincing, from the point of view of actual achievement. Nevertheless, many of the knowledge representation schemes that we currently take for granted were derived during this time, for example, Quillian's paper, which gave rise to semantic nets (see Chapter 4). Without this decade of imaginative exploration, which had its share of spectacular failures, it is doubtful that expert systems would exhibit the variety of functions and structures that they do today.

The whole notion of 'computer understanding' is entirely problematic, of course. It is simply not clear under what conditions one would be prepared to assert that a machine understood anything. However, even if one is unsure about what would constitute sufficient grounds for understanding, one can at least list some of the necessary grounds. The first is the ability to represent knowledge about real or imaginary worlds, and reason using these representations. Expert systems exhibit this ability, insofar as they possess an explicit representation of knowledge about some domain, and are capable of applying this knowledge to solve real problems. However, like the Winograd program, their outlook is strictly circumscribed, and their behaviour does not exhibit any of the more global aspects of understanding, such as the ability to perceive analogies and learn from experience, that we associate with human beings. Until we have some theory of how humans achieve and exercise such cognitive skills, our chances of programming machines to exhibit them seem to be remote.

A representative sample of papers from the latter half of this period can be found in Winston (1975); Minsky's paper on a knowledge representation formalism called 'frames' is particularly worth reading in the present context. Also worth consulting are both volumes of Winston and Brown (1979), which summarize much of the work done at the Massachusetts Institute of Technology during the 1970s. They contain a number of important papers on such topics as natural language processing, computer vision, robotics and symbolic computation, which I shall neglect here.

1.1.3   The Modern Period: techniques and applications

What I shall call the 'Modern Period' stretches from the latter half of the 1970s to the present day. It is characterized by an increasing self-consciousness and self-criticism, together with an orientation towards techniques and applications. For evidence of the former, see the papers in Haugeland (1981), and for the latter Coombs (1984).

The flirtation with psychological aspects of understanding, which never really got going in the UK, is somehow less central than it was, even in the US. This is partly due to the reappraisal of strong claims made by certain people for certain programs that were supposed to model aspects of human cognition. For theoretical treatments of the relationship between human reason and artificial intelligence, the reader is referred to Dreyfus (1972), Simon (1976), Boden (1977) and Searle (1981).

The disillusionment with general problem-solving methods, such as heuristic search, has continued apace. Researchers have realized that such methods overvalue the concept of 'general intelligence', traditionally favoured by psychologists, at the expense of the domain-specific ability that human experts possess. Such methods also undervalue simple common sense, including the ability of humans to avoid, identify and correct errors.

The conviction has grown that the heuristic power of a problem solver lies in the explicit representation of relevant knowledge that the program can access, and not in some sophisticated inference mechanism or some complicated evaluation function. Researchers have developed techniques for encoding human knowledge in modules which can be activated by patterns. These patterns may represent raw or processed data, problem states or partial problem solutions. Early attempts to simulate human problem solving (e.g. Newell and Simon, 1972) strove for uniformity in the encoding of knowledge and simplicity in the inference mechanism. Later attempts to apply the results of this research to expert systems have typically allowed themselves more variety.

It became clear that there were advantages attached to the strategy of representing human knowledge explicitly in pattern-directed modules, instead of encoding it into an algorithm that could be implemented using more conventional programming techniques.

1. The process of rendering the knowledge explicit in a piecemeal fashion seemed to be more in tune with the way that experts store and apply their

knowledge. In response to requests as to how they do their job, few experts will provide a well-articulated sequence of steps that is guaranteed to terminate with success in all situations. Rather, the knowledge that they possess has to be elicited by asking what they would do in typical cases, and then probing for the exceptions.

2. This method of programming allows for fast prototyping and incremental system development. If the system designer and programmer have done their jobs properly, the resultant program should be easy to modify and extend, so that errors and gaps in the knowledge can be rectified without major adjustments to the existing code. If they haven't done their jobs properly, then changes to the knowledge may well have unpredictable effects, since there may be unplanned interactions between modules of knowledge.

3. Researchers realized that a program doesn't have to solve the whole problem, or even be right all of the time, in order to be useful. An expert system can function as an intelligent assistant, which does some of the tedious enumeration of alternatives in the search for a solution, and rules out some of the less promising ones, leaving the final judgement, and some of the intermediate strategic decisions, to the user. We shall see an example of just such a program in Chapter 2: the DENDRAL system for helping chemists discover the structure of an unknown compound.

The Modern Period has seen the development of a number of systems that can claim a high level of performance on non-trivial tasks. Some these are described in detail in later chapters, e.g. the MYCIN system for treating blood infections (Chapter 6), the R1 system for configuring the VAX range of computers (Chapter 9), and the MECHO system for solving problems in Newtonian mechanics (Chapter 11). A number of principles have emerged which distinguish such systems from both conventional programs and earlier work in AI (Davis, 1982).

The part of the program which contains the representation of domain-specific knowledge, the 'knowledge base', is generally separate from the part of the program which performs the reasoning, the 'inference engine'. This means that one can make at least some changes to either module without necessarily having to alter the other. Thus one might be able to add more knowledge to the knowledge base, or tune the inference engine for better performance, without having to modify code elsewhere.

Practitioners try to use as uniform a representation of knowledge as possible. This makes the knowledge easier to encode and understand, and helps keep the inference engine simple. However, as we shall see in Chapter 7 and beyond, uniformity can pose problems if different kinds of knowledge are forced into the same formalism.

Unlike more conventional problem-solving programs, which employ methods more algorithmic and numerical that those typically encountered in expert systems, knowledge-based programs attempt to offer the user some kind of explanation as to how the conclusions were arrived at. Given a uniform knowledge representation and a simple inference engine, this usually involves presenting a trace of which modules of knowledge became active in which order. Typically such traces leave a good deal to be desired, and so improving the quality of explanations remains a topic for research.

Present-day expert systems technology appears to work best in domains where there is a substantial body of empirical knowledge connecting situations to actions. A deeper representation of the domain, in terms of spatial, temporal or causal models, is often avoided, or deemed unnecessary. Problems which require something closer to the 'computer understanding' researched in the Romantic Period tend to be passed by.

One can see from this sketch that surrounding the core of expert systems practice that has been built up over the last 15–20 years, there is a less stable and more speculative fringe of research topics which are at the heart of mainstream artificial intelligence. It's hard to tell at the present time whether the goal of computer understanding has been abandoned, postponed or deemed somehow irrelevant to practical applications. The next section looks at some of these research areas with a view to pointing the interested reader in the direction of the literature.

1.2 Research topics in expert systems

Given that expert systems research has grown out of more general concerns in artificial intelligence, it is not surprising that it maintains strong intellectual links with related topics in its parent discipline. Some of these links are outlined below. There are also references to chapters of this book which have a bearing on the various topics.

1.2.1 Knowledge acquisition

Buchanan *et al.* (1983) define knowledge acquisition as 'the transfer and transformation of potential problem-solving expertise from some knowledge source to a program'. This topic, to which we shall return in Chapters 2, 7 and 13, relates to the subfield of AI known as 'machine learning' (see, for example, Michalski *et al.*, 1983). Learning programs associated with expert systems differ considerably in the extent to which the program learns by being told, by modifying or manipulating what it already knows, by induction from some set of examples, or by discovering new concepts.

For example, expert system shells like EMYCIN (Van Melle *et al.*, 1981) are simply told about new rules by the expert, although the TEIRESIAS package (Davis, 1977) attempts to ensure that new rules reference relevant attributes and do not introduce redundancy or inconsistency into the rule base. Rule generation and modification programs like META-DENDRAL (Buchanan and Feigenbaum, 1978) cooperate with an expert in devising and testing new rules to account for data, while heuristic learning programs like AM and EURISKO (Lenat, 1982) set out to discover new concepts and relationships.

1.2.2 Knowledge representation

As we have seen, knowledge representation is a substantial subfield in its own right on the borderline between AI and cognitive science. It is concerned with the way in which information might be stored in the human brain, and the (possibly analogous) ways in which large bodies of knowledge can conveniently be stored in data structures for the purposes of symbolic computation. By symbolic computation I mean non-numeric computations in which the symbols can be construed as standing for various concepts and relationships between them.

Several conventions for coding knowledge have been suggested, including rule sets (Davis and King, 1977), generalized graphs (Findler, 1979) and predicate logic (Kowalski, 1979). Most expert systems use one or more of these formalisms, and their pros and cons are still a source of controversy among theoreticians, although a more pragmatic approach is often adopted for the practical purposes of implementation. The problems of knowledge representation form the subject matter of Chapters 3, 4 and 5, and a number of software tools for constructing such representations are reviewed in Chapter 12.

1.2.3 Knowledge application

This relates to the issues of planning and control in the field of problem solving. Expert systems design involves paying close attention to the details of how knowledge is accessed and applied during the search for a solution (Davis, 1980). Knowing what one knows, and knowing when and how to use it, seems to be an important part of expertise; this is usually termed 'meta-knowledge', i.e. knowledge about knowledge. *meta-knowledge is knowing*

Different strategies for bringing domain-specific knowledge to bear will *when & how* generally have marked effects upon the performance characteristics of *to use* programs. Most knowledge representation formalisms can be employed *information* under a variety of control regimes, and expert systems researchers are continuing to experiment in this area. The systems reviewed in Chapters 5–10 have been specially chosen to illustrate the many different ways in which such problems can be tackled. Each has something to offer the student of expert systems research.

1.2.4 Generating explanations

The whole issue of how to help a user understand the structure and function of some complex piece of software relates to the comparatively new field of human/computer interaction, which is emerging from an intersection of AI, engineering, psychology and ergonomics (see, for example, papers in Coombs, 1984). The contribution of expert systems researchers to date has been to place a high priority upon the accountability of consultation programs, and to show how explanations of program behaviour can be systematically related to the chains of reasoning employed by rule-based systems. Ongoing contributions include attempts to separate out the different kinds of structural and strategic knowledge implicit in expert performance (Clancey, 1983), and attempts to make explicit and accessible the design decisions associated with the specification of consultation programs for the purposes of generating better explanations and automatic programming (Swartout, 1983).

This issue sometimes goes under the name of 'transparency', i.e. the ease with which one can understand what the program is doing and why. The expert systems reviewed in this book are all examined from the point of view of their ability to explain their behaviour, and a résumé of this field is included in Chapter 14. Transparency from the knowledge engineer's point of view is considered in Chapters 12 and 13.

1.2.5 Educational applications

The possibility of using an expert system as an educational tool relates to the field of 'intelligent teaching systems', which has strong links with both psychology and computer-assisted learning (see papers in Sleeman and Brown, 1982). Given that an expert system embodies what an expert knows about some domain, it seems reasonable to suppose that such a program could provide a basis for individualized instruction at a computer terminal. However, research has shown that it is by no means straightforward to adapt a running expert system as an intelligent tutor (Clancey, 1982).

The reasons for this include our ignorance of: what makes for a productive tutorial dialogue; what constitutes a good explanation for pedagogical purposes; and how to mix conventional telling and testing with the more exploratory modes of learning by experiment and discovery. The section on NEOMYCIN in Chapter 7 deals with some of the issues involved in trying to harness knowledge-based programming to the ends of intelligent computer-aided instruction.

1.3 A word of warning

The reader will have realized by now that many of the more interesting aspects of expert systems technology are inextricably tied up with ongoing research issues. However, there is a tendency in the commercial press to present as 'state of the art' many techniques which are imperfectly understood, and whose efficacy is far from being established. This places the expert systems researcher in an embarrassing position for two reasons: (a) she appears to be researching 'solved problems'; and (b) his cautionary statements will appear negative and in conflict with the widespread optimism of persons who wish to create markets for new technology.

Undoubtedly there are those for whom the field of expert systems has all but engulfed the rest of artificial intelligence, insofar as expert systems seems to be its most commercially viable branch. However, it would be quite wrong to suppose either that expert systems would have developed in their present form without the nutrient context of related areas in AI, or that it will continue to flourish in the absence of input from its parent discipline. Thus, although I have had to neglect other areas of artificial intelligence (such as planning, belief systems and natural language processing) it is unquestionably the case that the more advanced expert systems applications of the future will need to draw upon the results of such research.

What is certain is that the practical experience of implementing programs which demonstrate expertise in some domain of realistic complexity will ultimately benefit the theory and practice of artificial intelligence. Such projects serve to promote interdisciplinary cooperation between domain specialists, computer scientists and social scientists with an interest in information processing. Commercial interest in expert systems is also having the positive effect of helping to promote partnerships between industrial concerns and academic 'centres of excellence'.

1.4 Exercises

1.1 Search is a central topic in artificial intelligence. As we saw earlier in this chapter, problem solving programs generally work by reducing problems, of whatever kind, into search problems which are solved by traversing some appropriate space of possible solutions. First, we shall look in more detail at some of the search methods outlined in the text.

Figure 1.1 gives algorithms for performing depth-first search and breadth-first search, written in a functional notation resembling, but not identical to, the syntax of LISP. The inset tree diagrams show the order in which nodes are visited by the corresponding algorithm.

Depth-first search

```
dfs (G, C, L)
    IF C = G THEN success
    ELSE [LET L = succ (C) + L
          IF L = () THEN fail
          ELSE dfs (G, first (L),
          rest (L))]
```

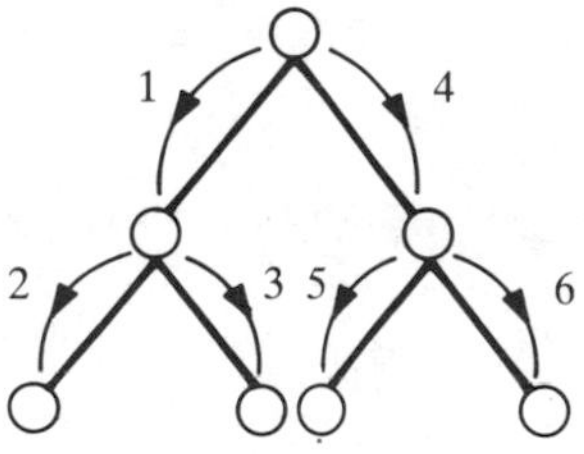

Breadth-first search

```
bfs (G, C, L)
    IF C = G THEN success
    ELSE [LET L = L + succ (C)
          IF L = () THEN fail
          ELSE bfs (G, first (L),
          rest (L))]
```

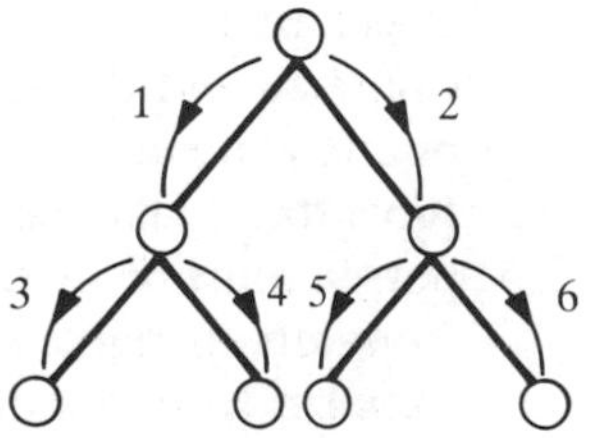

Figure 1.1 Exhaustive search strategies.

G is the node representing the goal, C the current node (initially the start state), and L a list (initially empty). succ is a function which returns the successors of a node, first a function that returns the head of a list, such that first(a b c) = a, and rest a function that returns the tail of a list, such that rest(a b c) = (b c). '+' signifies an append operation upon lists, such that (a b c) + (d e f) = (a b c d e f).

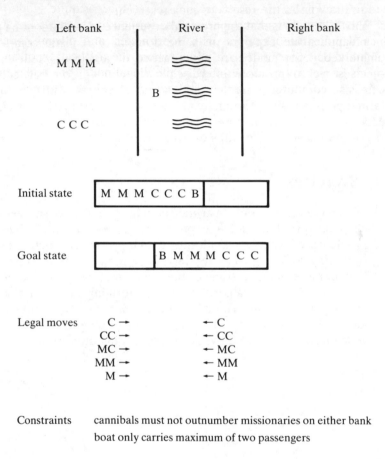

Figure 1.2   The missionaries and cannibals puzzle.

Consider the 'missionaries and cannibals' puzzle, shown in Figure 1.2. This puzzle can be stated as follows. There are three missionaries, three cannibals and a boat on the left bank of a river (initial state), and to solve the puzzle you must transport all six persons to the right bank, using the boat (goal state). The boat only carries two persons at a time, and at least one person must bring the boat back. Thus the legal moves are: one cannibal from left to right, two cannibals from left to right, a missionary and a cannibal from left to right, two missionaries from left to right, and one missionary from left to right, plus the inverse moves from right to left.

The following complication acts as a further constraint upon move application: if the cannibals ever outnumber the missionaries on either bank, then they will devour them. A solution to this problem is therefore a sequence of moves which leads from the start state to the goal state without violating this constraint.

It is possible to solve this problem by either of the search methods given above, since the underlying search space is quite small. Figure 1.3 shows how that search space can be formed by the recursive application of applicable operators, with 'loop nodes' and 'illegal nodes' clearly marked. Loop nodes are nodes where the application of an operator leads back to an earlier state, while illegal nodes are nodes that fail to satisfy the stated constraint; neither are developed further.

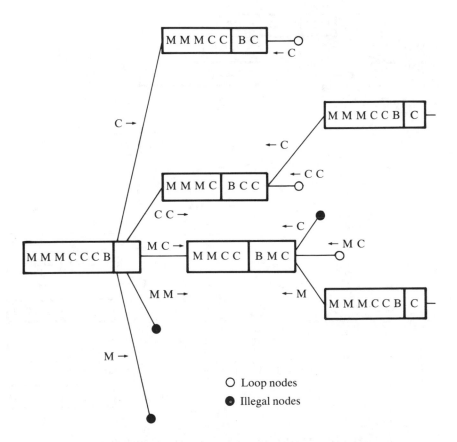

Figure 1.3 Developing the missionaries and cannibals search space.

Figure 1.4 shows the complete search space for depth-first search, with moves being tried in the order in which they are listed in Figure 1.2. The search develops 22 nodes and the success path is 11 nodes long; therefore we say that the penetrance of the search is 11/22 = 0.5.

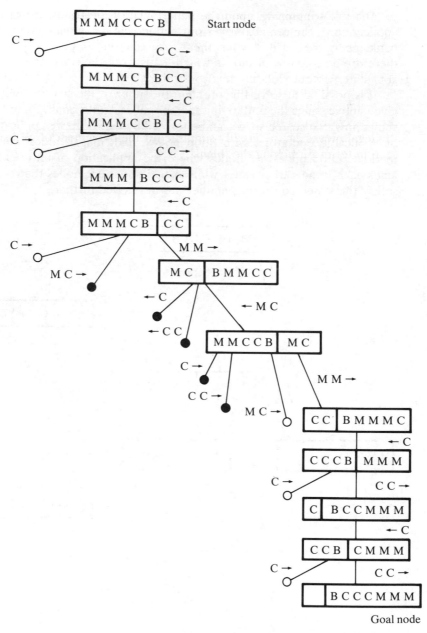

Figure 1.4   The complete search space by depth-first search.

a) Choose a representation for the state of the river banks, and write
programs which solve this problem by depth-first search and breadth-
first search. Consult Amarel (1968) concerning the different ways in
which this problem can be represented, and note the savings that can be
derived from using more efficient representations of states.

b) Attempt to improve upon the penetrance of exhaustive depth-first search by changing the order in which moves are considered at each state.

1.2 Another classic problem is that posed by the 8-puzzle. Here, eight moveable tiles are arranged in a 3×3 framework, and the goal is to get from some arbitrarily chosen jumbled configuration of the tiles to some arbitrarily ordered state (see Figure 1.5). Note that the specification of the legal moves can be greatly simplified if the movement of all tiles is seen in terms of moving the 'blank'.

2	8	3
1	6	4
7		5

Initial state   as above (say)

Goal state

1	2	3
8		4
7	6	5

Legal moves   move blank   up
                            down
                            left
                            right

Constraints   no diagonal moves

Figure 1.5   The 8-puzzle.

Unlike the missionaries and cannibals problem, the 8-puzzle is not soluble in a reasonable time by exhaustive search methods. This is because the puzzle has 9! (over 300 000) possible states. Consequently an evaluation function must be used to augment generate-and-test with hill-climbing.

Devise an evaluation function for this problem and write a program which attempts a best-first search of the underlying space. Do you notice any plateau effects, or local maxima? Is your evaluation function sensitive enough?

1.3 For the classical AI approach to problem solving to work, the problem formulation must identify the start state, a set of legitimate operators for transforming one state into another, and an agreed goal state with an associated test which can be used to decide unequivocally whether or not the goal has been achieved. Are there many real world problems that can be formulated in this way?

Chapter 2 Heuristic Search in DENDRAL and META-DENDRAL

In Chapter 1 we saw that researchers had, for the most part, become disillusioned with the so-called 'weak methods' of problem-solving, such as generate and test, and hill-climbing. Various technical problems were noted with the discovery and use of evaluation functions, and it was felt that such methods undervalued domain-specific knowledge and common sense, and overvalued the notion of general intelligence. It is unlikely that expert systems as a field of research would exist today, at least in its present form, had these attempts to develop general-purpose problem-solving programs been successful.

In attempting to relate the theory and practice of artificial intelligence to the emerging technology of expert systems, it seems sensible to start with a description of the DENDRAL project, which began at Stanford University in 1965, and demonstrates that it is possible for a program to rival the performance of domain experts in a specialized field. The task is to determine the molecular structure of an unknown organic compound, and the method that the system uses is a modified form of generate and test. DENDRAL can be seen as a kind of stepping-stone between the older, general-purpose problem-solving programs and more recent approaches involving the explicit representation of domain knowledge.

In order to help the reader understand what the program does, it is first of all necessary to say a little about the domain: nothing more than high school chemistry is assumed, however!

2.1 Structure elucidation of organic compounds

Imagine that you are a chemist who has been presented with an unknown chemical compound which has been isolated from some source such as a terrestrial or marine organism. It is your job to find out the molecular structure of this compound, which involves determining which atoms are in the compound, and how they are connected together to form the molecule. Both the source and the procedures used to isolate the compound from the source may give you some clues as to what kind of molecule to expect. Additional evidence can be gained by subjecting the compound to physical, chemical and spectroscopic tests. Heuristic DENDRAL is concerned with the interpretation of data obtained from a mass spectrometer, and so this device needs to be explained.

A mass spectrometer is a piece of laboratory equipment for chemical analysis which produces a set of peaks called a spectrum from a small sample of a given compound supplied in a gaseous form. This spectrum is characteristic of the compound, and can therefore be used as a 'fingerprint' to help identify it. Chemists would like to be able to both predict the mass spectrum of a given compound, and derive the molecular structure of a compound given its spectrum.

The instrument works by bombarding the chemical sample with a beam of electrons, which causes the compound to fragment and its components to become rearranged. A molecule can be considered as a connected graph, in which case fragmentation corresponds to the breaking of edges in the graph which stand for chemical bonds. Atom migrations correspond to the detachment of nodes from one subgraph and their attachment to another subgraph.

Positively charged fragments are then collected by mass, by passing the pieces through a magnetic field, and are displayed in a histogram which plots mass against relative abundance. In other words, the machine finds the mass of each of the resulting molecular fragments and then produces a spectrum in which the mass of each detected fragment is represented by a spectral peak. The intensity of each peak is determined by the relative number of fragments having that mass.

The problem is that any complex molecule can fragment in more than one way, i.e. different bonds can be dissolved as a result of the bombardment, accompanied by different patterns of migration. So, unlike other techniques such as x-ray crystallography, mass spectrometry does not give an unambiguous result. The mapping of spectral peaks to the molecular fragmentations which cause them is one-to-many, because there are usually many ways to break up a molecule and obtain fragments of any given mass.

It can therefore be seen that the theory of mass spectrometry is incomplete. Nevertheless, some predictions can be made concerning which bonds in a given molecule are likely to break and therefore contribute to peaks in the mass spectrum. Figure 2.1 represents a prediction to the effect that, if the substructure shown on the left appears in a molecule, then the bonds between atoms 8 and 14, and between atoms 11 and 12, will break under the electron bombardment, as indicated by the two structures on the right.

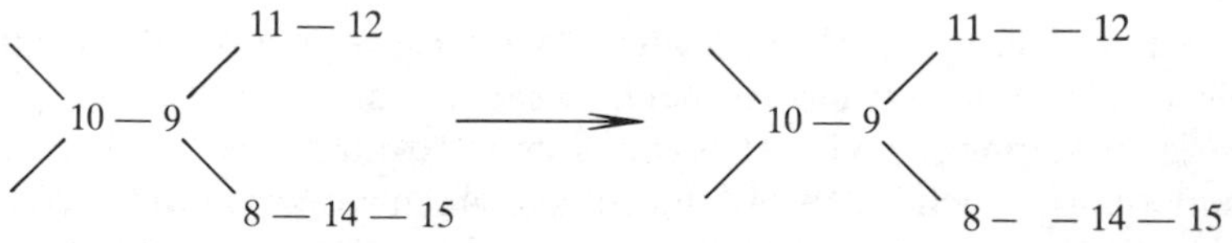

Figure 2.1   Fragmentation under electron bombardment.

However, when you are working in the other direction, from peaks representing fragmentations to the original molecule, life is more difficult. The best that the chemist can hope for is to identify some of the compound's substructure, and then derive a set of constraints that the other subparts must satisfy. In other words, given that spectroscopy and other tests have allowed you to deduce the chemical formula of the compound, and the presence or absence of certain substructural features, you are left with the problem of discovering the actual arrangement of atoms and molecules in three-dimensional space. The conclusions you have drawn so far are called constraints because they serve to restrict or rule out many of the possible arrangements which could result in structural variants (isomers).

Given that you have some systematic way of enumerating all the possible arrangements, one way to proceed would be to generate them one after the other and then discard those that failed to satisfy the constraints. However, this would be very expensive in terms of computer time and processing power. It is preferable to constrain the initial generation of candidates, and consider only a fraction of the possible arrangements.

The DENDRAL Planner is a program that can be used to assist with the process of deciding which constraints to impose. More specifically, it applies knowledge of spectral processes to infer constraints from instrument data. There are two kinds of constraint, called 'required' and 'forbidden'. The required constraints are based upon the conclusions that we have already drawn, and the requirement that candidates exhibit the requisite features. Forbidden constraints rule out possibilities either because they fail to fit the data, or because the resultant structures would be chemically unstable (given what we know about valency and electron configuration).

These constraints can be supplied in various ways, for example, by giving the program a structural skeleton which the atoms have to fit into, or by supplying rules which say how you expect the compound to fragment. The program associates peaks in the spectrogram with fragments in this skeleton, and then handles the combinatorics of finding consistent ways of fitting the substructures into the skeleton. The output from the Planner is a list of incomplete structural hypotheses that have been developed as far as the data and fragmentation rules will allow.

2.2   CONGEN: a constrained generator

CONGEN is a program which constructs complete chemical structures by manipulating symbols. It receives as its input a molecular formula, represented as a list of atoms that it uses as building blocks, together with a set of constraints which serve to restrict the possible interconnections among atoms. Its output is a list of all possible ways of assembling the atoms into molecular structures, given the constraints imposed.

So CONGEN assists the chemist by allowing him to specify various kinds of structural constraint and then generating an exhaustive and non-redundant list of complete structural hypotheses. The latter step employs a structure generation algorithm to determine all topologically unique ways of assembling a given set of atoms into molecular structures. This is an iterative process, during which the chemist can impose further constraints, suggested either by new evidence or by the hypotheses themselves.

There are a number of representational problems associated with the generation process, and these are described in Carhart (1979). One is that some of the symbols manipulated by the structure generation algorithm stand for 'superatoms', i.e. polyatomic fragments such as benzene rings, instead of genuine atoms such as carbon or hydrogen. The superatom is then considered as a single atom with a valency equal to the sum of the available bonding sites. In order to generate 'final structures', the program has to re-expand the superatoms in the 'intermediate structures', and this process is called 'imbedding'. The imbedder determines all the unique ways in which this re-expansion can take place and generates the appropriate structures.

Giving CONGEN a superatom is rather like giving it a constraint, of course, since this will limit the ways in which the atoms and molecular fragments can be arranged. The main difference is that constraints may overlap arbitrarily, whereas specifying one superatom will have consequences for the specification of others. Many constraints refer to unexpanded superatoms, and the user can decide when imbedding occurs.

The user sets up a CONGEN problem using a program called EDITSTRUC, which gives the chemist a language for building structures of arbitrary complexity and associating arbitrary names with them. There are commands to construct rings and chains of atoms, and give them properties, such as aromaticity, in addition to their names. There is also a library of common structures, such as methyl and hydroxyl groups.

A session begins with the definition of a molecular formula, e.g. $C_{15}H_{26}O$. Then, typically, the user defines superatoms, such as chains or rings of carbon atoms with associated hydrogens. Free valencies can be used by CONGEN to link such structures to other structures; in Figure 2.2, the carbon atom labelled C2 has one valence free, while the one labelled C3 has two.

ATOM#	TYPE	NEIGHBORS	HRANGE
1	C	2	3-3
2	C	1 3 4	0-0
3	C	2 4	0-0
4	C	2 3	2-2

```
        H
        |
  H — C1 — H
        |
      C2 — C3
        |
(a)  H — C4 — H    (b)
```

Figure 2.2 (a) A molecule with free valencies, and (b) connections between the atoms.

The SHOW command can be used to display a table of the current set of atoms and their connections; the information for Figure 2.2 (a) would be shown as in (b).

The HRANGE column displays the range of the number of hydrogen atoms associated with an atom in the substructure. There is a command called

HRANGE which can be used to associate any range of hydrogens with an atom that is consistent with its free valencies. In the case shown above, the exact number of hydrogens is specified; this therefore prevents any of the unsaturated electrons from bonding with further hydrogens.

When the user has finished defining superatoms for the moment, he can go on to specify constraints. For example, he could specify that the hypotheses must contain a ring of a certain size, or that particular superatoms are only allowed a certain number of internal bonds. Having done this, he can run the CONGEN program on the problem, and the structure generation algorithm will produce hypotheses consistent with both the specified superatoms and the constraints.

CONGEN may generate hundreds of structures. Consequently, the user may wish to display some of them to see if he has left out important constraints. He may also wish to imbed various superatoms, and this imbedding process may reveal duplications in the hypothesis list which CONGEN will automatically remove.

DENDRAL also has programs to help the user rule out some hypotheses and order the others by using knowledge of mass spectrometry to make testable predictions about candidate molecules. Thus the program MSPRUNE eliminates candidates which are not worth considering because the fragmentations one would expect them to undergo are not found in the spectral data. MSRANK orders the remaining candidates according to the number of predicted peaks which appear in the data and the number of peaks not found. The scores for the presence and absence of these features are weighted according to the importance of the underlying spectral processes. This is basically a strategy of 'hypothesize-and-test', whereby initial data suggest some space of hypotheses, which in turn predict the presence or absence of certain other data, and can be verified or eliminated as a consequence.

After each iteration through the candidates, new substructures can be specified, and additional assertions about free valencies can be made. Such pieces of information enable the program to prune the list of candidate structures still further. This process is repeated until the chemist has succeeded in narrowing down the number of hypotheses, perhaps by running additional experiments on the compound to derive further constraints.

2.3 Rule induction in META-DENDRAL

META-DENDRAL can be distinguished from DENDRAL in the following way. DENDRAL is a program which uses a set of rules to reason about the domain of mass spectrometry. META-DENDRAL is a program which reasons about the rules that DENDRAL uses to perform this task. There is clearly a distinction to be made between reasoning with rules and reasoning about the rules you reason with. The latter is an example of what is usually called 'meta-level reasoning' (see, for example, Davis, 1976).

The role of META-DENDRAL is to help a chemist determine the relationship between spectral processes and the structural features of compounds. It is intended as an aide which attempts to form general rules of mass spectrometry by correlating the two. Working together, program and chemist decide which data points are interesting, and then look for processes which might explain them. Finally, the program tests and modifies the derived rules, rather as a chemist would.

The rules of mass spectrometry that chemists use to describe a fragmentation, such as that depicted in Figure 2.1, can also be expressed symbolically as what artificial intelligence programmers call 'production rules'. A thorough discussion of this kind of rule will have to wait until Chapter 3, but the basic idea is that the rule has two parts, a left-hand side and a right-hand side, and that the left-hand side specifies conditions under which the right-hand side becomes 'active' or 'true'. Thus the following rule would be a way of encoding the fact that a particular molecule fragments in a particular way in a mass spectrometer, assuming that '—' stands for a bond and '*' stands for a break:

$$N - C - C - C \longrightarrow N - C * C - C$$

The left-hand side of such a rule describes a structural feature, while the right-hand side describes a spectral process. META-DENDRAL aims to aid a chemist in the task of deriving such rules. The input/output pairs which constitute its training instances are respectively: a molecular structure, and a point from the histogram of the relative abundances of fragment masses, i.e. a spectral peak.

It is important to realize that although the 'vocabulary' for describing atoms in subgraphs is small, and the actual 'grammar' for constructing subgraphs is simple, the number of subgraphs that can be generated is very large. The basic source of the combinatorial explosion is, of course, the connectivity of the subgraph. However, in addition to this, there are up to four dependent attributes associated with each atom – atom type, number of non-hydrogen neighbours, and number of hydrogen neighbours (as we have already seen), plus the number of doubly bonded neighbours. Buchanan and Feigenbaum (1978) point out that the size of the search space for subgraphs containing 6 atoms, each with any of 20 attribute-value pairs, is 20^6 possible subgraphs. Similarly, the right-hand sides of rules can contain many combinations of actions, involving one or more bonds breaking and zero or more atom migrations.

In coping with this potential for combinatorial explosion, META-DENDRAL (like DENDRAL) attempts a problem-solving strategy of plan, generate and test. Thus META-DENDRAL has a planning phase, involving a program called INTSUM, which stands for the interpretation and summary of data. Its job is to propose plausible processes which might occur in a set of known compounds which constitute the training instances. The output of INTSUM goes to a heuristic search program called RULEGEN. RULEGEN is like CONGEN, except that it generates candidate rules, rather than candidate chemical structures. Like

CONGEN, RULEGEN uses knowledge of the domain and heuristics to constrain the generation of candidates. Once candidate rules have been generated, the last phase of META-DENDRAL, called RULEMOD, tests and modifies them. The division of labour between RULEGEN and RULEMOD is that RULEGEN does a comparatively coarse search of the rule space, for reasons of efficiency, while RULEMOD performs a finer search to refine the candidates. We shall now look at each of these programs, INTSUM, RULEGEN and RULEMOD, in a little more detail.

2.3.1 INTSUM: data interpretation and summary

Given a set of molecules, INTSUM uses chemical knowledge to generate the spectral processes that might occur. The breakages and migrations are associated with bonds which belong in a particular portion of molecular structure, chosen because it is common to the molecules in the set. One can think of this substructure as a pattern or skeleton that could be found in a number of different compounds. INTSUM then examines the spectra of these molecules, looking for positive evidence for each hypothesized process. It is important to remember that there is scope for ambiguity in the association of processes with data points. For example, a process which produces a $CH_3 CH_2$ fragment will cause a peak in the spectrum at mass 29. However, this fragment could have been detached from either end of a molecule like $CH_3 CH_2 CH_2 NH CH_2 CH_3$.

In using INTSUM to derive a working model of mass spectrometry, the user has a considerable amount of freedom to incorporate his own assumptions about what kinds of rule would be appropriate in the identification of the current set of compounds. This model will determine (a) the vocabulary to be used in constructing the rules, (b) the syntax of the rules which map chemical structures into spectral processes, and (c) semantic constraints which serve to rank or prune rule hypotheses. Thus, a chemist might specify that only certain atomic components are to be considered, or decide to place some upper limit on the complexity of chemical structures or of spectral processes which are featured in the rules.

2.3.2 RULEGEN: generating rule hypotheses

RULEGEN is a heuristic search program, like CONGEN, except that it generates rules by investigating the fragmentations proposed by INTSUM. Molecular features at the site of spectral processes are combined into a subgraph which becomes the left-hand side of a rule hypothesis. The right-hand side will simply be the process that INTSUM suggests for that site.

Given a rule hypothesis, the program then goes to work, searching through a space of such subgraph descriptions, looking for more specific subgraphs supported by better sets of evidence. It makes subgraphs more specific by systematically adding feature descriptions, such as atom type and number of hydrogen neighbours, thereby generating 'successors' to more general characterizations of molecular structures. Each attribute which has a value for which there is supporting evidence generates a new successor.

For reasons of efficiency, RULEGEN performs only a coarse search. In other words, not all of the intermediate subgraphs are considered, partly because not all of the attributes will be important on all atoms near the fragmentation site. Also, RULEGEN only considers the positive evidence for associating structural features and spectral processes.

2.3.3   RULEMOD: refining and testing the rules

The role of RULEMOD is to evaluate and modify the rule hypotheses generated by RULEGEN. In particular, it considers the negative evidence available, i.e. the cases where candidate rules predict processes which are not found in the data. It then operates on the rules to make them either more general or more specific.

The RULEMOD program performs five basic tasks:

1. Removing redundancy. The data may be overdetermined, i.e. many rule hypotheses generated by RULEGEN may explain the same data points. Usually only a subset of the rules is necessary, and there may also be rules which make incorrect predictions.

2. Merging rules. Sometimes a set of rules, taken together, explain a pool of data points that could be accounted for by a single, slightly more general, rule which includes all the positive evidence, but does not introduce any negative evidence. If such a rule can be found, the overlapping rules are deleted and the compact rule retained.

3. Making rules more specific. Often rules are too general, and therefore make incorrect predictions. RULEMOD tries adding feature descriptions to atoms in each rule to try and delete the negative evidence, while retaining the positive evidence of correct predictions.

4. Making rules more general. Given that RULEGEN is reasoning from particular cases, it frequently makes rules that are more specific than they should be. RULEMOD will try and make rules more general, so that they cover the same data points, perhaps including new data, without making any incorrect predictions.

5. Selecting the final rules. It is possible that redundancies may have been introduced by the generalization and specialization operations of RULEMOD. Consequently, the selection procedure of step (1) is applied again to remove them.

The stages of selection, merging, deletion and so on can be applied iteratively until the user is reasonably satisfied with the rule set.

2.4   Evaluating DENDRAL and META-DENDRAL

The DENDRAL program runs on the SUMEX computing facility at Stanford University in California, and is available over the TYMNET computer network. It supports hundreds of international users every day, assisting in structure elucidation problems such as antibiotics, marine sterols and impurities in manufactured chemicals. When applied to published structure elucidation problems to check their accuracy and completeness, the program found a number of plausible alternatives to the published solutions.

The quality of rules generated by META-DENDRAL can be assessed by testing them on structures not in the training set, by consulting mass spectroscopists, and by comparing them with published rules. The program has succeeded in rediscovering known rules of spectrometry that had already been published. Also, its ability to predict spectra for compounds outside the original set of instances is impressive. However, it should be pointed out that, unlike DENDRAL, META-DENDRAL is not in routine use. It is CONGEN rather than RULEGEN which has proved to be the most useful tool for practising chemists.

At the beginning of the chapter, I described DENDRAL as a stepping-stone between general-purpose problem-solving programs and more recent developments in expert systems, for two reasons. Firstly, DENDRAL uses a weak method, generate and test, to traverse the search space of alternative structures, but unlike earlier programs it takes advice from the human expert into account as it generates candidates for testing. Thus it is able to benefit from the real world knowledge of the chemist expressed as a set of constraints that candidate solutions must meet. In addition, it has access to an explicit representation of knowledge, in the form of fragmentation rules, which augments the algorithmic base for enumerating graph structures. However, it does not have some of the more advanced features for controlling inference found in more recent systems such as MYCIN (see Chapter 6); control over the program's iteration through the candidates remains in the hands of the user.

It is perhaps worth asking why DENDRAL is such a success story, and what lessons about the limitations of current expert systems technology can be learned from the project.

- DENDRAL sets out to be an expert's assistant, rather than a stand-alone expert in its own right. This enables the system designer to allocate functions between man and machine which draw upon their different strengths, rather than exposing their respective weaknesses. Thus the heuristic search technique is constrained by the domain knowledge (and the 'hunches') of the human expert.

- The heuristic search program has an algorithmic base for the enumeration of chemical structures considered as planar graphs. Thus the generation phase of the 'plan, generate and test' strategy is founded on a procedure with proven mathematical properties. Further, the implementation of this algorithm is both efficient and well understood.

- The successful ascent to the meta-level is made possible by the well-defined syntax and semantics of the language for representing and recursively elaborating chemical structures. In other words, there are rules for making new symbol structures out of old, and for interpreting the result. Thus it is known, for any combination of symbols, whether or not it describes a possible structure and what it actually means.

It would be going too far to say that these three features are either necessary or sufficient for a successful expert systems application. There are interesting and useful programs which do not meet all of the above criteria, and the possession of these features is no guarantee of a happy outcome to the knowledge engineering effort. Nevertheless, getting the right allocation of function between man and machine, availing oneself of existing algorithms, and using a representation language whose syntax and semantics are strictly specified, are important points to bear in mind when setting out to apply artificial intelligence techniques to any real world problem.

In the next three chapters, considerable attention will be devoted to the problem of choosing a knowledge representation language. As I have hinted earlier, knowledge representation is a controversial area of artificial intelligence. Researchers typically disagree about what features a knowledge representation language should have, and whether any of the current languages meet those needs. Here I shall concentrate on examining the issues and describing the main methods, rather than foisting a particular set of opinions on the reader.

Chapter 3 **Production Systems**

A representation has been defined as 'a set of syntactic and semantic conventions that make it possible to describe things' (Winston, 1984). The syntax of a representation specifies a set of rules for combining symbols and arrangements of symbols to form expressions in the representation language. The semantics of a representation specify how expressions so constructed should be interpreted, i.e. how meaning can be derived from form.

In the field of expert systems, knowledge representation implies some systematic way of codifying what an expert knows about some domain. However, it would be a mistake to suppose that representation is the same thing as encoding, in the sense of encryption. If one encodes a message by transposing its constituent symbols in some regular fashion, the resultant piece of code would not be a representation of the contents of the message from an AI point of view, even if the code were machine-readable and easy to store in the memory of the machine. For one thing, the code would preserve any lexical or structural ambiguities of natural language inherent in the message. Thus the message, 'Visiting aunts can be a nuisance' is just as ambiguous in its encrypted form as it is in English. In other words, the coded text is no more comprehensible than the clear text. Secondly, representation implies organization. A representation of knowledge should render that knowledge accessible and easy to apply via more or less natural mechanisms. This means that the store of knowledge should be addressed by content, rather than by location.

Of course, whatever notational system is used, ultimately a computer must be able to store and process the corresponding codes. This is not a very constraining requirement, however, given the power of current languages for symbolic computation. The main criteria for assessing a representation language are logical adequacy, heuristic power and notational convenience.

Logical adequacy means that the formalism should be capable of expressing the knowledge you wish to represent. For example, it is not possible to represent the idea that every drug has some undesirable side-effect unless you are able to distinguish between the designation of a particular drug and a particular side-effect, e.g. aspirin aggravates ulcers, and the more general statement to the effect that 'for any drug you care to name, there is an undesirable side-effect associated with it'. The commonest way of achieving this is to use variables of quantification, along the lines of 'for all x, if x is a drug then there exists a y, such that y is an undesirable side-effect associated with x'. Note that values of y are constrained by values of x, but not conversely. That is to say, the choice of a drug to exemplify x constrains the choice of a side-effect to exemplify y. Any representational scheme which is intended to codify such statements must be capable of making this distinction with regard to what logicians call the 'scope' of variables (see Chapter 5).

should be able to solve problems

Heuristic power means that as well as having an expressive language with a well-defined syntax and semantics, there must be some means for using representations so constructed and interpreted to solve problems. It is often the case that the more expressive the language, in terms of the number of different kinds of semantic distinction it can make, the more difficult it is to control the drawing of inferences during problem solving. Many of the formalisms that have found favour with practitioners may seem quite restricted in terms of their powers of expression when compared with English or even standard logic, but they frequently gain in heuristic power as a consequence, i.e. it is relatively easy to bring the right knowledge to bear at the right time.

Should be declarative

Notational convenience is a virtue because most expert systems applications require the encoding of substantial amounts of knowledge, and this task will not be an enviable one if the conventions of the representation language are too complicated. The resulting expressions should be relatively easy to write and to read, and it should be possible to understand their meaning without knowing how the computer will actually interpret them. The term 'declarative' is often used to describe code which is essentially descriptive and can therefore be understood without knowing what states a real or virtual machine goes through at execution time.

production rule, structured objs, predicate logic implemented as

3.1 Pattern-directed inference systems

Three main formalisms have found favour with expert systems designers: production rules, structured objects and predicate logic. These formalisms are normally implemented as what are called 'pattern-directed inference systems' (Waterman and Hayes-Roth, 1978). The resultant programs consist of a number of relatively independent modules (e.g. rules, structures or clauses) which are matched against incoming data and which manipulate data structure.

There are three essential ingredients to any such system:

1. A collection of modules which are capable of being activated by incoming data which matches their 'trigger' patterns.

2. One or more dynamic data structures that can be examined and modified by an active module.

3. An interpreter that controls the selection and activation of modules on a cyclic basis.

The way that these ingredients work together will become more apparent when the formalisms are examined in more detail. However, it is important to bear in mind that, even within the bounds of particular formalisms, there is substantial variation in terms of both implementation detail and overt behaviour. The survey below is intended to give a clear impression of how such systems typically work, and the kinds of thing that they can be made to do.

Recent AI research has concentrated upon a number of topics related to pattern-directed inference:

1. The efficient implementation of such interpreters.
2. Turning relatively 'pure' formalisms with some mathematical basis into practical, high performance systems.
3. Experimenting with mixed formalisms.

Chapters 3, 4 and 5 describe the different kinds of system in more depth. Implementation details have been suppressed in much of the text for ease of reading by non-programmers. The discussion of systems which use more than one representation of knowledge is deferred until Chapters 10 and 12.

3.2 Production rules

Production rules are a formalism which saw some use in automata theory, formal grammars and the design of programming languages, before being pressed into the service of psychological modelling (Newell and Simon, 1972) and expert systems (Buchanan and Feigenbaum, 1978). In the expert systems literature, they are sometimes called 'condition-action rules' or 'situation-action rules', for reasons that will become apparent. Their principal use is in the encoding of empirical associations between patterns of data presented to the system and actions that the system should perform as a consequence.

A production system consists of a rule set (sometimes called 'production memory'), a rule interpreter that decides how and when to apply which rules, and a 'working memory' that can hold data, goals or intermediate results.

3.2.1 The syntax of rules

Rules consist of premise-action pairs, for example:

if P_1 & ... & P_n,
then Q_1 & ... & Q_n.

with the reading 'if premises P_1 and ... and P_n are true, then perform actions Q_1 and ... and Q_n'. The P_i are sometimes called 'conditions', and the Q_i 'conclusions', since the commonest action is to conclude that a certain proposition is true (often with some degree of confidence). Another piece of terminology is that the premise is sometimes called the 'left-hand side' of the rule, while the action is called the 'right-hand side', for reasons that should be apparent.

The conditions are usually 'object-attribute-value' triples, for example:

(Peter age 36)

would signify that Peter's age was 36, i.e. that the 'value' of the age 'attribute' for the 'object' Peter was 36. One can imagine a rule that includes this condition. For example

> [rule1]   if (Peter age 36) &
>   (Peter employment none),
>   then (Peter claim UB).

signifies that if Peter is 36 years old and unemployed, then he should claim unemployment benefit. This is not a very general rule, since it only applies to Peter at a certain age. Suppose we want to make the somewhat wider statement that anyone between the ages of 15 and 65 years old who is unemployed should claim unemployment benefit. This requires that we introduce variables which do not denote particular objects or values, but can be seen as 'place holders' that will match against suitable values and become 'bound' to them. In the following expression, variables are prefixed by a star (*):

> [rule2]   if (*person age *number) &
>   (*person employment none) &
>   (*number greater-than 15) &
>   (*number less-than 65),
>   then (*person claim UB).

There are a number of obvious but essential points that need to be made about the above expression. Firstly, the three occurrences of the *number variable in the premise must be instantiated to the same value when the rule is interpreted. Secondly, the two occurrences of the *person variable, one in the premise and one in the action, stand for the same entity and so, regardless of which one is instantiated first, the other must take the same value.

3.2.2 The working memory

The most basic function of the working memory (WM) is to hold data, often in the form of object-attribute-value triples. These data are used by the interpreter to 'drive' the rules, in the sense that the presence or absence of data elements in the working memory will 'trigger' some rules, by satisfying their activation patterns. An example will make this clear.

If the working memory is a list containing the following triples:

> WM = ((Peter age 36) (Peter employment none))

then at the next cycle the interpreter will look to see which rules in production memory have conditions which are capable of being satisfied. If a condition contains no variables, then it is satisfied only if an identical expression is present in working memory. If a condition contains one or more variables, i.e. if it is a pattern, then it is satisfied only if there exists an expression in working memory which 'matches' it in a way that is consistent with the way in which other conditions in the same rule have already been matched.

In this context, a simple match is just an assignment of constants to variables which, if applied as a substitution, would make the pattern identical to the expression that it matched against. Thus, (Peter age 36) satisfies the condition (*person age *number) in [rule2] with substitution 'Peter' for '*person' and '36' for '*age'. Let us agree to write this substitution as the set of pairs {Peter/*person, 36/*age}.

Subsequent attempts to match conditions in [rule2] will now be constrained by the substitution derived above. Thus (*person employment none) can no longer be satisfied by (John employment none) because '*person' has already been assigned a value. If we let the original match for (*person age *number) stand, then only (Peter employment none) will do.

Of course, there may be situations in which working memory contains many elements, some of which will give rise to assignments which only satisfy some of the conditions. Consider

WM = ((John age 25) (Peter age 36)
       (John employment lecturer) (Peter employment none)).

In this case, an attempt to satisfy the conditions of [rule2] might well lead to the assignment {John/*person, 25/*age} in the first instance, so that any subsequent attempt to match (*person employment none) against (John employment lecturer) with '*person' bound to 'John' would fail. Thus the pattern matcher must be capable of 'backtracking' (undoing a losing decision, such as the variable bindings obtained above) and exploring other alternatives. Performing such a many-to-many match can be very expensive if implemented in a naïve way, although special algorithms have been developed for this purpose (Forgy, 1979), as we shall see in Chapter 9.

3.2.3 The behaviour of the interpreter

The interpreter for a set of production rules can be described in terms of what is called the 'recognize-act cycle', consisting of the following sequence of steps:

1. Match the calling patterns of rules against elements in working memory.
2. If there is more than one rule that could fire, then decide which one to apply; this is called 'conflict resolution'.
3. Apply the rule, perhaps adding a new item to WM or deleting an old one, and then go to step (1).

It is typically the working memory that supplies both the data for the rules to match their premises against in step (1), and the data structure which the actions modify in step (3). Usually, a 'start-up' element is inserted into the WM at the beginning of the computation to get the cycle going. The computation halts if there is a cycle in which no rules become active, or if the action of a fired rule contains an explicit command to halt.

In step (2), the system has a set of pairs consisting of rules and the variable bindings derived from pattern matching; these pairs are called 'instantiations'. Conflict resolution corresponds to the system 'making up it's mind' which rule to fire. Of course, it is possible to design a rule set such that, for all configurations of data, only one rule is ever eligible to fire. Such rule sets are called 'deterministic', i.e. you can always determine the 'right' rule to fire at any point in the computation. Most of the rule sets in which we are interested from an expert systems point of view will be non-deterministic, i.e. there may often be more than one piece of knowledge that might apply at any given time.

The conflict resolution strategy employed will tend to have a marked effect upon system behaviour, so it should be chosen with care. Good performance from an expert systems point of view depends on both sensitivity and stability. Sensitivity means responding quickly to changes in the environment reflected in working memory, while stability means showing some kind of continuity in the line of reasoning (McDermott and Forgy, 1978; Brownston *et al.*, 1985, Chapter 7). Conflict resolution mechanisms vary from system to system, but three are very popular, and are often used in combination.

1. Refractoriness. A rule should not be allowed to fire more than once on the same data. The obvious way of implementing this is to discard from the conflict set instantiations which have been executed before. A weaker version only deletes the instantiation which fired during the last cycle. The latter is used specifically to prevent loops. If a loop is what you want, there is sometimes a 'refresh' function that will allow you to explicitly override refractoriness whenever you wish.

2. Recency. Working memory elements are often time-tagged so that you can tell at which cycle an item of data was added to WM. The recency strategy ranks instantiations in terms of the recency of the elements that took part in the pattern matching. Thus rules which use more recent data are preferred to rules which match against data which has been loitering in WM for some time. The idea is to follow the 'leading edge' of the computation, if possible, rather than doubling back to take another look at old data. Such doubling back may, of course, occur if the current line of reasoning fails.

3. Specificity. Instantiations which are derived from more specific rules, i.e. rules which have a greater number of conditions and are therefore more difficult to satisfy, are preferred to more general rules with fewer conditions. Thus, given that one could fire either $P \& Q \& R \rightarrow S$ or $P \rightarrow S$, one chooses the former, because it takes more of the current data into account. This strategy can be used to deal with exceptions to general rules, along the lines of

> [rule3]   if (*X is-a bird)
>   then (*X can fly).
> [rule4]   if (*X is-a bird) &
>   (*X is-a emu)
>   then not(*X can fly).

The production rule language OPS5, discussed later in this chapter (and in Chapter 9) uses all three strategies to good effect. Without such aids, production systems would have no simple methods for dealing with non-determinism, handling exceptions or focusing the program's attention on the problem in hand. In other words, the representation would lack heuristic power, in that the behaviour of such programs would be very hard to control.

3.3 Further aspects of control

Controlling the behaviour of rule-based systems poses non-trivial problems. There are two general approaches to this: global and local control. Global control regimes tend to be domain-free, in that the strategy employed does not use domain knowledge to any significant extent. Local control regimes tend to be domain-dependent, in that special rules are required which use domain knowledge to reason about control. Global techniques are usually 'hard-coded' into the interpreter, and therefore difficult for the programmer to change, while local techniques are often 'soft-coded' in the sense that the programmer can write explicit rules to create particular effects.

3.3.1 Forward and backward reasoning

At the global level of control, production rules can be driven forward or backward. We can chain forward from those conditions that we know to be true, towards conclusions which the facts allow us to establish, by matching data in working memory against the left-hand sides of rules, as described above. However, we can also chain backward from a conclusion that we wish to establish, towards the conditions necessary for its truth, to see if they are supported by the facts. In this case, we match special goal statements in WM against the right-hand side of rules. Modifications to working memory then manipulate these goal statements (e.g. replacing them with subgoals), as well as modifying patterns of data. An example of an expert system using forward chaining is R1 – the program that configures VAX computers (see Chapter 9). An example of backward chaining is provided by the MYCIN system for diagnosing blood infections (see Chapter 6).

One can make a distinction between forward and backward chaining and forward and backward reasoning. The mode of chaining describes the way in which the rules are activated, e.g. by matching WM elements against one side and then processing the other side. The mode of reasoning describes the way in which the program as a whole is organized, i.e. the problem solving strategy that the programmer had in mind. Thus, one could implement a backward-reasoning strategy using forward chaining: R1 does just this. It is worth explaining this distinction in a little more detail.

Roughly speaking, R1's problem solving strategy is one of top-down refinement. There is a main goal, such as configuring a system, which can be decomposed into subgoals, such as configuring the central processing unit, the unibus modules, the panelling and so on. However, the way the program actually works is wholly bottom up, i.e. it begins with a set of components and tries to achieve a configuration that satisfies each subgoal.

This distinction highlights a common problem in talking about the way in which AI programs work. Most complex systems, whether they are pieces of software, physical devices or some combination of the two, can be understood at various levels of description. Although these levels are related, they can be considered as being self-contained for the purposes of explanation and exposition. Thus R1 appears, at a certain level of abstraction, to be reasoning backward from its main goal via subgoals, even though the program, when running, is forward chaining on production rules.

An AND/OR tree is a useful device for representing the behaviour of a production system that works by problem decomposition, i.e. by splitting high-level goals into a series of subgoals that must be achieved, each of which may have their own associated subgoals, and so on. The nodes in the tree correspond to states of working memory, while links correspond to possible rule applications. The root node of the tree is the start state of the problem, while we assume that leaf nodes contain candidate solutions. Non-terminal nodes, on the other hand, will be of two kinds: AND nodes and OR nodes. AND nodes correspond to rule applications which rewrite a goal as a conjunction of subgoals, while OR nodes correspond to alternative rule applications. Thus, in the

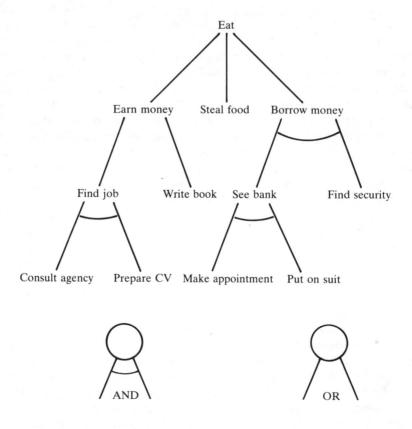

Figure 3.1   An AND/OR tree.

terminology introduced in Chapter 1, the possible rule applications generate a search space and determine its underlying structure as shown in Figure 3.1, an AND/OR tree for attaining the goal of eating.

In order to eat, one must either earn money, borrow money, or steal food. To earn money, one can either find a job or write a book (the former is easier). To find a job, one must consult an employment agency and prepare a curriculum vitae. (The 'steal food' subgoal is not expanded, for moral reasons.) To borrow money one must see one's bank and find some security to offer for the loan. To achieve the 'see bank' goal, one should make an appointment and put on a suit (since in order to borrow money, you must look as if you don't really need it).

It can be seen from the above that rule-based programming does not abolish combinatorial explosion, since the AND/OR tree for any problem may branch exponentially. Of course, it is possible to write a deterministic rule-based program in which there are no alternative rule applications at any cycle. But, in the more general case, it is hoped that the conflict resolution strategy employed by the interpreter at step (2) of the cycle will always choose a rule that leads to a reasonable solution.

3.3.2 Reasoning about control with meta-rules

Now the code for each production rule is meant to be self-contained, so that one rule never directly calls another, and all necessary context for rule activation is provided by the premises. Rule R at cycle C may facilitate the subsequent firing of rule S at cycle D, but this is only via the changes it makes to the contents of working memory. However, some production system interpreters allow the programmer to write 'meta-rules'. Meta-rules can be distinguished from ordinary domain or 'object-level' rules in that their role is to direct the reasoning required to solve the problem, rather than actually perform that reasoning. Thus, one might have meta-rules which reason about which object-level rule to apply next, thereby performing conflict resolution, rather than actually coding the conflict resolution mechanism in the interpreter itself.

In both meta- and object-level rules, the code of conditions and conclusions is usually stylized so as to have a very restricted syntax. This makes it easy for the system to examine its own rules, and to generate natural language translations of them, but it can also limit their expressive power. In other words, you cannot usually make all the semantic distinctions of predicate logic (see Chapter 5) in production rule languages.

Meta-rules can either be relatively domain-specific or domain-free, although the former is more usual. A domain-specific meta-rule is one that encodes a particular piece of strategic knowledge about the domain, e.g. in medical diagnosis, one might wish to encode the fact that special groups of patients, such as alcoholics or people suffering from burns, are especially prone to particular kinds of infection, and write meta-rules which point the program in the direction of those rules which seem most applicable to such cases. A relatively domain-free meta-rule might be one which advises the program to consider rules which generate small search spaces before rules that generate larger ones.

However, it is important not to be misled by this distinction, as a lot depends upon the level of abstraction at which the knowledge is expressed. For example, a meta-rule such as 'if x is an alcoholic, then consider rules for determining this disease before rules for determining that disease' could be abstracted along the lines of 'if x is some reason for believing that y is of category z, and there are special rules associated with category z, then apply those rules before trying other applicable rules'. The latter is less domain-dependent, insofar as it could be applied to a greater variety of problem-solving situations. A particular domain-specific application of this principle, such as the example concerning alcoholics, could be regarded as an instantiation of a more general meta-rule. At the present time, there is considerable interest in the possibility of identifying abstract problem solving principles capable of being applied in different domains by such a process of instantiation (e.g. Clancey, 1983).

We shall return to meta-rules and problem solving principles in Chapter 7, while examples of MYCIN meta-rules can be found in Chapter 6.

The following section is for readers who have found the above too abstract for their taste. It contains an introduction to rule-based programming in the production system language OPS5. The intention is to illustrate some of the concepts introduced in the text, rather than to impart an encyclopaedic knowledge of the language, for which the interested reader is referred to Brownston *et al.* (1985).

3.4 Programming in OPS5

OPS5 is a production rule language which has been implemented in both BLISS and LISP. The sample program below runs in the FRANZ LISP version. Running OPS5 in this version involves loading OPS5 into LISP, and then calling it, more often than not, from the top level of the LISP interpreter.

3.4.1 A simple OPS5 program

Here is a simple OPS5 program whose sole function is to take bricks from a heap and order them in decreasing size. Such a program does not encode a wealth of human expertise, but it is small enough to be taken in at one glance. A more advanced application of OPS5 is described in detail in Chapter 9.

```
(strategy mea)
(external wm)
(literalize goal task index)
(literalize brick name size place)
```

```
(p begin
    (start)
    -->
    (make brick ^name A ^size 10 ^place heap)
    (make brick ^name C ^size 30 ^place heap)
    (make brick ^name B ^size 20 ^place heap)
    (remove 1)
    (make goal ^task add ^index 1)
)

(p pick-up
    (goal ^task add)
    (brick ^size <size> ^place heap)
    - (brick ^size { > <size> } ^place heap)
    -->
    (modify 2 ^place hand)
)

(p holding
    (goal ^task add)
    (brick ^place hand)
    -->
    (modify 1 ^task put-down)
)

(p put-down
    (goal ^task put-down ^index <rank>)
    (brick ^place hand)
    -->
    (modify 2 ^place <rank>)
    (modify 1 ^task add ^index (compute <rank> + 1))
)

(p stop
    (goal ^task add)
    - (brick ^place heap)
    -->
    (remove 1)
    (call wm)
    (halt)
)

(defun rerun nil
    (remove *)
    (make start)
    (run))
```

An OPS5 program is somewhat different in appearance from a program in a more conventional, block-structured language, such as PASCAL. The syntax and semantics are both a good deal simpler than PASCAL, although this simplicity is not always reflected in program behaviour, as we shall see. A walk through the above program will not take very long.

The first statement, (strategy mea), is a declaration which selects a particular conflict resolution strategy. The two options are MEA and LEX. Both are a mixture of refractoriness, recency and specificity as described in Section 3.2.3. They are discussed in more detail in Chapter 9, but the basic difference between them is that MEA has an extra test which emphasizes the very first condition element in a rule when considering recency. It can be used to factor the rules according to the kind of goal statement that they exhibit in their first conditions. Thus, in the sample program, there are rules for getting started (begin), rules for adding bricks (holding, pick-up and stop), and rules for placing bricks (put-down).

(external wm) declares the function wm to be an external function which OPS5 is going to call from LISP. wm is in fact a LISP function provided by the OPS system for exhibiting the contents of the working memory. Had wm been a user-defined LISP function, the declaration would have been the same.

The literalize statements declare data structures that will be implemented as LISP vectors. The first declares that a goal has two attributes: a task and an index. The task is just an identifier, like add for 'add a brick to the row' or put-down for 'place a brick in the row'. The index attribute stores a number representing the position in the row that the program is trying to fill at any one time. Thus the attributes are rather like fields in a record, except that they are not strongly typed, as they are, say, in PASCAL. (In other words, you can have any kind of symbol you like as a value for any attribute. Most programming languages don't allow you to do this, and require that you say in advance what kind of entity the value will be, e.g. real number, character string or user-defined data type.)

Then there are the production rules themselves. Each rule is of the general form

```
(p <identifier>
    <condition>*
    -->
    <action>*)
```

where angle brackets denote place-holders for particular identifiers, conditions, etc. and the asterisks indicate that there can be one or more occurrences of conditions and actions.

Finally, there is a little bit of LISP to get things going. Most LISP functions have the general form

```
(defun <identifier> <argument list> <s-expression>*)
```

where an s-expression is a list structure in which the first element is usually a function name and the other elements are the arguments supplied for that function call. The LISP code in the above program is trivial and need not daunt the non-LISPer. rerun is a function of no arguments – it needs no input data because it always does the same thing.

(remove *) clears working memory for the current run of the program. (make start) adds the token (start) to WM so that the begin rule can fire. (run) simply runs the program.

3.4.2   The left-hand sides of rules

Condition elements in the left-hand sides of OPS5 rules are simply templates to be matched against working memory elements (WMEs). The matching conventions in OPS5 are more flexible than those described earlier in Section 3.2.1. Thus, a template like (goal ∧task add) will match a WME like (goal ∧task add ∧index 1), since the data in the WME satisfies the pattern of the template, even if the index attribute and its value are left over. However, if pattern and data are swapped over, so that (goal ∧task add ∧index 1) is a condition and (goal ∧task add) is the data, then the condition is not satisfied, because there is insufficient data.

Condition elements in more complex programs will typically contain variables, as in the put-down rule. <name> and <rank> are both variables, as denoted by the use of angle brackets. The first condition will match WMEs like (goal ∧task put-down ∧index 1), while the second will match WMEs like (brick ∧name A ∧place hand). One can place restrictions on the value assigned to such a variable by using curly brackets, as in the pick-up rule. The restriction placed on the value of the size attribute in the third condition is that it should be larger than the binding for <size> achieved in the matching of the second condition. For example, if the second condition is matched by the WME (brick ∧name B ∧size 20 ∧place heap), then only bricks with size greater than 20 can match the third condition.

The third condition of pick-up is further complicated by the fact that it is a negated condition. A condition of the form $-C$ is only satisfied if there is no WME that matches the template specified by C. Thus, the net effect of the conditions of pick-up are to select the biggest brick from the heap.

3.4.3   The right-hand sides of rules

Action elements are typically executed to alter working memory, perform incidental computations, or do input/output. The three main actions for altering WM are make, remove and modify. make and remove add and delete WMEs respectively.

The result of an action such as

(make brick ∧name A ∧size 10 ∧place heap)

in the begin rule is to add the vector

(brick ∧name A ∧size 10 ∧place heap)

to WM. Thus the head of the list is the command to be carried out, while the tail of the list specifies the contents of the new vector.

remove, on the other hand, is usually given a number as its argument, as in the begin rule. (remove n) means 'remove from working memory the element which matched with the nth condition in the current rule'. This obviously saves typing, and allows the system to sort out which condition to delete. On the other hand, this can be a source of bugs. If you add conditions to a rule at some later stage, and forget to change the number in the remove statement, the wrong WME may subsequently get deleted!

The net effect of a modify is the same as a combined make and remove. It is used to alter one or more fields in an existing WME. The general form of modify is

```
(modify n ^attr1 value1 ...)
```

where n references the WME that matched the nth condition in the current rule, as with remove, and the rest of the list specifies some number of attribute-value pairs. When the modify is executed, the new values are assigned to the attributes, and working memory is adjusted accordingly.

The easiest way to see how it works is to look at the put-down rule, which has two modify statements in its right-hand side.

```
(p put-down
    (goal ^task put-down ^index <rank>)
    (brick ^place hand)
    -->
    (modify 2 ^place <rank>)
    (modify 1 ^task add ^index (compute <rank> + 1)) )
```

The first modify action changes the place attribute of the vector representing the brick in hand to the current rank in the row, while the second changes the goal task from put-down to add and updates the rank by simply adding 1 to the index attribute of the current goal vector.

For example, suppose that WM contains the elements

```
{(goal ^task put-down ^index 1)
 (brick ^name C ^size 30 ^place hand)}
```

This will satisfy the left-hand side of the put-down rule, with the variable binding {1/<rank>}. After the right-hand side of the rule has been executed, WM will have changed to

```
{(goal ^task add ^index 2)
 (brick ^name C ^size 30 ^place 1)}
```

The second modify action also exemplifies the use of compute to perform incidental computations in the right-hand side of rules. For an example of an input/output action, the reader is referred to the second action in the stop rule. Just before the program halts, we use call to invoke the system function wm and print out the contents of working memory.

3.4.4 Synopsis of the program

The program only knows about two kinds of entity, one abstract and one concrete. Firstly, there are goals, which have mnemonic task names like add and put-down, and which focus upon particular positions in the row the program is trying to build. Secondly, there are bricks, which have arbitrary distinguishing names, as well as size and place attributes. The value of the size attribute remains constant throughout the program run, but the value for the place attribute changes as the brick is notionally moved about. These are both declared and represented in exactly the same way, as are all attributes. In other words, no distinction is made between abstract or concrete objects, or between attributes whose values are fixed and those that can be altered by program behaviour. Such distinctions exist solely in the mind of the programmer (if they exist at all).

The LISP function rerun is needed to get things started, by clearing WM in case it contains elements from a previous run, entering the start token (start), which doesn't need to be literalized as it is not a vector, and then calling OPS5 with (run).

The make statement in rerun enables the begin rule to fire. The first three actions of begin create three WMEs representing three blocks of different sizes, each of which is located in a place called heap. The remove action deletes (start) from working memory, while the make action initializes the goal statement with the task add and the index 1.

WM is now

```
{(goal ^task add)
 (brick ^name B ^size 20 ^place heap)
 (brick ^name C ^size 30 ^place heap)
 (brick ^name A ^size 10 ^place heap)}.
```

This state of working memory enables the pick-up rule to fire with variable binding {C/<size>}. C is the only binding for <size> such that there is no other larger brick on the heap. The modify action 'moves' C from heap to hand.

WM is now

```
{(goal ^task add)
 (brick ^name B ^size 20 ^place heap)
 (brick ^name C ^size 30 ^place hand)
 (brick ^name A ^size 10 ^place heap)}.
```

In the first two cycles only one rule was able to fire, i.e. the size of the conflict set was one in each case. At the third cycle, both pick-up and holding rules are able to fire. In other words, the program doesn't realize that it cannot pick up another brick with its notional hand full. After all, there is no reason why it should. The program only possesses as much knowledge as I have given it, and I omitted to encode this fact in any form.

As it happens, conflict resolution will do the right thing. Because the modify action has made (brick ^name C ^size 30 ^place hand) the most recent

WME, rules which match against it are preferred. Thus `holding` is preferred to another firing of `pick-up`. Note that refractoriness would not inhibit `pick-up` because it would be firing on new data. Note also that although `pick-up` is more specific, in that it has more condition elements than `holding`, `holding` still wins because recency criteria are applied before specificity criteria.

As you can see, making such calculations is not exactly trivial, especially with large rule sets. In general, it is best to keep the conflict set small by making the conditions more detailed. Thus, an additional negative condition could be added to `pick-up` along the lines of

```
- (brick ^place hand)
```

to check that there is no brick currently in hand. Ideally, one ought to be able to add this condition anywhere in the left-hand side of the rule, since it does not depend on variable bindings in any other condition, and creates no variable bindings of its own. Such is not the case. If you make it the first condition, OPS5 will complain bitterly, because the first condition in any rule must be a positive one. If you make it the second condition, you had better remember to change the `modify` in the right-hand side, because the resulting bug may not be instantly obvious when you run the program again. Anywhere else is acceptable, although last would be best. (If you insert this test between the two tests concerning the relative sizes of bricks, it will make the rule harder to read.)

In any event, `holding` will fire, changing the task to `put-down`. This will cause the `put-down` rule to fire next, not because of the fortuitous agreement in name between the task and the rule, but because WM will satisfy the rule's conditions, and no other rule has put-down as a goal. Putting goal statements first capitalizes on the MEA strategy, as described above.

The actions of `put-down` change the position of the brick from hand to the current row index, reset the task to `holding` and update the row index. This cycle of `pick-up`, `holding` and `put-down` continues in an entirely predictable way until there are no bricks left on the heap or in the hand. At this point, the stop rule succeeds, removes the now redundant goal statement, prints out the contents of working memory, and then halts.

WM is now

```
{(brick ^name C ^size 30 ^place 1)
 (brick ^name B ^size 20 ^place 2)
 (brick ^name A ^size 10 ^place 3)}
```

which is the solution to our simple problem.

3.4.5 The pros and cons of OPS5

Brownston *et al.* (1985, Chapter 1) give a good summary of the potential advantages and disadvantages of using a production system as a model of computation. Advantages cited include expressiveness, simplicity, modularity and modifiability. Let us look at each of these a little more closely from the knowledge representation point of view.

In the seriation program, we noted that there is nothing in the syntax which helps the programmer make and maintain certain semantic distinctions, such as that between 'essential' properties of an object, that cannot change during a program run, and 'accidental' properties that can and will change. Making such distinctions explicit can help program design, debugging and modification, especially in large systems that will be worked on by many people. On the other hand, there will be some overhead in terms of declarations and restrictions which have to be specified.

The last point is relevant to the issue of simplicity. Whatever the shortcomings of OPS5 may be, it is certainly an easy language to learn, and program texts often have a pleasing economy about them. However, we saw that the conflict resolution strategy needs to be considered when writing the rules, and this detracts from the simplicity of program behaviour. There seems to be a trade-off between knowledge-based programs which are easy and quick to write, and those which are easy to understand and debug. In other words, would you rather spend your time typing in extra declarations (some of which might affect the flow of control), or puzzling over the behaviour of the interpreter at run time?

On occasion, I have written fair-sized PASCAL programs that have compiled at the first or second attempt and subsequently run without trouble. I have never written an OPS5 program of more than a couple of pages which has run first or even second time. This suggests that the interactive and unrestricted nature of OPS discourages me from sitting down with a pencil and paper, and so I don't plan OPS programs so carefully, while the restrictive and batch-mode nature of PASCAL encourages me to take pains over the code I write.

The speed with which one can get OPS code running is therefore a two-edged sword. On the one hand, it facilitates fast prototyping and experimental programming of all kinds. On the other hand, if you want to build a serious program that will be both reliable and easy to extend, you will need to take just as much care as with any other language.

Another point about simplicity is that some conventional constructs, such as bounded loops and recursion, are tricky to handle in production systems. The 'pick-up holding put-down' loop in the seriation program is not too hard to follow, but both tighter and looser loops could be hard to engineer and understand. Brownston *et al.* (1985, Chapter 5) show both recursive and iterative programs for computing factorials in OPS5; I find the iterative program the easier to understand, but consider both of them more difficult than more conventional definitions. OPS is simply not designed to deal with nested structures of any kind, either control structures or data structures. The two usually go together, as in LISP, where function application is guided by the recursive structure of data.

3.5   Some problems with rule-based programming

A comparison of production systems with other knowledge representation formalisms is attempted at the end of Chapter 5, when other schemes have been considered. For the moment, one can make the following observations about the strengths and weaknesses of rule-based programming.

Firstly, such methodology as presently surrounds rule-based programming has been slow to evolve. There is a good deal more to writing an effective rule-based program than formulating a set of rules which capture the generalizations used by an expert, and encoding them in a production rule language. Even in the case where the rules do make true categorical statements about the domain, there is no guarantee that your program will perform in the way that you expect. Unless the rules have been carefully written with the conflict resolution strategy used by the interpreter kept constantly in mind, the first run of your program will almost certainly contain some surprises. It is usually difficult to predict the outcome of competition between the pattern-directed modules for the attention of the interpreter at each recognize-act cycle. As mentioned earlier, this is often a critical consideration when adding new rules to the system.

A second criticism that can be levelled at production systems is the fact that representing knowledge as an unordered and unstructured set of rules has certain disadvantages which, taken together, probably outweigh the often stated advantage that one can easily add another rule to the set and let the conflict resolution sort out when it should fire. This convention imposes no discipline whatever upon the programmer, in terms of encouraging him to differentiate between rules or sets of rules that perform different functions or address different aspects of the problem. It also fails to take advantage of whatever explicit structure the domain possesses in terms of taxonomic, part-whole or cause-effect relations that hold between objects and between classes of objects.

Finally, although production rules seem well suited to encoding empirical associations between situations and actions of the general form 'if these conditions hold, then do this', they appear to be less effective as a means of expressing more subtle forms of knowledge which can be used to reason about the fundamental nature and causes of interesting phenomena. For example, in the management of chronic illnesses, such as pulmonary dysfunction, the history of the patient is extremely important if the development of the disease is to be understood and an accurate prognosis arrived at.

Production rules in the service of knowledge-based programming can often suffer from the short-sightedness that afflicts evaluation functions in the service of heuristic search. Decisions are made using only a limited amount of local information, with the basic control regime of the interpreter supplying the only global guidelines. In Chapter 9, we shall examine a rule-based expert system which has been designed with control problems in mind.

Notwithstanding these criticisms, there is little doubt that rule-based programming will remain popular as an implementation vehicle for expert systems for some years to come. The main reasons for this include the fact that many experts find it relatively easy to express their knowledge in this way, and many programmers find it relatively easy to encode in this form. Some of the vices of rule-based programming can be ameliorated by combining rules with other representational devices, as we shall see in Chapter 10.

3.6 Exercises

3.1 Production systems have been used with some success in the psychological modelling of simple cognitive skills (see, for example, Newell and Simon, 1972). Such a task makes an appropriate exercise for applying rule-based techniques to problem solving, and it is also useful as an exercise in incremental programming.

a) Encode the following set of rules for subtraction as a production system in OPS5. Start-up code is provided below which gives you all the declarations and LISP you need. The first two rules are also provided, which get the computation going and read in the two numbers to be subtracted. The last rule to fire is also given, which prints out the sum in a recognizable form.

The input/output in read is a bit tacky. The user has to separate the tens and units of each number input with a carriage-return line-feed (crlf). The obvious thing would be to have two modify statements, instead of one, each with an accept. However, this doesn't work, because each modify creates a different copy of the original working memory element, instead of modifying the most recent copy.

In other words, two modifications of

```
(number ^name minuend ^tens unknown ^units unknown)
```

along the lines of

```
(modify 2 ^tens (accept))
```

and

```
(modify 2 ^units (accept))
```

would result in two copies of the original working memory element residing in working memory, as follows:

```
(number ^name minuend ^tens X ^units unknown)
(number ^name minuend ^tens unknown ^units Y)
```

where X is the first accepted digit, and Y is the second.

Because of this somewhat counter-intuitive state of affairs, both the tens and the units must be modified at the same time. Fancier input/output could be achieved by writing LISP, but I have avoided this here.

Here is the code, with the remaining rules sketched in.

```
(strategy mea)

(literalize goal is)
(literalize number name tens units)

(p start
    (start)
    -->
    (make goal ^is read)
    (make number ^name minuend
                ^tens unknown
                ^units unknown)
    (make number ^name subtrahend
                ^tens unknown
                ^units unknown)
    (make number ^name answer
                ^tens unknown
                ^units unknown)
    (remove 1)
)

(p read
    (goal ^is read)
    (number ^name minuend)
    (number ^name subtrahend)
    -->
    (write (crlf) Give minuend tens (crlf))
    (write (crlf) Give minuend units (crlf))
    (modify 2 ^tens (accept) ^units (accept))
    (write (crlf) Give subtrahend tens (crlf))
    (write (crlf) Give subtrahend units (crlf))
    (modify 3 ^tens (accept) ^units (accept))
    (modify 1 ^is units)
)

(p easy-units
        if goal = units &
            subtrahend units <= minuend units
        then do the subtraction for that column &
            goal := tens
)

(p hard-units
        if goal = units &
            subtrahend units > minuend units
        then goal := borrow
)
```

```
(p borrow
        if goal = borrow
        then add ten to the minuend units &
             do the subtraction for that column &
             goal := pay-back
)

(p pay-back
        if goal = pay-back
        then add 1 to subtrahend tens &
             do the subtraction for that column &
             goal := write
)

(p tens
        if goal = tens
        then do the subtraction for that column &
             goal := write
)

(p write
    (goal ^is write)
    (number ^name minuend ^tens <A> ^units <B>)
    (number ^name subtrahend ^tens <C> ^units <D>)
    (number ^name answer ^tens <E> ^units <F>)
    -->
    (write (crlf) (crlf) (tabto 3) <A> (rjust 2) <B>
           (crlf) - (tabto 3) <C> (rjust 2) <D>
           (crlf) (tabto 3) ---
           (crlf) (tabto 3) <E> (rjust 2) <F>
           (crlf))
    (halt)
)

(defun rerun nil
    (remove *)
    (make start)
    (run))
```

b) Common errors that children make when learning subtraction by this method are:

- forgetting to 'pay back' the borrowed units;
- always taking the smaller digit in any column from the larger one, regardless of which is minuend and which is subtrahend;
- always borrowing, whether needed or not.

Modify your OPS program so that it duplicates these errors. Refer to Young and O'Shea (1978) for inspiration.

c) It is assumed that the two numbers are two-digit numbers, and that the subtrahend is smaller than the minuend. Subtracting a larger number from a smaller one will not give the right result. You might try extending the program to fix this.

d) The program fragment given above is not a very general solution to the problem of subtraction, since it treats the tens and units differently. It would be inelegant to extend this program design to deal with arbitrarily large numbers, since one would have to have rules for 'hard' and 'easy' tens, hundreds, thousands, and so on, all doing very much the same thing. Redesign and reimplement the program so that it will deal with numbers of any size in a sensible fashion.

3.2 We saw in Chapter 3 that pattern-directed inference systems all work by matching incoming data against stored templates. Being able to see that one symbol structure is in some sense an instance of another is fundamental to artificial intelligence programming.

In constructing any pattern matcher, you first have to decide what kind of variables you want. In this example, we will just use variables that match against single expressions, and distinguish them by prefixing with a '?'. The simple behaviour we want is the following:

```
match((a b c), (a ?x c)) = true
match((a b c), (a ?x b)) = false
```

where the first argument to match is the sample to be matched, and the second argument is the pattern to be matched against.

It would also be nice to have matching with assignment, so that pieces of sample which match against pattern variables get assigned to those variables. For example

```
match((a b c), (a ?x c)) binds x to b
```

Note that the assignment, once made, must be adhered to for the rest of the match, so that

```
match((a b c b d), (a ?x c ?x d)) = true
```

but

```
match((a b c e d), (a ?x c ?x d)) = false.
```

Note also that samples and patterns may be arbitrarily embedded lists, so that

```
match((a (b c) d), (a (b ?x) d)) = true
```

although we insist that pattern variables match against atoms, and not lists, so that

```
match((a (b c) d), (a ?x d)) = false.
```

Program such a matcher in your favourite AI language.

3.3 Use the pattern matcher you have just created as a basis for a simple forward-chaining production rule interpreter. Do the many/many match between working memory elements and condition elements in the naïve way, i.e. simply loop through the working memory for each condition element. Experiment with different conflict resolution strategies, such as refractoriness, recency, specificity and their combinations.

3.4 In any workshop manual for any car, you will find fault-finding rules that can be formulated in the following way.

IF	the engine won't turn over &
	there is no current at the starter motor
THEN	check the battery
IF	the engine turns over &
	the engine won't start &
	there is no spark at the plug
THEN	check distributer cap for dampness
IF	the engine turns over &
	the engine won't start &
	there is no fuel at the jets
THEN	check there is petrol in the tank
IF	the engine starts &
	the engine misfires &
	the spark at the plugs is intermittent
THEN	check the ignition leads for looseness

Find such a manual and code a set of such rules in OPS5 or your own production rule language. Restrict yourself to a subclass of faults, such as those involving the ignition system. Document the problems encountered as you develop the system. Test it by constructing sets of symptoms that seem to you to be representative of the kinds of trouble you have had with cars in the past, and persevere until the program's advice seems reasonable to you. Now – how easy is this business of incremental programming?

Chapter 4 **Structured Objects**

I follow Nilsson (1982) in using the generic term 'structured object' to refer to any representational scheme whose fundamental building blocks are analogical to the nodes and arcs of graph theory or the slots and fillers of record structures. I shall systematically contrast these with schemes which have been derived either from the rewrite rules of formal grammars or the well-formed formulae of various logics. All structured object representations are essentially ways of grouping information in a more or less 'natural' way that allows it to be applied for particular purposes.

4.1 Graphs, trees and networks

The terminology of graph theory has been imported into artificial intelligence and computer science to describe certain kinds of abstract data structure. The following definitions are phrased in such a way as to reflect their current usage in describing structured objects, rather than their original definitions in their home discipline. All of them assume that there exist primitive entities called 'nodes' and 'links'. The nodes are the sources and destinations of links, and they usually have labels to distinguish them. The links may or may not have labels, depending upon whether or not there is more than one kind of link. Nodes are sometimes called 'vertices', and links are sometimes called 'edges'.

If N is a set of nodes, then any subset of $N \times N$ is a general graph, G. If the order of the pairs in $N \times N$ is material, then G is also a digraph (directed graph). If we outlaw self-loops by adding the restriction that the pairs must contain distinct nodes, then the result is a simple graph (or simple digraph). If we outlaw circuits as well, i.e. paths through the graph which begin and end with the same node, then G is a forest.

If G is a simple graph on n nodes with $n-1$ links and no circuits, then G is also a tree. It follows from this that G will be 'connected', in the sense that there will be a path from any node in the structure to any other node. In other words, a tree is a connected forest. It is usual to designate one of the nodes as the 'root' of the tree. The rest of the nodes form a loop-free, branching structure consisting of successors of the root. Nodes with no successors are called terminals, or 'leaves' of the tree, while the rest are non-terminals.

In graph theory, a network is simply a weighted digraph, i.e. a directed graph with numerical labels associated with links. These labels are normally indicators of the cost of traversing the link, or sometimes of the distance between links, as in a road map. In AI, the labels can stand for anything at all; they signify arbitrary relations between nodes. Indeed, researchers have often been castigated for designing networks in a rather careless fashion (e.g. Woods, 1975). The following definition is probably closer to current practice than the original one: if L is a set of labelled links and N is a set of nodes as before, then any subset of $N \times L \times N$ is a network. This implies that two nodes can be connected by more than one labelled link. One could use this to represent the fact that two objects stand in more than one relation to each other.

Simple graphs are useful for analogical representations of spatial and temporal relationships. They are also used to represent more abstract relationships, like causal connections. Accessing such information therefore involves graph search, for which various algorithms are already available.

Trees, on the other hand, are useful for representing classification hierarchies and discrimination nets. For example, one might wish to classify different kinds of disease according to organ location. The resulting tree would have the set of all diseases as its 'root' node, and the successors of this node would be nodes standing for such categories as heart disease, liver disease, kidney disease, and so on. Each of these nodes could have successors which specialize their ancestor node in different ways, and so on. Terminal nodes might stand for actual diseases that one can diagnose and treat, e.g. a liver disease like Hepatitis B.

'Semantic nets' (somewhat misleadingly named) are a kind of network commonly used to structure more general kinds of information. These are constellations of nodes and links in which the nodes stand for concepts and the links stand for relationships between them. They got their name because they were originally employed to represent the meaning of natural language expressions. The term 'associative nets' is better, being more neutral with regard to what the network will be used for. The use of some form of network for the modelling of concepts and relations is so widespread in AI systems of all kinds, including expert systems, that it is worth looking at their underlying assumptions in more detail.

4.2   The rise of associative networks

The systematic use of networks for knowledge representation begins with Quillian's (1968) work on language understanding. This paper is well worth reading today, even though it raises more problems than it solves. It is not an exaggeration to say that the assumptions and intuitions expressed therein had a powerful effect upon the direction of related research in the 1970s, and traces of these ideas can be found in present attempts to give the next generation of expert systems a deeper understanding of the domains with which they deal.

4.2.1 The quest for computer understanding

Quillian questioned the notion that our ability to understand language can be characterized, even in principle, by a set of basic rules. He viewed text understanding as involving 'the creation of some mental symbolic representation'. Such an outlook contrasts quite sharply with theories of language processing whereby understanding somehow involves retracing the steps that the speaker or writer took when generating the utterance or inscription; for example, the 'analysis by synthesis' arguments put forward in Miller and Chomsky (1963).

The fundamental idea is that the message content can be considered on an autonomous conceptual level which is one step removed from the details of the way in which the message is expressed. Thus, in contrast with the work of Chomsky (1965), Quillian's approach lays far more stress upon the role of semantics in natural language understanding, and far less upon the role of syntax. This led directly to a concern with how the meanings of words might be stored so that a computer could make human-like use of them.

The relevance of this work to knowledge representation for expert systems is not hard to see. It is obvious that verbal reports from human experts regarding how they do their jobs cannot be fed directly into a computer. Neither is the knowledge representation task one of simple translation from natural language into some formal language. Such a translation would not, in any case, be a simple matter, and even if it were the knowledge would still need to be systematized and structured in some way. Ideally, the resultant code should be economical in terms of storage, and remain human-readable as well as machine-readable.

Quillian was not the first to stress the importance of real world knowledge in natural language understanding. Earlier work on machine translation had made it abundantly clear that human use of word meanings could not be captured adequately by giving the computer access to nothing more than a machine-readable dictionary. However, he was among the first to suggest that the relevant aspects of human memory could be modelled in terms of a network of nodes representing concepts, and propose a processing model for the retrieval of semantic information from such a memory.

4.2.2 The type-token distinction and cognitive economy

There are two aspects of Quillian's memory model that are particularly relevant to subsequent semantic net systems, and so I shall emphasize these in the following description at the expense of other features. Firstly, there is a 'type-token' distinction made between concept nodes. The type node for a concept is connected to a configuration of tokens of other concept nodes which constitute its definition. This is rather like a dictionary, in which each entry is defined in terms of other entries, which are defined elsewhere in a similar fashion. Thus the meaning of token nodes is derived with reference to the corresponding type node, just as, in order to understand a word used in a dictionary definition, you may need to refer to the entry for that word. Thus there need to be links that connect all the tokens of a type to the type node where the definition can be found.

Quillian suggested that each type node and its associated configuration of defining tokens could be thought of as a 'plane' in the memory. Every token lies in one such plane, and has both a pointer back to its type node and links to other tokens in that plane. The full description of the concept, as distinguished from the definition that derives from the plane associated with its type node, includes all the type and token nodes that can be reached from the initial type node by tracing within-plane, token-to-token links. So the idea is that in addition to the dictionary definition of the concept, there is access to a hierarchy of related concepts, with those closest in meaning being near the top of the hierarchy. An example adapted from Quillian's paper will help to clarify this.

One might choose to define the meaning of 'machine' as an assembly of connected components which transmit force to perform work. This would require connecting the type node for 'machine' to tokens representing 'assembly', 'components' and so on. In addition to links within this definitional plane, there will be paths to other tokens, such as those standing for 'typewriter' and 'office', which represent knowledge to the effect that typewriters are a kind of machine for office use. Retrieving the definition of 'machine' involves little more than accessing the plane associated with the type node. However, in order to access real world knowledge about the kinds of things that machines are typically used for, one would have to follow links from the type node to other planes, such as those containing tokens for 'office' and 'typewriter'.

Another interesting feature of the memory model is usually referred to as 'cognitive economy'. Here one is concerned with representing the properties associated with concepts in the most economical way. Thus, if we know that a machine is an assembly of interconnected parts, and we know that a typewriter is a machine, then we can deduce that a typewriter is an assembly. It doesn't make sense to store this information explicitly by attaching it to the type node for 'typewriter'. If we allow 'typewriter' to have the property of being an assembly by virtue of its standing in a certain relation to 'machine', we can save a some storage space and still get the information that we need, so long as we can draw the right inference. Needless to say, this small saving is multiplied a hundred fold if we want to store information about a hundred different kinds of machine.

This convention, known today as the 'inheritance of properties', is extremely widespread in knowledge representation schemes which employ any kind of structured object. As we shall see later in this chapter, a number of extra features have been added to this facility in later years, but the basic idea remains the same. Inheritance of properties is a particularly clear example of the storage space versus processing speed trade-off that the designers of knowledge representation schemes need to consider.

4.2.3 Evaluating the process model

The basic information retrieval operation in the processing model which goes with the memory model can be described as an 'intersection search'. The idea is that if you want to know whether or not a typewriter is a machine, then 'activation' of some kind will spread out in all directions from both the 'machine' type node and the 'typewriter' type node. At some point, this spreading activation will intersect, establishing that there is indeed a relationship between these two concepts, since there is a path from each to the other. The nature of this relationship will naturally depend upon the links that were traversed in establishing the intersection. For example, one can conceive of a subnet in which 'typewriter' is linked to 'office equipment' by a link of the kind which states 'X is a kind of Y', while 'office equipment' is similarly linked to 'machine'. Given the transitivity of the relation 'is a kind of', the correct inference can be drawn.

It is interesting to note that Quillian's ideas enjoyed only a limited success as a psychological model of human memory organization and functioning. Collins and Quillian (1969) tested the model by measuring the time that human subjects took to answer questions about category membership and properties of concepts, and found that response time did increase with the number of assumed nodes involved in the intersection search. However, this result only held for positive responses. There were indications in the data that negative responses would cause trouble for the theory, and subsequent experiments by other researchers showed that this was indeed the case.

These results do not detract from Quillian's contribution to research in knowledge representation, however. His work anticipated a decade of research into network-based formalisms for conceptual encoding; the reader is referred to Findler (1979) for a representative selection of papers. Although modern associative nets differ substantially from the original conception in their overall structure, and are often employed to ends other than natural language understanding, many of the basic principles derive from the ideas described above.

4.3 Frame systems and prototypical knowledge

During the 1970s, various critiques of network-based formalisms were published, of which the most influential was probably that of Woods (1975). Using nodes and links to represent concepts and relations may sound straightforward, but experience has shown that it is strewn with pitfalls for the unwary. The limitations of the basic approach quickly became apparent, although it took some time for many of the implications to be recognized.

A thorough critique of this area is beyond the scope of an introductory text on expert systems; however, a number of salient points are worth mentioning.

4.3.1 The trouble with nets

In the first place, some network architects were not entirely scrupulous in the way in which they assigned meanings to nodes. Thus, faced with a type node labelled 'typewriter', it was often unclear as to whether it stood for the concept of a typewriter, or the class of all typewriters, or a typical typewriter. Similarly, token nodes were open to many interpretations, such as a particular typewriter, an indefinite singular typewriter, an arbitrary typewriter, and so on. Different interpretations support rather different sets of inferences, and so these are not idle distinctions.

Secondly, it is important to realize that reducing inference to intersection search does not abolish the problems associated with the combinatorial explosion noted in Chapter 1. Hence it was felt that a memory organization in terms of constellations of nodes with spreading activation as the main retrieval process resulted in a system whose behaviour was insufficiently constrained. For example, negative responses to queries seemed to involve extravagant amounts of search, since it is only after the activation has spread as far as it will go that you can be sure that two concepts do not, in fact, stand in the hypothesized relation.

Thus it was realized that many associative network formalisms were lacking in two respects: logical and heuristic adequacy. They were logically inadequate because they could not make many of the distinctions that logic can make, e.g. between a particular typewriter, at least one unspecified typewriter, all typewriters, no typewriters, and so on. They were heuristically inadequate because searches for information were not themselves knowledge-based. In other words, there was no knowledge in such systems which told you how to search for the knowledge that you wanted to find. These two shortcomings interacted in unpleasant ways; for example, if you were unable to represent negation or exclusive alternation (logical inadequacy), this led to gaps in your knowledge as to when you could safely terminate a failed search (heuristic inadequacy).

Various formalisms and mechanisms were proposed to deal with these problems, but few of them were widely adopted. For example, many network systems were enriched so that they were closer to various logics in their expressive power, thus making it possible to represent some of the distinctions described earlier. Others were given enhanced heuristic power by attaching procedures to nodes which could be executed whenever the nodes became active. Nevertheless, the basic organization of the memory in terms of nodes and links remained the same, even in cases where extra structures, such as partitions of nodes, were added. The resulting systems were often unwieldy; the original simplicity was lost with very little gain in capability.

4.3.2 Frames for representing stereotypical situations

Frames, by contrast, are a way of grouping information in terms of a record of 'slots' and 'fillers' (Minsky, 1975). This record can be thought of as a complex node in a network, with a special slot filled by the name of the object that the node stands for, and the other slots being filled with the values of various common attributes associated with such an object. This is a useful way of representing rather more subtle aspects of real world knowledge, like expectations and assumptions.

Minsky himself describes frames as 'data structures for representing stereotyped situations' to which are attached various kinds of information, including how to use the frame. The intuition was that conceptual encoding in the human brain is less concerned with defining strictly and exhaustively the properties that entities must possess in order to be considered exemplars of some category, and more concerned with the salient properties associated with objects that are somehow typical of their class. Such objects have been called 'prototypical objects' or 'prototypes'. Thus a prototypical bird, like a sparrow, can fly, and so we think of this as being a property of birds, even though there are birds, like the emu, which cannot fly. Thus a sparrow is a better exemplar of the bird category than an emu, because it is more typical of the class.

Frame systems attempt to reason about classes of objects by using prototypical representations of knowledge which hold good for the majority of cases, but which may need to be deformed in some way to capture the complexities of the real world where exceptions abound and there are often rather fuzzy boundaries between classes. The fundamental idea is that properties in the higher levels of the frame system are fixed, insofar as they represent things which are typically true about the object or situation of interest. The lower levels have slots that must be filled with actual data, and these slots have many different kinds of specification attached to them. For example, they can specify conditions that must be met by prospective fillers, they can specify procedures that can be called to provide fillers, they can inherit 'default' fillers from further up the hierarchy, i.e. fillers that are assumed to be correct unless they are explicitly known to be inappropriate.

4.3.3   An introduction to frame notation

Consider the following simple frame system, which is really no more than a record structure.

```
[PERSON is a kind of THING with
   AGE
   HEIGHT
   WEIGHT]
[PROPERTY is a kind of THING with
   UNITS
   RANGE]
[AGE is a PROPERTY with
   UNITS:   YEARS
   RANGE: 0 – 120]
```

```
[HEIGHT is a PROPERTY with
   UNITS:   FEET
   RANGE: 0 – 7]
[WEIGHT is a PROPERTY with
   UNITS:   POUNDS
   RANGE: 0 – 300]
[PETER is a PERSON with
   AGE:    36
   HEIGHT: 6
   WEIGHT: 150]
```

The frame representing 'person' can be considered as a kind of declaration, insofar as it says what kind of attributes a person has, such as age, height and weight, and then places certain restrictions upon the values that these attributes can take. For example, a person's age in years should be a number between 0 and 120; we expect his height to be under 7 feet, and his weight to be under 300 pounds. Note that the attributes themselves are represented explicitly by frames, and can have properties of their own.

The 'is a kind of' relation, sometimes abbreviated to 'ako', relates subclasses to their superclasses, and is analogous to the subset relation of set theory. The 'is a' relation, often written 'isa', relates members to classes, and is therefore analogous to the set theory's membership relation. Members of classes are usually called 'instances', while subclasses are often called 'kinds'.

As an example of default reasoning, consider the following fragment of frame system about cars.

```
[CAR is a kind of THING with
   COUNTRY-OF-MANUFACTURE
   MILES-PER-GALLON
   RELIABILITY]
[COUNTRY-OF-MANUFACTURE is a PROPERTY with
   RANGE: (BRITAIN, FRANCE, GERMANY, ITALY)]
[MILES-PER-GALLON is a PROPERTY with
   RANGE: 0 – 100]
[RELIABILITY is a PROPERTY with
   RANGE: (LOW, MED, HIGH)]
[BMW is a kind of CAR with
   COUNTRY-OF-MANUFACTURE: GERMANY
   RELIABILITY: HIGH]
[BMW 320 is a kind of BMW with
   MPG: 28]
[HSG 622T is a BMW 320 with
   MPG: 20
   RELIABILITY: MED]
```

The prototypical car is too heterogeneous to have any of the properties listed above already filled in. However, the prototypical BMW is a reliable car made in Germany; its petrol consumption depends upon the model. The prototypical 320 has a petrol consumption of 28 miles per gallon, but my 320 has a lower figure because it is an automatic, and it isn't so reliable because it has done a lot of miles. Thus the frame for my 320 inherits its country of manufacture from the BMW frame, as the BMW 320 frame does, but it overwrites both the MPG filler inherited from BMW 320 and the RELIABILITY filler inherited from the BMW frame. Thus it remains an instance of its class, with access to properties further up the hierarchy, even though it violates some of the typical property values in the class structure.

It should be clear from the above that the subclass relation implicit in such a hierarchy is not identical to the subset relation of set theory; neither is the instance relation identical to set membership. Rather the subclass relation constitutes a process of specialization, whereby the class object stands for a more restricted prototype, and the instance relation is closer to exemplification. One is interested, not in sets and their members, but in trying to capture the relationships between generic and individual concepts. A language for dealing with concepts is not obliged to conform to the axioms of set theory; however, it is obliged to capture something of the informality of human reasoning. Minsky's frame theory attempts to provide mechanisms for such important aspects of everyday thought as assumptions and expectations.

There is some psychological evidence to support the use of prototypical objects in human reasoning. A discussion of this work is well beyond the scope of this text; the interested reader is referred to Rosch (1973, 1975). Neisser (1976), in his controversial book, attempts to relate frame theory to broader issues in the psychology of memory and perception.

4.4 Object-oriented systems

Many experimental knowledge representation languages have been produced in the last 10 years, and many of them are frame-based. The fundamental organizing principle in such schemes is the packaging of both data and procedures into structures related by some form of inheritance mechanism. In this section we look at two of the precursors of today's expert systems tools, KRL and FLAVORS, with a view to understanding why these systems developed as they did. Then we see how some of the difficulties associated with this style of programming are handled in a more modern system, LOOPS.

4.4.1 Prototypes, perspectives and procedural attachment in KRL

KRL (Bobrow and Winograd, 1977) was a self-conscious attempt to integrate much of what had been learned from earlier work on structured objects into a single system that was both theoretically defensible and of practical utility. The building blocks of the representation were called 'conceptual objects' and were similar to Minsky's frames in that they stood for prototypes and their associated properties. Their basic idea is well described by the following quotation from their 1977 paper:

'to explore the consequences of an object-centred factorization of knowledge, rather than the more common factorization in which knowledge is structured as a set of facts, each referring to one or more objects.'

This orientation led to a declarative, description-based language, in which conceptual objects are viewed, not in isolation, but from the perspective of other (usually prototypical) objects. The fundamental intuition is that the properties of an object that appear relevant, interesting and so on are a function of how you perceive the object and for what purpose. Thus, if you are to play a piano at a concert, you are interested in the quality of the sound and whether or not it is in tune, whereas if you are to carry a piano upstairs, you are interested only in its size and weight, and you couldn't care less about its musical properties! Your perception of the piano depends to some extent on what you see it as exemplifying at a particular point in time. The pianist sees it as an example of a musical instrument, while the removal man sees it as a piece of furniture.

Seen in this light, description can be viewed as a process of comparison, in which one specifies a new entity by saying in what way it is similar to, but different from, existing objects. Thus a van is very like a car except that it has no seats or windows in the rear. This is a rather wholistic view of representation, rather than a reductionist one. In other words, a complete constellation of concepts can be defined in terms of each other, rather than in terms of some smaller set of primitive ideas. The trouble with the use of primitives in semantic representations is that no-one can ever agree on which are the primitive concepts, or how they should be combined to form more complex ideas.

The procedural aspect of KRL also constituted a departure from more conventional programming methods. It is customary to attach procedures to particular operations that need to be performed. Infrequently, these procedures will be 'polymorphic', in the sense that they can be given different classes of data that have to be manipulated differently, but they can still be relied upon to do the right thing. An example would be procedures which 'know' how to deal with both fixed and floating point numbers. However, procedures are usually more strongly typed, in that the formal parameters will only accept actual parameters of a particular class; otherwise, the procedure body must take the alternative data classes into account.

In KRL, procedures are attached to classes of objects. Bobrow and Winograd integrated this kind of procedural attachment with the underlying frame structure, and made it possible for subclasses to inherit procedures as well as data from their associated superclasses. The intuition here is that it is useful to be able to program in terms of 'generic operations' whose implementation details can be defined differently for different classes of objects. Just as abstract data types allow the programmer to forget about the details of how data are actually stored in the machine, so generic operations allow him to forget about how operations on such data objects are actually implemented. An example will help make this clear.

Suppose you are Commander-in-Chief of a combined forces operation. You have at your disposal tanks, ships, and aircraft, awaiting your order to attack. When you ask different units to attack, they will respond in totally different ways – aircraft may drop bombs, ships may fire missiles, and so on. However, underlying this variety of attacking behaviour, implemented in terms of various lethal devices being unleashed, is a very general concept, namely that of attack. As Commander-in-Chief, you are only interested in a particular level of description; you want implementation decisions about which buttons to press, and so forth, to be made locally in the units themselves.

The notion of attack is even more general than this, of course. If we read that one politician has attacked another, we assume a verbal attack, rather than a punch on the nose, and we are right (most of the time). Our interpretation of the use of generic concepts, such as attack, is extremely dependent upon context. Our linguistic behaviour and patterns of thought are so riddled with this kind of phenomenon that we rarely pay any attention to it. It is one of the things that makes it so difficult to program 'natural language understanding', and it is one of the reasons why natural language processing is such an important field in AI.

To return to KRL, the idea behind an object-centred organization of procedures was to try to learn from studies of human information processing how more naturalistic styles of reasoning might be programmed. In particular, it was assumed that the control of inference would be done locally, in contrast with the more global regimes associated with both structured objects and automatic theorem proving. In other words, as well as knowing how to implement generic operations, classes of objects would also know when to invoke the various procedures to which they had access.

KRL had other features of interest, such as scheduling agendas and process frameworks, which are less central to the present discussion, although they were equally influential. The reader is referred to the original paper for more details. Lehnert and Wilks' (1979) critique of KRL is also worth looking at, as is Bobrow and Winograd's (1979) reply. KRL was really a vehicle for research into the theoretical foundations of knowledge representation; next we look at a system with a more practical orientation.

4.4.2 FLAVORS on the Lisp Machine

FLAVORS is a representation language embedded in ZETALISP which both incorporates many of the features of object-centred programming described above and extends the basic paradigm to handle non-hierarchical modes of inheritance.

This style of programming is particularly suited to problems that require detailed representations of real world objects and dynamic relationships between them. The classic application is simulation. Given a complex system consisting of interacting parts, simulation can play an important role in various kinds of problem solving. For example, the design and diagnosis of electronic devices gave rise to LORE, the forerunner of LOOPS. Similarly, SMALLTALK (Goldberg, 1981; Goldberg and Robson, 1983) has seen application in office systems which support the 'desk-top metaphor', in which icons on the screen represent familiar pieces of office equipment.

The central notion is that the whole program is built around a set of objects, each of which has a set of operations defined over it. Instead of representing such objects in terms of passive data structures, object-oriented systems permit representational units a more active role, in which they are capable of interacting with other units by passing messages. The resultant emphasis is therefore less upon the design of a global control structure that will invoke procedures in the ordinary way (as in PASCAL, say) than upon the specification of the objects themselves, and the roles that they are allowed to perform.

These units have their own internal representations of data, with their own mechanisms for updating and using the information so encoded. They are also armed with private procedures, which are often local implementations of generic operations. The following example, taken from the *Lisp Machine Manual* (Moon *et al.*, 1983), illustrates this quite well.

Here is one way of representing 'ship' as a conceptual object; I have simplified the actual FLAVORS code.

```
(defflavor (ship)
  x-position
  y-position
  x-velocity
  y-velocity
  mass)
```

defflavor is a LISP function whose invocation will create a LISP object to stand for ship and associate with it the properties x-position, y-position, x-velocity, y-velocity and mass. The following procedure could then be defined to calculate the speed of any ship so represented:

```
(defmethod (ship speed)
  (sqrt (+ (^ x-velocity 2)
           (^ y-velocity 2))))
```

All this definition states is that the speed of a ship can be calculated by taking the square root of the sum of the squares of its velocities with respect to the *x*- and *y*-coordinates. Such a procedure belongs to the abstract data type representing ship, and is often called a 'method' of the class ship. The idea is that as well as encoding declarative knowledge about ships, i.e. attributes commonly associated with the prototypical ships, we are also able to encode procedural knowledge, i.e. methods for using declarative knowledge to solve problems.

This seems very straightforward, but as a programming style it only works if certain conventions are observed.

Firstly, programs designed in this way must institute and observe a 'contract' between objects, such that each object only communicates with others in a well-understood way. In other words, the interface between such units must be properly designed and then strictly adhered to. The best way to see this is by example.

Suppose we have created an instance of `ship`, called `Titanic`, by executing the LISP expression

```
(setq Titanic (make-instance ship))
```

which simply assigns the LISP object returned by the call to `make-instance` to the LISP variable `Titanic`. In order to access the *x*-position of the *Titanic*, the program must send a well-formed request to the object representing the *Titanic*, saying 'tell me your *x*-position'. How the *x*-position is actually stored is that object's business and nobody else's. Neither objects in other classes, nor the non-object parts of the program need to know this. Indeed, they should be forbidden from knowing the storage and access mechanisms, in case they use them instead of going through the `Titanic` object itself.

Secondly, it is clearly redundant to define separate methods for calculating the speeds of different classes of object moving in the same coordinate system. The method defined above for ships will do just as well for aircraft, say, since calculating the speed of such objects constitutes a generic operation. Therefore it makes sense to associate this method with a superordinate class, like `modes of transport`, and have instances of the class `ship` and `aircraft` inherit this method from higher up the hierarchy.

This is little more than 'cognitive economy' extended to the procedural side of things. Performing a generic operation is thus assimilated into the message-passing paradigm, with both the name of the operation and the arguments to the operation being transmitted according to the protocols defined. Sending a message is not the same thing as procedure invocation, because it gets things done without the caller having to know which method will be employed, or where it will be inherited from. All the caller knows is the name of the generic operation and the arguments to that operation. The data determines which function is actually used.

Finally, the novelty of the FLAVORS system lies in the ability to mix 'flavors', i.e. to support multiple inheritance and combined methods (Cannon, 1982). This extension allows objects to have more than one parent, and therefore to inherit data and procedures from more than one place. Thus the organizing principle is no longer a hierarchy of objects, but a heterarchy – it is a lattice rather than a tree. Why would you want to do this? Consider the following example.

The window-oriented display of the Lisp Machine is in fact implemented in the object-centred style. That is to say, windows on the screen are represented internally as LISP objects, which record both properties of windows, such as length, breadth and position, and procedures for opening, closing and drawing windows. These windows come in a variety of designs – with and without borders, with and without labels, and so on.

Thus the class `window with border` is a subclass of `window`, and so is `window with label`. In a hierarchical system, these would each be disjoint subclasses of the same superordinate class. They would inherit certain methods, such as `drawing` from the `window` class, and have more specialized methods of their own, for drawing borders or labels, as appropriate.

What happens if you want a bordered window with a label? This new class, representing `window with border and label`, could be treated as a subclass of `window` in a hierarchical system, disjoint from either the `window with border` or `window with label` subclasses, which would be its siblings in the tree structure. However, this would be wasteful, as well as counter-intuitive. What we really want is to mix two existing 'flavors' of window to get a new 'flavor'. We would like this new kind of window to inherit from both its parents, `window with label` and `window with border`, and combine the properties and methods so derived in the right way.

The question is: how do you achieve this, so that the mix does what you want? The problem is in two parts:

1. Find suitable methods higher up in the hierarchy.
2. Combine them to get the desired effect.

One mechanism that works well is to have 'before' and 'after' code that can be executed on either side of the main method. Thus, in the example of the windows given above, you could compose a method for drawing a window with border and label by having instances of the mixed class inherit the `draw` method from `window` itself, via either parent, and then inherit more specialized 'after' methods from each of its parents. The combined method would then consist of executing the more general method from `window` first, and then executing both the `border` and `label` specializations afterwards (in that order) to get .a labelled, bordered window.

All this requires some extra machinery, of course, which makes the basic inheritance mechanism for methods more complicated than the original conception; just as allowing default values to overwrite inherited data complicated the simple model of cognitive economy. This calls for rather careful organization of the system architecture, with clear conventions for the programmer to observe in designing the behaviour of his object-oriented system. The next section looks at the use of objects in a modern knowledge engineering environment, LOOPS, with a view to seeing how such things are typically done.

4.4.3 Multiple inheritance in LOOPS

As Cannon (1982) noted, it is relatively easy to combine behaviours if they don't interact. The whole idea of hierarchical inheritance systems was that in creating new classes and instances, you only ever added LISP code. Either old values and procedures would automatically be inherited by new objects, or they would completely overwrite them. Therefore the process of expanding a knowledge-based system was one of incremental programming. You simply told the system about more objects, and as long as you placed these new objects at the right point in the hierarchy, inheritance would always do the right thing.

However, it is often the case that behaviours do interact. Thus, when redrawing a labelled bordered window, the basic window needs to be drawn first, then the border, then the label. Get the order wrong, and the display is spoiled.

Often it is only necessary to augment an inherited method. This is the case when you only want a window with a border, or a window with a label, but not a window with both. LOOPS provides a special method invocation mechanism, called <-Super for doing this (Bobrow and Stefik, 1983, Chapter 6). This will invoke the next more general method of the name supplied, so that the more specialized method can combine it with local code, along the lines of

```
(BorderedWindow.Refresh
    [LAMBDA (self)
        (<-Super self Refresh)
        (<- (@ :border) Display)
        self])
```

This is an INTERLISP procedure which invokes the more general method returned by <-Super, before executing local code to draw the border. The details of the syntax are less important than the principle of getting a more general method from elsewhere and executing it, before doing something more specialized, defined locally. However, it is possible to write more complex code, e.g. using INTERLISP conditionals and iterative constructs, if you really want to revel in the baroque intricacies of that language!

Inheriting one method, the 'nearest' one up the hierarchy, may not be enough however. Given a class like window with border and label, you may want to inherit methods from each super class. The function <-SuperFringe is like <-Super, except that it invokes the next more general method of the same name for each of the superclasses of the current class. These superclasses are kept in a list associated with the current class, and inheritance proceeds depth-first and left-to-right.

LOOPS also provides a more general method invocation function, called Do-Method, which is even more powerful than the above. Using Do-Method one can invoke a method from anywhere in the heterarchy and execute it in the context of the current object. This facility is potentially dangerous, of course, since it does not conform to the conventions outlined earlier. The authors advise that it should only be used as a last resort, i.e. when only an axe will do.

4.5 Some problems with structured objects

One can see that structured object representations were first developed in accordance with a very simple intuition, namely that one could devise ways of representing the world that were much more analogical than either production rules or predicate logic. As is so often the case, much of the attractive simplicity of these ideas has been lost at the implementation stage, as researchers have attempted to use these formalisms to solve complex problems. Nevertheless, there is still something appealing about the way in which frame- and object-based systems seem to handle the more idiosyncratic aspects of human reasoning.

The main problem is that, in dedicating their efforts to dealing with defaults and exceptions, some of the architects of such systems appear to have undermined what little formal underpinnings structured objects ever possessed. As Brachman (1985) points out, if you allow unrestrained over-riding of inherited properties, it becomes impossible to represent either definitional conditions (such as 'all squares are right-angled quadrilaterals with equal sides') or contingent universal statements (such as 'all the flowers in my garden are roses'). Many frame systems do not incorporate any distinction between 'essential' properties (those that an individual must possess in order to be considered an instance of a concept) and 'accidental' properties (those that all the instances of a concept just happen to possess). Instead, instances usually inherit 'typical' properties, which are susceptible to cancellation or alteration anywhere in the hierarchy. This makes it impossible to express universal truths, or even to construct composite concepts out of simpler conceptual units in a reliable way.

This is very bad news, because it undermines the whole idea of representation via structural correspondance, which is after all what such systems are supposed to be about. It also leaves the door wide open to inconsistency, especially where multiple inheritance paths are involved. Appeals to 'typicality' don't work, because they lead to counter-intuitive results. Thus, although one would want to use such a scheme to represent the fact that a platypus is a mammal, it certainly isn't a typical mammal, in the way that a horse or a cow is. Nor does it make sense to say that a typical Indian elephant is a typical elephant; rather we want to capture the intuition that all Indian elephants are elephants, regardless of whatever properties idiosyncratic instances may possess.

Thus the anti-formality inherent in the use of structured objects appears to be coming under fresh attack. Frames and objects were intended to remedy some of the shortcomings of semantic nets, by adding extra structure and providing a clearer semantics based on the notion of typicality. However, it seems that, without further work on their epistemological foundations, their theoretical contribution to knowledge representation will remain open to question.

There is plenty of room for opinion here. It is at least arguable that frames and objects offer the knowledge engineer powerful facilities at the implementation level, in that they provide some useful mechanisms for combining declarative and procedural knowledge. The trouble is that they leave the programmer with difficult decisions to make with regard to the epistemological status of the properties so encoded and their associated inheritance paths.

Modern programming tools, like LOOPS, do tend to make a distinction between 'class variables', which contain information about the class as a whole, and 'instance variables', which contain information specific to an instance. This would appear to take some of the force out of Brachman's argument. On the other hand, LOOPS gives the user few guidelines about how to avoid some of the epistemological pitfalls outlined above, and hence provides no safeguards against the creation of incoherent structures. Yet this is also true of structured objects and predicate logic! It is just as easy to generate meaningless representations (representations which cannot be interpreted consistently) in structured objects like OPS5 and PROLOG-based systems as it is in LOOPS.

So what do we make of all this? The most cynical interpretation is that our so-called 'knowledge representation languages' are really just high-level programming languages, and that their epistemological foundations are, in fact, quite shallow. A more charitable interpretation is that such languages do provide data and control structures which are more flexible than those associated with conventional languages, and they are therefore more suited to the simulation of human reasoning than anything we had before. These two interpretations are not mutually exclusive, in that one can hold them both to be true at the same time. People typically divide up depending upon how worried they are about this state of affairs, i.e. whether they feel that the knowledge representation problem has somehow been solved by the development of sophisticated tools, or whether they suspect that further work on the foundations is essential for real progress.

4.6 Exercises

4.1 Here is start-up code for a simple frame system, written in FRANZ LISP. All it does is create data types with associated access and update functions for each slot. Converting it to a frame system requires that data types can be organized into a specialization hierarchy with an inheritance relation between subnodes and their superordinates.

```
; -------------------- Sketch of frame system ----------------------

; deftype - defines an abstract data type by declaring slots and
; defining associated functions for put and get operations.

; a recognizer function of the form is-<type> is also defined
;  automatically.

; For example, to define 'dog' as a datatype with 'owner' and 'breed'
; slots that one can 'put' and 'get' values to, type

; (deftype dog (owner put get) (breed put get))

; This automatically defines 5 Lisp functions:
; is-dog, put-owner, get-owner, put-breed and get-breed.
```

```
(defmacro deftype (type &rest slots)
    `(progn (addprop ',type (defrecognizer ,type) 'methods)
          (mapc '(lambda (each)
                          (addprop ',type (car each) 'slots)
                          (mapc '(lambda (every)
                                          (addprop
                                              ',type
                                              (defmethod every
                                                      (car each))
                                              'methods))
                                  (cdr each)))
              ',(reverse slots))
          ',type))

(defmacro defrecognizer (type)
    `(defun ,(concat "is-" type) (arg) (eq (get arg 'type) ',type)))

(defun addprop (object value attribute)
    (putprop object (cons value (get object attribute)) value))

; deftoken - creates a token of a type with values for slots
; indexing is from tokens to types and types to tokens

; For example, to create a dog called 'sacha' with owner 'peter' and
; breed 'spaniel', type

; (deftoken dog sacha (owner . peter) (breed . spaniel)).

; (is-dog 'sacha) should return 't'
; (get-owner 'sacha) should return 'peter'
; (get-breed 'sacha) should return 'spaniel'.

(defmacro deftoken (type token &rest values)
    `(progn (mapc '(lambda (pair)
                          (putprop ',token (cdr pair) (car pair)))
              ',values)
          (putprop ',token ',type 'type)
          (addprop ',type ',token 'tokens)
          ',token))

; ----------------------- Defining methods ---------------------------

; defmethod - creates methods of the form <key>-<slot>
```

```
(defun defmethod (key slot)
    (caseq key
            (get (make-get-fun (hyphenate 'get slot) slot))
            (put (make-put-fun (hyphenate 'put slot) slot))
            (t (msg N "unknown operation: " key N))))

(defun make-get-fun (name slot)
    (eval `(defun ,name (id)
                    (get id ',slot))))

(defun make-put-fun (name slot)
    (eval `(defun ,name (id val)
                    (putprop id val ',slot))))


(defun hyphenate (word1 word2)
    (concat word1 (concat '- word2)))
```

a) Define add and rem methods for slots which assume that the fillers of the slots are lists and which respectively add and remove an item from the slot. Use the definitions of make-get-fun and make-put-fun to guide you.

b) Design a specialization hierarchy for such data types and modify the code so that it
   i) supports simple inheritance, and
   ii) allows default properties to be overwritten. Does this cause problems when you try to express definitions? If so, try to distinguish between properties that must be true of all members of a class and those which are merely default properties that members can overwrite.

As an example, consider the hierarchy shown in Figure 4.1.

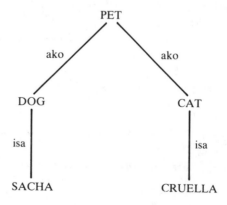

Figure 4.1 A simple hierarchy.

The 'ako' link indicates a 'kind of' link between classes and their superclasses, while the 'isa' link indicates an 'instance of' link between individuals and the classes to which they belong.

The properties 'owner' and 'breed' are common to both dogs and cats and should therefore be defined in the PET frame. However, properties which are peculiar to dogs and cats should be defined in the appropriate frame. For example, the property 'amount of exercise needed' applies to dogs but not to cats, since they do not need to be taken for walks. Defining properties as high in the hierarchy as possible is a way of implementing the idea of cognitive economy. However, it requires the interpeter for such a system to know where to look for such information.

In order to look up the hierarchy for methods and values, each class should have a special slot that holds the name of its superclass. Looking up the hierarchy then involves following this trail of pointers until the method or value is found. Default values allow 'typical' values associated with classes higher up the hierarchy to be overwritten lower down. Thus PET might have a CUDDLY property with the value TRUE. The SNAKE subclass of PET might overwrite this property with the value FALSE, while DOG and CAT inherit their values from PET.

c) Use the pattern matcher you created in Exercise 3.2 to program a simple natural language front end to your frame system, so that you can ask questions like 'Who is the owner of Sacha?' and, 'Is Sacha a dog?'.

4.2 Read the paper by Hayes in Brachman and Levesque (1985). Are frames no more than an implementation device for first-order logic, or do they capture genuinely extra-logical aspects of human reasoning?

4.3 Read Brachman's (1985) critique of frame systems.

a) Should expert systems architects worry about these issues or not?

b) Should the purveyors of frame systems build in integrity constraints of various kinds, or simply provide the tools for users to design their own?

Chapter 5 **Predicate Logic**

There are a number of different usages of the word 'logic'. Firstly, there is logic as a field of study and research, whose primary concern is with the soundness or unsoundness of arguments. Secondly, there is logic as a kind of formal language, namely a calculus with syntactic rules of deduction.

An argument consists of a number of statements or propositions from which some other proposition or statement 'follows'. The initial statements are called the premises, while the latter is called the conclusion. We have already met this terminology in the section on production rules, and these terms derive from the literature on logic.

In saying that a logic is a formal language, one means that one can say, for any sequence of symbols whatsoever, whether or not it conforms to the rules for constructing expressions of the language. If a sequence of symbols does so conform, we say it is a 'well-formed formula' of the language. The fact that we are able to say, unequivocally, whether or not this is the case implies that we have a finite set of rules which completely describes the syntax (the external appearance in terms of form, structure or shape) of well-formed expressions.

Formal languages are usually contrasted with natural languages, such as French and English. The latter are to some extent 'informal', in the sense that we do not have a complete set of rules which is capable of generating all and only the acceptable sentences of these languages. It has been argued that natural languages are just very complicated formal languages; this is a controversial issue which we shall not get involved with here.

In saying that a logic is a calculus with syntactic rules of deduction, one is saying (roughly speaking) that the meaning, value or outcome associated with an expression in the language depends solely upon its external form, and not upon any extraneous associations or ideas that might attach to the symbols in the mind of someone reading or writing them. Taking arithmetic as an example of a formal language, the value of the expression '3 + 5' is given by certain rules which have nothing to do with the fact that three is the number of the Trinity, or that five is the number of fingers on a person's hand. Similarly the value of 'P & Q' in the propositional calculus is defined by certain rules which have nothing to do with the fact that P comes before Q in the alphabet, or that P is the first letter of 'Peter'. In fact, the value of 'P & Q' doesn't even depend upon the fact that the logician who writes this sequence of symbols as part of a proof has in mind that P stands for 'Socrates is a man' and Q stands for 'Socrates is mortal'. This is because the attachment between the symbols and the propositions is entirely in the mind of the logician, and has no counterpart in the rules of the calculus. This will become clearer when we see what these rules are like.

5.1   The propositional and predicate calculi

Propositional calculus is the logic of unanalysed propositions in which propositional variables, like P and Q, can be thought of as standing for the sense of expressions like 'Socrates is a man' and 'Socrates is mortal'. Propositions can, of course, be compound, as in 'Socrates is a man and Socrates is mortal', which we might represent by 'P & Q'. The following are rules for constructing well-formed formulae (wffs) of the propositional calculus.

If P is atomic, then P is a wff.

[~]   if P is a wff, then so is $\sim P$.
[&]   if P and Q are wffs, then so is $(P$ & $Q)$.
[v]   if P and Q are wffs, then so is $(P$ v $Q)$.
[→]   if P and Q are wffs, then so is $(P \rightarrow Q)$.
[≡]   if P and Q are wffs, then so is $(P \equiv Q)$.

Nothing is a wff, unless derived from these rules. Thus the expression

$$((\sim P \ \& \ (Q \rightarrow R)) \equiv \sim(S \ v \sim\sim T))$$

is well-formed, since we can trace the following rule applications:

[→]   to Q and R
[~]   to P
[&]   to $\sim P$ and $(Q \rightarrow R)$
[~]   to T
[~]   to $\sim T$
[v]   to S and $\sim\sim T$
[~]   to $(S$ & $\sim\sim T)$
[≡]   to $(\sim P$ & $(Q \rightarrow R))$ and $\sim(S$ v $\sim\sim T)$.

However,

$$(\sim\& \ ))P \ P \ P) \equiv (Q \ (R$$

is not well-formed, because there is no rule that will produce the concatenation of '$\sim$' and '&', for example.

The meaning of expressions in a formal language is as strictly defined as their form; in fact, the two are closely correlated. Thus, the statement 'P & Q' means that 'P is true and Q is true' – no more and no less. The meaning of ampersand is therefore completely given by the following 'truth table', which signifies that $(P$ & $Q)$ is true just in case both P is true and Q is true, otherwise it is false. In the truth tables given below, I observe the convention of writing the truth value associated with a complex expression under the main connective for that expression.

P	&	Q
T	T	T
T	F	F
F	F	T
F	F	F

In other words, the value of $(P \& Q)$ depends upon the values we assign to P and to Q, i.e. whether we consider them to be true or not. An assignment of truth values to propositional variables is sometimes called an 'interpretation'. However, there are certain other propositions whose truth does not depend upon such an assignment. For example, $((P \& Q) \to P)$ is true under all interpretations; such propositions are called 'theorems' of the calculus.

(P	&	Q)	$\to$	P
T	T	T	T	T
T	F	F	T	T
F	F	T	T	F
F	F	F	T	F

The propositional calculus has some nice properties, which I shall describe informally here; the reader is referred to Lemmon (1965, Chapter 2) for a more formal treatment.

- Completeness. If P is a theorem of the propositional calculus, then it can be derived using only the rules of inference.
- Soundness. There is no P such that P and $\sim P$ are theorems. In other words, it is not possible to derive a contradiction by using the inference rules.
- Decidability. For any P, there is an effective procedure for showing whether P is in fact a theorem or not.

However, the propositional calculus has its limitations. You can't deal properly with general statements of the form 'All men are mortal', e.g. you can't derive from the conjunction of this and 'Socrates is a man' that 'Socrates is mortal' follows. To do this, you need to analyse propositions into predicates and arguments, and deal explicitly with quantification, i.e. expressions of the form 'for all x, x has the property F', 'for some x, x has the property F', and so on.

Predicate logic provides a formalism for performing this analysis of propositions and additional methods for reasoning with quantified expressions. The term 'predicate logic' derives from the fact that we analyse propositions into predicate-argument compositions. Thus, instead of representing the proposition that an object, a, has some property, F, by the propositional constant P, we typically represent it by placing the predicate in front of the thing that it is predicated of: Fa. A similar arrangement applies to the expression of a relationship, R, between n objects, $a_1, ..., a_n$. This would be rendered: $Ra_1...a_n$. Common notational variants include parenthesizing the arguments, with or without commas separating them, e.g. $F(a)$, $R(a_1, ..., a_n)$, or parenthesizing the whole expression, with the understanding that the first item in the list is always the predicate, while the rest are its arguments, e.g. $(F\ a)$, $(R\ a_1\ ...\ a_n)$. These conventions make expressions containing real predicates and arguments (as opposed to meta-variables like F, R, a, etc.) easier to read. I shall use the convention of parenthesizing the whole expression for the rest of this chapter.

Relations can take any number of arguments, and these arguments can be listed in any order, so long as the conventions adopted are adhered to throughout. Thus 'John gave Fido to Mary' could be represented by (gave John Fido Mary) or (gave John Mary Fido), assuming that the usage is consistent.

The real power of predicate logic becomes apparent when we wish to represent more general statements, such as 'John gave Mary everything'. The translation into predicate logic is (all x (gave John Mary x)), i.e. for any thing you care to name, let's agree to call it x, John gave it to Mary. The variable x is understood to range over some domain of appropriate objects. The fact that it is governed by the operator 'all' signifies that it is 'universally quantified'. The embedded expression, (gave John Mary x), is said to be within the 'scope' of the quantifier 'all', and x is sometimes said to be 'bound' in (gave John Mary x).

Contrast this with another kind of quantification, as in 'John gave Mary something'. The translation into predicate logic is (some x (gave John Mary x)), i.e. there is some thing, let's agree to call it x, such that John gave it to Mary. Here, the variable x still ranges over a domain of appropriate objects, but the fact that it is governed by the operator 'some' signifies that it is 'existentially quantified'.

Quantifier scopes aren't always so easy to determine, however. Many statements involving the quantifiers 'all' and 'some' are potentially ambiguous to a machine, even if they appear to be unambiguous to us. For example, the statement 'Everyone loves someone' would generally be interpreted as (all x (some y (loves x y))) by a human listener, rather than (some x (all y (loves x y))). The first rendering could be retranslated as: for any person you care to name, let's agree to call him or her x, there exists at least one person, let's agree to call him or her y, that x loves. Thus the person filling the role of y could be different for each value of x. The second rendering could be retranslated as: there exists at least one person, let's agree to call him or her

y, such that any person you care to name, let's agree to call him or her x, loves y. Thus the beloved is the same in each case. These two (retranslated) statements can be seen to make rather different claims. The fact that one of these (the former) represents the reading preferred by most English speakers is an interesting phenomenon which serves to illustrate the maxim that human thought processes are not strictly logical.

The good news, then, is that predicate logic can be used as an analytic tool to represent facts, such as (mortal Socrates), general statements, such as (all x (man $x \rightarrow$ mortal x)), vague statements, such as (some x (gave x Socrates hemlock)), and complex relationships, such as (all x (some y (person x & computer $y \rightarrow$ uses x y))).

The bad news is that the nice property of decidability doesn't carry over into the extended logic; there is a complex proof of this that we won't bother with here. Completeness and soundness do carry over, though, so long as you only quantify over individuals, like Socrates; this is called 'first order logic'. If you quantify over predicates, like 'man', then you are in second order logic, and it appears that you lose completeness too (see Boolos and Jeffrey, 1980, Chapter 18).

5.2 Theorem proving, logic programming and knowledge representation

Automatic theorem proving refers to the generation of proofs in mathematical logic by machine, while logic programming refers to the use of logic as a programming language. These are distinct but related activities, since both involve the mechanization of inference. The use of logic for knowledge representation also involves inference; however, one is less interested in the possible theoremhood of propositions than the (albeit related) question of what inferences you can draw from a given set of propositions, and which of those inferences will lead to the solution of a given problem.

One of the problems with applying logic to problem solving is that logic doesn't tell you which inferences you should draw at any given point in your search for a solution; it only tells you which inferences you are entitled to draw according to the rules. Roughly speaking, the more you know, the more inferences you are capable of drawing if you so desire. Unless you have some more or less reliable criteria for choosing what to infer next, the more knowledge you have, the greater your search problem, and the less likely you are to find the solution!

It is clear that human information processing is not typically hampered in this way. That is to say, the more knowledge I have about a domain, the more likely I am to be able to solve problems to which my knowledge is relevant. This suggests that, in addition to object-level knowledge expressed as statements in one's logical language, one needs either particular strategies built into the interpreter, or else expressions which serve to direct the drawing of inferences, rather as meta-rules serve to direct the selection of object-level rules in production systems.

In the past, applications of logic to AI have been hampered by problems of this kind. Thus Green's (1969) question-answering system QA4 could handle relatively simple queries, but failed to cope with more difficult ones, thanks to the combinatorial explosion inherent in resolution theorem-proving. Systems which replaced resolution theorem-proving with more procedural methods of inference, such as PLANNER (Hewitt, 1972), attempted to give the programmer more control over the way in which inferences were drawn. However, procedural deduction languages of this kind are typically quite limited in expressive power, as Moore (1975) has pointed out. Even today, the trade-off between logical and heuristic adequacy, mentioned in Chapter 3, is not well understood.

The remaining subsections go into the syntax, semantics and pragmatics of logic for knowledge representation in more detail. Readers should feel free to skip these at first reading, if they find them heavy going.

5.2.1 Normal forms

In automatic theorem-proving, logic programming and knowledge representation, one often aims for maximum uniformity and standardization in the syntax, avoiding the full syntactic variety of the propositional and predicate calculi. The main reason for this is that the more variety there is in the syntax, the more inference rules you need. For example, in natural deduction systems such as that described by Lemmon (1965), ten rules are required to deal with the connectives of the propositional calculus. If one can reduce the complexity of the syntax in terms of the number of connectives, the degree of embedding and the significance of order, then corresponding reductions in the complexity of the inference rules are possible. Such reductions can also lead to a reduction in the size of the resultant search space.

The three main syntactic schemes employed are conjunctive normal form (CNF), full clausal form, and the Horn clause subset. Rules which will turn propositional calculus expressions into their normalized equivalents can easily be specified.

Conjunctive normal form

In CNF, conditionals and biconditionals are eliminated in favour of disjunction and negation, using the following equivalences:

$$[E\equiv] \quad (P \equiv Q) \equiv ((P \to Q) \,\&\, (Q \to P))$$
$$[E\to] \quad (P \to Q) \equiv (\sim P \lor Q)$$

Then negation is driven in, so that it governs only atomic formulae (propositions containing no logical operators), using the following equivalences:

$$[D{\sim}\&] \quad {\sim}(P \& Q) \equiv ({\sim}P \lor {\sim}Q)$$
$$[D{\sim}\lor] \quad {\sim}(P \lor Q) \equiv ({\sim}P \& {\sim}Q)$$
$$[D{\sim}{\sim}] \quad {\sim}{\sim}P \equiv P$$

Finally disjunction is distributed over conjunction, using the following equivalence:

$$[D\&\lor] \quad (P \lor (Q \& R)) \equiv ((P \lor Q) \& (P \lor R))$$

It is customary to reduce the nesting of parentheses by making '&' and 'v' operators of variable arity (allowing occurrences of them to govern any number of operands), using the following equivalences:

$$[D\lor] \quad (P \lor (Q \lor R)) \equiv (P \lor Q \lor R)$$
$$[D\&] \quad (P \& (Q \& R)) \equiv (P \& Q \& R)$$

Both the disjunction sign and the conjunction sign can now be dropped without ambiguity, and resulting expression treated as an implicit conjunction of disjunctions. An example will make this clear.

$$\sim(P \lor Q) \to (\sim P \& \sim Q)$$
$$[E{\to}] \quad {\sim}{\sim}(P \lor Q) \lor (\sim P \& \sim Q)$$
$$[D{\sim}] \quad (P \lor Q) \lor (\sim P \& \sim Q)$$
$$[D\&\lor] \quad (\sim P \lor (P \lor Q)) \& (\sim Q \lor (P \lor Q))$$
$$\{\{\sim P, P, Q\}, \{\sim Q, P, Q\}\}$$

Expressions within inner brackets are either atomic formulae (atoms) or negated atomic formulae. Such expressions are called 'literals', and from a logical point of view their order is immaterial, hence the use of the curly brackets from set theory. Literals in the same clause are implicitly disjoined, while clauses within outer brackets are implicitly conjoined.

Clausal form

Clausal form is very similar to CNF, except that the positive and negative literals in each disjunction are grouped together on different sides of an arrow and the negation symbols are dropped. Thus

$$\{\{\sim P, P, Q\}, \{\sim Q, P, Q\}\}$$

from the above example would become the two clauses

$$P\ Q \leftarrow P$$
$$P\ Q \leftarrow Q$$

and most people agree that this is more readable (for humans) than CNF.

Atoms on the left-hand side of the arrow are implicitly disjoined, while items on the right-hand side are implicitly conjoined. The syntax should be read in the following way: to show that the left-hand side is true, show that the right-hand side is true. In other words, the two expressions given above are equivalent to the more familiar

$$P \to (P \lor Q)$$
$$Q \to (P \lor Q)$$

A little thought will convince you that

$$\leftarrow P$$

is equivalent to $\sim P$, and that

$$P \leftarrow$$

is equivalent to plain P.

More precisely, a clause is an expression of the form

$$B_1, ..., B_m \leftarrow A_1, ..., A_n$$

where $B_1, ..., B_m, A_1, ..., A_n$ are atomic formulae, with $m \geq 0$ and $n \geq 0$. The A_i are the conjoined conditions of the clause, while the B_i are the disjoined conclusions.

If the clause contains variables, $x_1, ..., x_k$, then the correct interpretation is

> for all $x_1, ..., x_k$
> B_1 or ... or B_m if A_1 and ... and A_n.

If $n = 0$, i.e. if there are no conditions specified, then the correct interpretation is an unconditional statement to the effect that

> for all $x_1, ..., x_k$
> B_1 or ... or B_m.

If $m = 0$, i.e. if there are no conclusions specified, then the correct interpretation is the following denial

> for all $x_1, ..., x_k$
> it is not the case that A_1 and ... and A_n.

If $m = n = 0$, then we have the empty clause, whose correct interpretation is always falsity.

An atomic formula (sometimes called an 'atom') is a predicate-argument expression of the form

$$P(t_1, ..., t_m)$$

where P is an m-place predicate symbol, the t_i are terms and $m \geq 1$.

A term is either a variable, a constant symbol, or a function-argument expression of the form

$$f(t_1, ..., t_m)$$

where f is an m-place function symbol, the t_i are terms and $m \geq 1$.

The Horn clause subset

The Horn clause subset is just like the full clausal form, except that you are allowed one atom at most on the left-hand side. Thus the Horn clause equivalent of a rule will have the general form

$$P \leftarrow Q_1 ... Q_n$$

where the Q_i are implicitly conjoined. Write this as

$P :- Q_1, ..., Q_n.$

and you have the syntax of the PROLOG programming language.

PROLOG employs the 'problem-solving interpretation of Horn clauses' described in, for example, Kowalski (1979, pages 88–9). The fundamental theorem proving method that PROLOG relies upon is called 'resolution refutation', and is fully described in Robinson (1979). The following sections attempt to impart no more than the basic ideas and the rationale behind the method.

5.2.2   The resolution principle and the propositional calculus

The inference rules employed in computational logic are also significantly streamlined in comparison with the kinds of rules associated with more traditional methods of theorem proving. Instead of the dozen or more rules found in most natural deduction systems, AI theorem provers for clausal forms typically use only a single rule of inference: the resolution principle, first described by Robinson (1965). This can be regarded as a generalization of more familiar rules, such as *modus ponens* (deducing Q from $P \rightarrow Q$ and P), *modus tollens* (deducing $\sim P$ from $P \rightarrow Q$ and $\sim Q$) and chaining (deducing $P \rightarrow R$ from $P \rightarrow Q$ and $Q \rightarrow R$).

Consider the following example from the propositional calculus. Given two clauses, P and Q, which have already been transformed into CNF, where

$P = \{P_1, ..., P_i, ..., P_m\}$
$Q = \{Q_1, ..., Q_j, ..., Q_n\}$

and $P_i = \sim Q_j$ for $1 \leq i \leq m$, $1 \leq j \leq n$; then a new clause, R, can be derived by merging P' and Q' where P' is P less P_i and Q' is Q less Q_j. R is called the 'resolvent' of the resolution step, and P and Q are its 'parent' clauses. We say that P and Q 'clash' on the pair of complementary literals $\{P_i, \sim Q_j\}$, and the derivation of R corresponds to the drawing of a single inference.

Resolution is potentially powerful because it subsumes many other inference rules, as can be most clearly seen if we express more conventional rules in their conjunctive normal form. (From here on, I shall use lower case letters to stand for the literals inside clauses, and upper case letters to stand for whole clauses.)

Modus ponens:	$\{\sim p, q\}$ $\{p\}$	$\rightarrow \{q\}$
Modus tollens:	$\{\sim p, q\}$ $\{\sim q\}$	$\rightarrow \{\sim p\}$
Chaining:	$\{\sim p, q\}$ $\{\sim q, r\}$	$\rightarrow \{\sim p, r\}$
Merging:	$\{p, q\}$ $\{\sim p, q\}$	$\rightarrow \{q\}$
Reductio:	$\{\sim p\}$ $\{p\}$	$\rightarrow \{\}$

Notice that a contradiction gives the empty clause. This signifies that the set of (implicitly conjoined) clauses is inconsistent. Considered as a 'state description' of some world, we say that it is 'unsatisfiable'. The significance of this will become apparent shortly. For the moment, suffice it to say that the theorem prover at the heart of many AI programs is what is known as a 'resolution refutation system'. In order to prove that R follows from some set of propositions S, you assume $\sim P$ and then attempt to derive a contradiction from its conjunction with S. If you succeed in doing this, you are justified in asserting P, otherwise you aren't. If you fail, then it's important to realize that you haven't proved $\sim P$. You've simply failed to prove P.

Resolution is a rule of inference that allows you to derive new wffs from old. However, the logistic system described so far doesn't tell you how to do proofs. Theorem proving has its strategic as well as its systemic aspects.

Consider the following example:

Let $P = \{p\}$ be 'Fido is hungry'
Let $Q = \{\sim p, q\}$ be 'If Fido is hungry, he barks'

$R = \{q\}$, 'Fido barks', is a valid inference from the set of clauses $S = \{P, Q\}$, because P and Q clash on the pair of complementary literals $\{p, \sim p\}$. We say that S 'logically implies' R, and can therefore be added to S to form a new set $S' = \{P, Q, R\}$.

Many proofs will require more than one inference step, of course. For example, let S be $\{P_1, P_2, P_3\}$ where

$P_1 = \{p\}$ meaning 'Fido is hungry'
$P_2 = \{\sim p, q\}$ meaning 'If Fido is hungry, he barks'
$P_3 = \{\sim q, r\}$ meaning 'If Fido barks, John is angry'.

If we want to show that S logically implies $R = \{r\}$, 'John is angry', then we require two steps of resolution:

$P_1, P_2 \rightarrow \{q\}$
$\{q\}\ P_3 \rightarrow R$

Notice that in the first step we used a two clauses from the original S, but that in the second step we used a resolvent that we had added to S, producing $S' = \{P_1, P_2, P_3, \{q\}\}$, in order to complete the proof. Notice also, that we could have done the proof a different way, e.g.

$P_2, P_3 \rightarrow \{\sim p, r\}$
$P_1, \{\sim p, r\} \rightarrow R$

which results in a different resolvent being added to S to produce $S' = \{P_1, P_2, P_3, \{\sim p, r\}\}$. There is nothing in the logic which tells us which clauses we ought to select for clashing; it simply tells us which we may clash.

A number of problems arise in connection with this:

- If S is very large to begin with, and the proof we are attempting is long, it is conceivable that there might be many ways to prove our theorem, and that some will produce shorter proofs than others. Obviously, we would prefer the shorter proofs, if we can get them.

- S may support all kinds of inferences which have nothing to do with the proof of R. Yet how can we know in advance which inferences will lead to R?

- The whole process has a built-in potential for combinatorial explosion. S grows with each inference step, giving us more and more options. Some of these options might lead to circularity. For example, consider the following chain of inferences:

$$\{p\}\ \{\sim p, q\} \rightarrow \{q\}$$
$$\{q\}\ \{\sim q, p\} \rightarrow \{p\}$$
$$\{p\}\ \{\sim p, q\} \rightarrow \{q\} \ \ldots$$

The pattern of reasoning we have followed so far is usually referred to as forward reasoning. That is to say, you start from what you know and reason in the direction of what you are trying to prove (you hope). One way of tackling some of the problems listed above is to reason backward from the goal towards the evidence you need.

Suppose you want to derive $\{q\}$ from some set of clauses $S = \{..., \{\sim p, q\}, ..., \{p\}, ...\}$. It seems sensible to comb the set looking for clauses that have q as a literal, and then try and resolve the other literals away (if there are any). However $\{q\}$ doesn't clash with, for example, $\{\sim p, q\}$, since the pair $\{q, q\}$ aren't complementary.

First add the negation of what you are trying to prove, $\sim R$, to S, and then try and show that $S' = S + \sim R$ is unsatisfiable. Assuming that S was consistent in the first place, if S' is inconsistent it must be because S logically implies R. Let's consider this in more detail.

First negate the goal, e.g. turn $\{q\}$ into $\{\sim q\}$. Then attempt to resolve $\{\sim q\}$ with another clause in S'. There are only three possibilities. Either there is no clause containing q in S, in which case the proof fails; or S contains $\{q\}$, in which case the proof is immediate; or S contains a clause $\{..., q, ...\}$ that resolves with $\{\sim q\}$ to generate $\{...\}$, which contains one or more literals all of which need to be resolved away if we are to demonstrate the contradiction. These remaining literals can be thought of as subgoals that need to be solved if we are to solve our main goal, $\{q\}$. An example will make this clearer.

$P_1 = \{p\}$ meaning 'Fido is hungry'
$P_2 = \{\sim p, q\}$ meaning 'If Fido is hungry, he barks'
$P_3 = \{\sim q, r\}$ meaning 'If Fido barks, John is angry'
Goal = $\{r\}$

The proof is as follows.

$$\{\sim r\}\ \{\sim q, r\} \rightarrow \{\sim q\}$$
$$\{\sim q\}\ \{\sim p, q\} \rightarrow \{\sim p\}$$
$$\{\sim p\}\ \{p\} \rightarrow \{\}$$

This method of proving theorems is called 'resolution refutation', because it uses the resolution rule of inference, but adopts a refutation strategy. The use of resolution in backward reasoning is characteristic of the *modus tollens* of natural deduction systems, just as its use in forward reasoning is characteristic of *modus ponens*.

The main advantage is that reasoning backward from what you are trying to prove serves to focus the search for a solution, since inferences drawn are at least potentially relevant to the goal. Also, seeing the production of resolvents as the generation of subgoals is intuitively satisfying. However, it doesn't solve all the problems noted above. For example, it doesn't guarantee that you will find shorter proofs rather than longer ones. Neither does it abolish the combinatorial explosion inherent in the proof-generation process, although the 'attention-focusing' effect of goal-directed reasoning obviously prevents totally irrelevant inferences from being generated and added to the set of clauses.

5.2.3 The resolution principle and the predicate calculus

Like expressions in propositional calculus, predicate calculus expressions can be put into normal form, although we need to extend the rules of syntactic transformation. The sequence of rule applications is now as follows. For any expression, E:

1. Eliminate biconditionals and then conditionals.

2. Drive negation in.

3. Standardize variables apart. For example, if E is $(x)(F(x))$ & $(x)(G(x))$, it is sensible to give variables bound in the scope of different occurrences of quantifiers different names. Otherwise, when the quantifiers are eliminated, logically distinct variables might end up with the same name.

4. Eliminate existential quantifiers. Existential variables which occur outside of the scope of any universal quantifier can be replaced by Skolem constants (i.e. arbitrary names), while existential variables which occur inside the scope of one or more universal quantifiers must be replaced by Skolem functions, whose arguments are the universally bound variables within whose scope the existential occurs. A Skolem function is just an arbitrary function name that says 'the value of this variable is some function of the values assigned to the universal variables in whose scope it lies'.

5. Convert to prenex form. The remaining quantifiers (all of them universal) should now be moved to the 'front' of the expression, so that E is now a list of universally quantified variables followed by a 'matrix' in which no quantifiers occur.

6. Distribute disjunction over conjunction.

7. Drop the universal quantifiers. All free variables are now implicitly universally quantified variables. The existentials are either constants or functions of universal variables.

8. Drop the conjunction signs, as before, leaving a set of clauses.

9. Rename variables again, so that the same variable does not appear in different clauses.

The basic pattern-matching operation in resolution theorem-proving is called 'unification'. When matching complementary literals, we look for a substitution of terms for variables that makes two expressions identical. Let the early letters in the alphabet signify names and the later letters signify variables. Then

$F(x, a)$ and $F(b, y)$ have unifier: $\{b/x, a/y\}$

It is useful to derive the most general unifier, g, which has the property that, for any other unifier, s, there exists a substitution, s', which, when applied to the substitution instance derived from s, produces the substitution instance derived from g. An algorithm for this can be found in Nilsson (1982, pages 142–3).

Clauses which contain no variables, often called 'ground clauses', can be resolved as before. In order to resolve two non-ground clauses, you must first find a unifier for the complementary literals, then do the clash and then instantiate the resolvent with the unifier. For example,

$\{F(a, x), G(b, x, y)\}$

and

$\{\sim F(z, c), H(z)\}$

have unifier $\{a/z, c/x\}$ and generate the resolvent

$\{G(b, c, y), H(a)\}$.

Figure 5.1 is an example of resolution in predicate calculus using a forward-reasoning strategy. Given the following premises:

$\{dog(Fido)\}$	'Fido is a dog'
$\{\sim dog(x), \sim hungry(x), barks(x)\}$	'Every hungry dog barks'
$\{hungry(Fido)\}$	'Fido is hungry'

it can be seen that $\{barks(Fido)\}$ is a valid inference, because it can be derived from the axioms by two steps of resolution. Expressions on the same line resolve on complementary literals, generating a resolvent on the next line, labelled by the appropriate substitution.

Resolution refutation, using backward reasoning, is analogous to that for the propositional calculus, and is illustrated in Figure 5.2.

Resolution refutation is a complete theorem-proving strategy. That is to say, if any well-formed formula is a theorem of the predicate calculus, you can prove it by this method. However, the method is not a decision procedure for predicate calculus as truth tables were for propositional calculus. This is because it is not guaranteed to terminate on non-theorems. There is no decision procedure for predicate calculus, as was shown by Goedel (1931).

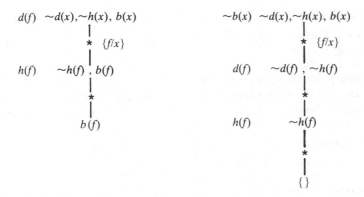

Figure 5.1 Forward reasoning   **Figure 5.2** Backward reasoning
with resolution.   with resolution.

It was suggested earlier that additional strategies are required to help resolution refutation deal with combinatorial explosion. Here is a brief survey of some of the main methods, together with their advantages and disadvantages.

- Breadth-first search. Compute all the first-level resolvents, then all second level, and so on. This strategy is complete, but grossly inefficient.

- Set of support strategy. At least one parent of every resolvent must be a descendant of the goal. This strategy is both complete and usually better than the above.

- Unit preference strategy. Use unit clauses as parents whenever possible. They generate resolvents with fewer literals, and therefore help the search focus upon the empty clause.

- Linear input form. Every resolvent has a parent in the base set. This strategy is not complete for the full clausal form of logic, but simple, efficient, and complete for the Horn clause subset. This is the strategy used by the logic programming language PROLOG.

A major focus of interest in logic programming is the control of deduction. There are a number of different strategies associated with resolution refutation systems, to do with the order in which steps of inference are performed, and these raise problems analogous to conflict resolution in production systems. Another important research area is that of developing techniques for the efficient implementation of interpreters for such languages.

5.3 Logic for knowledge-based systems

It is quite easy to emulate a backward-chaining production system in PROLOG. However, it is also possible to write a simple interpreter for forward chaining without very much effort. Either way, the ground literals function as the working memory, while the non-ground clauses function as rules. Modification of working memory is achieved by 'assert' and 'retract' operations. It is less easy to mimic the local flow of control associated with frame systems, although we shall see some examples of how this effect can be achieved in Chapter 11 (on MECHO). There are also ways of handling defaults and exceptions, although these take you somewhat outside the standard logic.

Logic programming languages give the knowledge engineer facilities for quantification and pattern matching which are generally more powerful than those afforded by production rule interpreters and semantic nets. Although there certainly exist rule and net systems which offer the power of first-order logic, such capabilities are usually purchased at the price of greatly complicating the original formalism. However, the power of logic-based systems is not purchased without price: theorem proving with full unification is computationally expensive in terms of both memory and CPU. For this reason, it was thought that resolution refutation was infeasible as a computational device for reasoning about problems of realistic complexity. Today, improvements in both the theory and practice of logic programming hold out more hope for the expert systems architect, although the current state of the art still leaves something to be desired.

It should also be pointed out that a purely logic-based approach is perhaps less tried and tested as a methodology for the construction of large-scale systems, when compared with frames and production systems. Possible problems include the specification of control, the principled use of 'side-effects' (i.e. destructive modifications of data structure), and the management of the interaction with the user. The lesson to be learned from MECHO is that applying logic to some knowledge-rich domain is a non-trivial enterprise.

5.4   Summary of the three formalisms

The three formalisms outlined in Chapters 3–5 do not constitute mutually exclusive choices with regard to the organization and implementation of expert systems. For example, a number of systems combine production rules with either semantic nets or frames. Also, relationships do exist between the syntax and semantics of the formalisms, and exemplars are sufficiently diverse to resist easy generalizations.

Having said that, here are some easy generalizations.

5.4.1   The pros and cons of production rules

Production systems typically do forward chaining, i.e. matching data in working memory against the left-hand sides of rules and then executing the right-hand sides. However, a more goal-driven effect can be achieved by having task statements in working memory and making the first condition of each rule a test for the current task. This 'layers' the rule set according to the particular task in hand, so that when one task is done, the right-hand side of the rule that concludes the task will usually set up the next task, and so on.

The working memory can be partitioned too, so that different kinds of rules look at different parts of the data structure. Programs which consist of large production rules representing different knowledge sources which look at different partitions are said to have a 'blackboard' architecture. This is because the different knowledge sources only communicate with each other by leaving messages in the appropriate partitions ('pigeon hole' might have been a better metaphor).

Most production rule interpreters do not support backtracking, since modifications to data structure are destructive, making it difficult to return to an earlier state of the computation. This is very efficient – it obviously saves space to surgically alter the representation of working memory at the end of each recognize-act cycle instead of stacking old states. Control mechanisms are global and context-free. This has simplicity on its side, but there are times when it is both inefficient and restrictive.

5.4.2 The pros and cons of structured objects

Frames are a good implementation device for exploiting inherent structure in rules and data. They also lend themselves to model-fitting approaches, e.g. looking for a best match between data and some hypothesis. Context-dependent interpretation and local flow of control can be very useful for certain applications.

Like production systems, frame systems do not usually support backtracking, and for the same reason (destructive modification of data structure). However, the whole idea of most of these systems is that the records contain enough information for the interpreter to be able to make sensible decisions about what to do next that will not normally need to be revoked. However, some systems do allow for a kind of iterative refinement, i.e. alternative hypotheses are processed in successive stages using different strategies until one of them wins.

Frames offer mechanisms for dealing with things like exceptions and defaults which are not easy to handle in standard logic. However, they are often criticized precisely because of this, as the cancellation and alteration of inherited properties makes it difficult to properly define anything in terms of anything else. Many people are unhappy with frame- and object-based systems because they seem to depart from logic and because their flexibility in matters of context and control can make their behaviour both hard to predict and difficult to understand.

It can be argued that this kind of complexity is the price you pay for a formalism that is both very general and potentially very powerful. However, the freedom that object-oriented programming gives you should be used wisely, resisting the temptation to create a new slot every time you come up against a new problem, and then filling it with some special piece of code that solves the problem in a less than principled way. Networks of communicating objects must be carefully designed, and their communication protocols strictly adhered to, if their behaviour is to be coherent and controlled.

5.4.3   The pros and cons of predicate logic

You get backtracking and pattern matching for free in a logic programming language like PROLOG. However, you may not want the backtracking as standard (in which case you have to disable it), and the pattern matching provided may not meet your precise requirements. For many applications, though, these facilities are welcome and useful.

It is not altogether trivial to structure rules and data according to your needs, although it can undoubtedly be done by an experienced programmer. The typical resolution refutation system deals with a set of propositions and uses only minimal indexing. Large non-deterministic programs really require some extra control features to be built into a special-purpose interpreter.

A logic program can act as a runnable program specification. That is to say, the program is designed by defining concepts and describing states of affairs in a declarative language which can then be given a procedural interpretation. However, it is a mistake to believe that programming in logic will automatically abolish all the pitfalls associated with frames and rules. Non-determinism is still there, and inconsistent or semantically anomalous descriptions of the world can still be composed. Thus logic does not solve the computational problems associated with knowledge representation and reasoning about control, and it is asking rather a lot to suppose that it should!

5.5   A word of warning

Some of the above is probably controversial. There is no widespread agreement in the literature as to the strengths and weaknesses of the various formalisms. Neither is there very much agreement as to which formalisms are best for which kinds of problems.

Many successful systems use more than one formalism, while others function perfectly well with one, and it's not altogether clear why this is the case. In Chapters 3, 4 and 5, I have treated these formalisms separately in order to try and clarify some of the basic issues. Chapters 10 and 12 deal in some detail with the question of mixed formalisms, and refine some of the above remarks, while Chapter 15 attempts a re-examination of the strengths and weaknesses of the various schemes with reference to the sample systems described in Chapters 6–11.

I admit that some the issues have been skated over. This is an introductory text on expert systems, and not an advanced text on knowledge representation, which is a topic worthy of study in its own right. Readers who wish to pursue this topic are recommended to consult the papers in Brachman and Levesque (1985).

5.6 Exercises

5.1 Here is a simple fault-finding problem that can be formulated in terms of deduction.

> 'If an engine misfires and the spark at the plugs is intermittent then the ignition leads are loose or the battery leads are loose. My engine misfires. The spark at my plugs is intermittent. My ignition leads are not loose.'

a) Translate these sentences into predicate logic.

b) Put the logical expressions derived above into conjunctive normal form.

c) Show that 'My battery leads are loose' follows as a logical consequence of this set of sentences using
  i) forward reasoning, and
  ii) backward reasoning.

5.2 Just to give you a taste of automatic theorem proving, we are now going to use the pattern matcher you built in Exercise 3.2 to drive a theorem prover for the proportional calculus, which uses what is known as Wang's algorithm. A brief explanation of this method is called for.

Well-formed formulae of propositional calculus, like

$$(p \ \& \ (p \rightarrow q)) \rightarrow q$$

can be considered as having left- and right-hand sides, rather like equations. In the above example, the split occurs around the dominant connective, the second occurrence of $\rightarrow$, which governs the other connectives occurring in the formula, including the other occurrence of $\rightarrow$ within parentheses. Thus

LHS: $p \ \& \ (p \rightarrow q)$
RHS: q

It is convenient to let the conjunction in the LHS be implicit, such that LHS will always be a list of premises, while RHS will always be a list of conclusions:

LHS: $(p \ (p \rightarrow q))$
RHS: (q)

Having split the formula in this way, we can apply the following syntactic rules of deduction. The object of applying these rules is to end up with an expression of the form

LHS: $p_1 \ldots p_i \ldots p_n$
RHS: $q_1 \ldots q_j \ldots q_m$

where the p_i are implicitly conjoined and the q_i are implicitly disjoined and $p_i = q_j$ for some i and j. If we end up with $p_i = q_j$ for some i, $1 \leqslant i \leqslant n$, and some j, $1 \leqslant j \leqslant m$, then we have proved the theorem. You will see how and why this works as we go through the algorithm.

First of all, expressions in the calculus are reduced to a particular syntactic subset, in which all conditionals and biconditionals have been eliminated in favour of disjunctions according to the following equivalences:

$p \rightarrow q$ is equivalent to $\sim p \vee q$, while
$p \equiv q$ is equivalent to $(p \rightarrow q) \mathbin{\&} (q \rightarrow p)$.

The next rule states that if a disjunction occurs on the LHS, we have to prove the theorem for both disjuncts. It's obvious when you think about it. If I say

$(p \vee q) \rightarrow r$

I am saying both that

$p \rightarrow r$

and

$q \rightarrow r$

i.e. that either of the premisses will do to demonstrate the conclusion. To show that this is in fact the case, you need to do two separate proofs. I shall say that the disjunct has been 'split'.

The situation with disjunctions on the RHS is somewhat different. You simply drop the disjunction and add both disjuncts to the list. Think about it; if you assert that

$p \rightarrow (q \vee r)$

you are saying that either

$p \rightarrow q$

or

$p \rightarrow r$

and you don't much care which. So you drop the disjunction and just add the disjuncts, hoping that one of them will eventually pair off with an expression on the other side, which gives you your proof. I shall say that such a disjunction has been 'spliced', i.e. it disappears, though its disjuncts remain.

Dealing with conjunctions now, the situation is somewhat reversed. If I say that

$(p \mathbin{\&} q) \rightarrow r$

I can drop the conjunction and just add the conjuncts to the LHS list, because its list elements are implictly conjoined, as noted earlier.

If, on the other hand, I say that

$$p \rightarrow q \ \& \ r$$

I am saying both that

$$p \rightarrow q$$

and that

$$p \rightarrow r$$

so I am committed to two separate proofs. Consequently, the RHS conjunct has to be split, and a proof done for each conjunct.

All we have to do now is deal with negation. The rule is that negations simply swap sides and change signs, rather like expressions in equations.

The easiest way to implement all this is using recursive rewrite rules. The top-level function, call it 'wang', should take a possible theorem as its input, split it into left- and right-hand sides and call a subsidiary function (say 'prove'), passing each side as a parameter, together with a stack for splitting conjunctions and disjunctions. In addition to the rules outlined above, all one needs is a terminating condition which states that the proof terminates with success if the left- and right-hand sides contain an identical expression.

Here is a sample output from my solution program on the three theorems listed below.

$$(q \rightarrow (p \rightarrow q))$$
$$(p \ (p \rightarrow q) \rightarrow q)$$
$$((p \rightarrow (p \rightarrow q)) \ p \rightarrow q)$$

The printout uses the following abbreviations to show which rule has fired.

A	means assumption
$\rightarrow$	means elimination of a conditional
vL	means a split disjunction on the left
vR	means a spliced disjunction on the right
nL	means a negation moved from left to right
nR	means a negation moved from right to left

A	$q \rightarrow (p \rightarrow q)$
$\rightarrow$	$q \rightarrow (\sim p \vee q)$
vR	$q \rightarrow \sim p \ q$

A	$p \ (p \rightarrow q) \rightarrow q$
$\rightarrow$	$p \ (\sim p \vee q) \rightarrow q$
vL	$\sim p \ p \rightarrow q$
nL	$p \rightarrow p \ q$
vR	$q \ p \rightarrow q$

A $(p \rightarrow (p \rightarrow q)) \, p \rightarrow q$

$\rightarrow$ $(\sim p \vee (p \rightarrow q)) \, p \rightarrow q$

∨L $\sim p \, p \rightarrow q$

∩L $p \rightarrow p \, q$

∨R $(p \rightarrow q) \, p \rightarrow q$

$\rightarrow$ $(\sim p \vee q) \, p \rightarrow q$

∨L $\sim p \, p \rightarrow q$

∩L $p \rightarrow p \, q$

∨R $q \, p \rightarrow q$

5.3 Kowalski once asserted that

'There is only one language suitable for representing information – whether declarative or procedural – and that is first-order predicate logic. There is only one intelligent way to process information – and that is by applying deductive inference methods.' (*SIGART Newsletter*, Special Issue on Knowledge Representation, No.70, February 1980).

a) Discuss this view in the light of Chapters 3 and 4, where alternatives to predicate logic are discussed.

b) Discuss this view again after reading Chapters 5–11, where expert systems employing a variety of knowledge representation schemes are described.

c) Read the papers by Furukawa *et al.* and Bobrow cited in Chapter 12. Is logic the answer to our knowledge engineering problems, or do we need multiple paradigms?

Chapter 6 MYCIN: Medical Diagnosis using Production Rules

The term 'medical computing' refers to the use of computer technology in the administration and practice of medicine. 'Computer-aided medical decision making' refers to any use of computers which contributes to the judgemental aspect of clinical practice. 'Medical expert systems' refers to the use of computers as advisors in the processes of diagnosis and treatment.

Problems for the medical profession include:

- enormous costs of modern methods;
- information explosion, both medical and managerial;
- geographic maldistribution of expertise and resources;
- increased demand on physician's time for quality care.

There is obviously a potential role for expert systems in providing diagnostic, prognostic, treatment planning and educational programs.

This chapter concentrates upon one particular expert system, MYCIN, describing its function, structure and run-time behaviour in a fair amount of detail. The idea of doing this is to illustrate certain ideas about representation and control, and specific techniques for implementing such ideas, without having to resort to abstractions and generalities. MYCIN is a good vehicle for teaching purposes because:

- it is typical of a broad class of consultation programs which perform diagnoses and offer advice;
- it satisfies to some extent the criteria of realistic complexity, fulfilling a need, high performance, reliability and usability that one associates with a successful expert system;
- it has given rise to a family of related programs which are either modelled on MYCIN, in that they use the same representational scheme and control structure applied to a different domain, or are complementary to MYCIN, in that they provide extra facilities which use MYCIN or which MYCIN can use.

6.1 Treating blood infections

An 'antimicrobial agent' is any drug designed to kill bacteria or arrest their growth. The term 'antibiotic' is often used as a synonym, although strictly

93

speaking this refers to any drug isolated as a naturally occurring product of bacteria or fungi, e.g. penicillin from penicillin mould. Some antibiotics are too toxic for therapeutic purposes, and there is no single agent effective against all bacteria.

The selection of therapy for bacterial infection is a four-part decision process:

- deciding if the patient has a significant infection;
- determining the (possible) organism(s) involved;
- selecting a set of drugs that might be appropriate;
- choosing the most appropriate drug or combination of drugs.

This task is by no means straightforward. The diagnosis of infection is complicated by the fact that the human body is normally populated by bacteria, e.g. skin and throat. Samples from normally sterile sites, e.g. blood and cerebrospinal fluid, may be contaminated subsequently in the laboratory. Initial diagnosis is therefore based on clinical criteria, e.g. fever and pain.

Samples taken from the site of infection are sent to a microbiology laboratory for culture, i.e. an attempt to grow organisms from the sample in a suitable medium. Early evidence of growth may allow a report of the morphological or staining characteristics of the organism. However, complete testing and definite identification can take 24–48 hours or longer.

Even if an organism is identified, its range of antimicrobial sensitivities may be unknown or uncertain. For example, *Pseudomonas* is normally sensitive to gentamycin, but resistant strains are emerging. Sensitivity data are typically not available until one or two days after a culture is obtained.

The physician must therefore select a drug based on

- the possible identities of the organism;
- the likely effectiveness of antimicrobial agents against this range of possibilities.

The effect of a drug on a particular patient will depend upon additional factors, such as age, sex and kidney status. The route of administration, e.g. oral, intravenous, or intramuscular, may also be dependent upon special considerations. Changes in dosage, or even changes in the drug(s) being administered, may become necessary as further information on the culture and the clinical status of the patient become available.

There is a good deal of evidence to suggest that help is needed with antimicrobial selection. Antibiotics date from the 1930s, with penicillin being discovered in 1943. As early as the 1950s, it became clear that they were being misused, e.g. practitioners were prescribing them for respiratory infections, whether viral or bacterial.

Despite attempts to educate doctors, the problem remains; few seem to go through the methodical decision process outlined above. Over-prescription in the US during 1972 was estimated at a factor of 10–20, so the annual cost to patients and hospitals is enormous. Furthermore, overprescription can result in the development of resistant strains of bacteria.

The purpose of MYCIN is to assist a physician who is not an expert in the field of antibiotics with the diagnosis and treatment of blood infections. Work on MYCIN began in 1972 as a collaboration between the medical and AI communities at Stanford. The most complete single account of this work is Shortliffe (1976).

There have been a number of extensions, revisions and abstractions of MYCIN since 1976, but the basic version has three components:

1. A consultation system which asks questions, draws conclusions and gives advice.

2. An explanation system which answers questions and justifies advice.

3. A rule acquisition system for adding new rules and changing existing ones.

6.2   The consultation system

The consultation system is that part of the program which generates a set of hypotheses with respect to the offending organisms, and then makes therapy recommendations based on these hypotheses. Note that the identity of the organisms does not have to be established with certainty for the recommendation of therapy to become feasible. MYCIN is often incorrectly described as a medical diagnosis program; it is really a program for treating blood infections.

The consultation system consists of a rule base, a set of static and dynamic data structures, and a control structure.

6.2.1   MYCIN's production rules

A simplified syntax for MYCIN's rules is given below. Terms in angle brackets denote descriptions of expressions, rather than actual expressions. : : = means 'is defined as', while | signifies disjunction. This grammar describes the way in which the rules are represented internally as LISP code. LISP is the high-level list-processing language in which MYCIN is implemented.

```
      <rule> ::= <premise> <action>
   <premise> ::= ($AND <condition> ... <condition>)
 <condition> ::= (<predicate> <context> <parameter> <value>)
                 | ($OR <condition> ... <condition>)
    <action> ::= <conclusion> | <instruction>
```

A rule is a premise-action pair, as described in Chapter 3. Premises are conjunctions of conditions, which may be disjunctions. Conditions are typically predications which evaluate to truth or falsehood with some degree of certainty. 'Certainty factors' are numbers associated with the data elements that match conditions, indicating the degree of belief or disbelief in the information represented.

Actions are either conclusions to be drawn with some appropriate degree of certainty, e.g. the identity of some organism, or an instruction to be carried out, e.g. compiling a list of therapies. Rules, as well as data, have a numerical weight, called a 'tally', associated with them. This number is meant to reflect confidence in the application of the rule, and the degree of confidence in the conclusion will be a function of both the tally of the rule and the combined certainties of the data matching the conditions of the rule.

The following is a typical MYCIN rule for inferring the class of an organism.

```
PREMISE: ($AND (SAME CNTXT GRAM GRAMNEG)
               (SAME CNTXT MORPH ROD)
               (SAME CNTXT AIR AEROBIC))
ACTION:  (CONCLUDE CNTXT CLASS ENTEROBACTERIACEAE TALLY .8)
```

However, the user never sees the LISP code. Prior to being displayed at the terminal, rules are translated into a kind of English. Thus the rule given above would appear as:

```
IF   1) the stain of the organism is gramneg, and
     2) the morphology of the organism is rod, and
     3) the aerobicity of the organism is aerobic
THEN there is strongly suggestive evidence (.8) that the
     class of the organism is enterobacteriaceae.
```

The only thing to notice about the LISP code at this stage is that it is highly uniform and stylized. This fixed rule format makes the translation relatively easy, and it also makes it easy for the program to examine its own rules. This is in keeping with LISP's tradition of treating programs as data. Because LISP programs are just list structures, they can be processed by the same primitive functions as those used to manipulate data. Imagine how comparatively difficult it would be to write a PASCAL program to examine and manipulate its own source code.

6.2.2 MYCIN's data structures

There are two main kinds of data structure used by the consultation system: static and dynamic.

Static data structures

The static structure stores definitional information which is kept separate from the inferential knowledge embodied in the rules, in the form of:

- simple lists, e.g. the ORGANISMS and STERILESITES lists, which enumerate all the organisms and sterile sites known to the system;
- knowledge tables, which contain records of certain clinical parameters and the values they take under various circumstances, e.g. the gramstain, morphology and aerobicity of every bacterial genus known to the system;

- a classification system for clinical parameters according to the context in which they apply, e.g. whether they are attributes of patients, cultures or organisms.

Much of the medical knowledge not contained in the rules resides in the properties associated with the 65 clinical parameters known to MYCIN. These parameters can be classified in various ways. The system distinguishes between three broad semantic types: yes/no, single-valued and multi-valued.

Yes/no parameters deal with attributes which an object either possesses or does not, e.g. the FEBRILE attribute of patients. Questions to the user which seek the value of such a parameter expect either a yes or a no for an answer.

Single-valued parameters deal with attributes which have a value which excludes all other values in the range, e.g. the IDENT attribute of organisms. If an organism has SALMONELLA as the value of its identity attribute, then it can't also have ARIZONA as that value.

Multi-valued parameters deal with attributes which can have more than one value, e.g. the INFECT attribute of patients. Clearly a patient can be suffering from more than one infection.

Parameters are assigned various properties by the system for various purposes; the main ones either help to monitor the interaction with the user, or help to guide the application of rules.

For example, each parameter has the following properties to facilitate interaction with the user:

- an EXPECT property which indicates the range of possible values for the attribute;

- a PROMPT property which gives an English sentence used by MYCIN when requesting the value of the parameter;

- a LABDATA property which indicates whether or not the parameter is a piece of primitive data which may be known with certainty;

- a TRANS property used for translating the parameter into its English representation.

In addition, there are two important properties which serve to relate clinical parameters to the rules which reference them:

- a LOOKAHEAD property which lists all the rules that mention the parameter in their premise;

- an UPDATED-BY property which lists all the rules which reference the parameter in their action, allowing a conclusion to be drawn about the value of that parameter.

Such properties are clearly useful in deciding which rules to apply, given that the system's current goal is to find out about a particular parameter.

Dynamic data structures

Dynamic data is held in a 'context tree', which serves to organize the information relating to a particular patient. Advice will obviously be based upon the cultures, organisms, prior operations and treatments associated with a patient, as well as personal characteristics like age and sex, and each of these can be considered as a different context. The tree serves to structure the clinical problem, and relate one context to another.

The relationship between rules in the knowledge base and the context tree is as follows. Rules are categorized according to the context types they deal with, e.g. some apply to organisms, some to cultures, some to treatments, and so on. Apart from this, the rules are not organized into any kind of decision tree or inference network.

The CNTXT symbol appearing in rules like the one shown above is really a variable which gets instantiated by the name MYCIN gives to the context node it is currently looking at, e.g. ORGANISM-1. So the premise evaluated in the context of ORGANISM-1 would be instantiated to

```
($AND (SAME ORGANISM-1 GRAM GRAMNEG)
      (SAME ORGANISM-1 MORPH ROD)
      (SAME ORGANISM-1 AIR AEROBIC))
```

before MYCIN attempted to find out if the conditions were true. Information about ORGANISM-1 is attached to the corresponding node in the context tree and stored in a kind of record structure. Suppose we have the following data:

```
ORGANISM-1
  GRAM  = (GRAMNEG 1.0)
  MORPH = (ROD .8) (COCCUS .2)
  AIR   = (AEROBIC .6) (FACUL .4)
```

with the following meaning:

the gram stain of ORGANISM-1 is definitely gram negative;
the morphology of ORGANISM-1 is rod with a certainty of .8 and
    coccus with a certainty of .2;
the aerobicity of ORGANISM-1 is aerobic with a certainty of .6 and
    facultative with a certainty of .4.

Thus (SAME ORGANISM-1 GRAM GRAMNEG) evaluates to 1.0, indicating certainty that this condition is true. The other two conditions evaluate to 0.8 and 0.6 respectively. $AND then takes the minimum value of these certainties, so that the value for the conjunction becomes 0.6; $OR would take the maximum value.

This use of min and max has an intuitive appeal: our certainty about P_1 & ... & P_n is as great as our certainty about the most doubtful proposition, while our certainty about P_1 ∨ ... ∨ P_n is as great as our certainty about the most certain proposition.

Any value greater than or equal to 0.2 is sufficient for the rule application to succeed. In this case, the following conclusion is drawn:

```
(CONCLUDE ORGANISM-1 CLASS ENTEROBACTERIACEAE .6 .8)
```

Notice that TALLY has been set to the CF for the premise of the rule, 0.6. This value is used to compute a CF for the conclusion of the action according to the simple formula:

$$CF<action> = CF<premise> * CF<rule>$$

so we conclude that ORGANISM-1 is an enterobacteriaceae with a certainty of 0.48.

6.2.3 MYCIN's control structure

The consultation system is essentially a backward-chaining production system. However, there are other control features in MYCIN which modify this basic behaviour. The mechanics of this will become apparent in the following sections.

Backward chaining

MYCIN has a top-level goal rule which defines the whole task of the consultation system:

> IF   there is an organism which requires therapy, and consideration has been given to the possibility of additional organisms requiring therapy
>
> THEN   compile a list of possible therapies, and determine the best therapy in this list.

A consultation session follows a simple two-step procedure:

1. Create the patient context as the top node in the context tree.

2. Attempt to apply the goal rule to this patient context.

The goal rule is therefore a PATRULE; it applies to the 'patient' context. Applying the rule involves evaluating its premise, which involves finding out if there is an organism which requires therapy. In order to find this out, it must first find out if there is indeed an organism present which is associated with a significant disease. This information can either be obtained from the user direct, or via some chain of inference based on symptoms and laboratory data provided by the user. Hence the system reasons backward from a problem statement, i.e. 'are there organisms which require therapy?' to relevant facts which give the values of clinical parameters, via rules which relate conclusions to evidence in the context of cultures and organisms, known as CULRULES and ORGRULES.

The consultation is essentially a search through a goal tree. The top goal at the root of the tree is the action part of the goal rule, i.e. the recommendation of a drug therapy. Subgoals further down the tree include determining the organism involved and seeing if it is significant. Many of these subgoals have subgoals of their own, such as finding out the stain properties and morphology of an organism. The leaves of the tree are fact goals, such as laboratory data, which cannot be deduced.

As noted in Chapter 3, this is called a backward-chaining control structure, since the program reasons backward from what it wants to prove towards the facts that it needs, rather than reasoning forward from the facts that it possesses towards the goal.

The system can ask the user for items of data as and when they are needed for the evaluation of a condition in the current rule. If the required information is not forthcoming, there may be rules which apply to the clinical parameter in question and which can be invoked in search of its value. If there are no such rules, then the current rule application will fail. The system knows which parameters it can ask about, because they have the LABDATA property mentioned above. Hence question selection and rule invocation alternate, with the associated procedures calling each other in a hidden recursion.

The two procedures involved are MONITOR and FINDOUT.

- MONITOR attempts to evaluate the premise of the current rule, condition by condition. If any of the conditions is false, or indeterminate due to lack of information, the rule is rejected, and the next rule on the list of applicable rules pending in the current context is tried. The rule application succeeds when all of the conditions in the premise are deemed to be true, and the conclusion of the rule is added to the record of the current consultation.

- FINDOUT gathers the information that will count for or against a particular condition in the premise of the rule under consideration. If the information required is laboratory data which the user can supply, then control returns to MONITOR and the next condition is tried. Otherwise, if there are rules which can be used to evaluate the condition, by virtue of the fact that their actions reference the relevant clinical parameter, they are listed and applied in turn using MONITOR.

This control structure is quite simple as AI programs go; there are only a few deviations from standard depth-first search:

1. The subgoal set up is always a generalized form of the original goal. So, if the subgoal is to prove the proposition that the identity of the organism is *E. coli*, then the subgoal actually set up is to determine the identity of the organism. This initiates an exhaustive search on a given topic which collects all of the available evidence.

2. Every rule relevant to the goal is used, unless one of them succeeds with certainty. This is because of the inexact character of many of the inferences drawn, necessitating the collection of evidence concerning more than one hypothesis. If the evidence about a hypothesis falls between -0.2 and $+0.2$, it is regarded as inconclusive, and the answer is treated as unknown.

3. The control structure encourages the program to ask for the values of parameters flagged as LABDATA before it attempts to deduce them.

While backward chaining is going on, the context tree and the consultation record are being elaborated. Nodes are added to the context tree as they are required by applicable rules which reference contexts not yet created. The consultation record, on the other hand, is updated after rule applications, and it keeps track of how the values of clinical parameters were obtained and why particular questions were asked.

The selection of therapy takes place after this diagnostic process has run its course. It consists of two phases: selecting candidate drugs, and then choosing a preferred drug, or combination of drugs, from this list.

The special goal rule given above does not lead to a conclusion, but instigates actions, assuming that the conditions in the premise are satisfied. At this point, MYCIN's THERULES come into play: therapy rules for selecting drug treatments. These are never invoked under the regular control structure by MONITOR and FINDOUT, because they do not apply directly to any of the clinical parameters. They contain sensitivities information for the various organisms known to the system. A sample rule is given in Figure 6.1.

IF	the identity of the organism is *Pseudomonas*	
THEN	I recommend therapy from among the following drugs:	
	1 – COLISTIN	(.98)
	2 – POLYMYXIN	(.96)
	3 – GENTAMICIN	(.96)
	4 – CARBENICILLIN	(.65)
	5 – SULFISOXAZOLE	(.64)

Figure 6.1   A MYCIN therapy rule.

The numbers associated with each drug are the probabilities that a *Pseudomonas* will be sensitive to the indicated drug.

The preferred drug is selected from the list according to criteria which attempt to screen for contra-indications of the drug and minimize the number of drugs administered, in addition to maximizing sensitivity.

The user can go on asking for alternative therapies until MYCIN runs out of options. When each set of recommendations is rejected, the program is simply run again with the recommended drugs removed from consideration.

Meta-rules, antecedent rules and the PREVIEW mechanism

MYCIN had about 200 such rules in its rule set at the time of the 1976 report. The rules are indexed by the clinical parameters appearing in their action parts. Thus it is easy to retrieve for consideration all of the rules which might apply in determining the value of a given parameter.

Since 1976, MYCIN has acquired more rules, and different kinds of rules. For example, there are now meta-rules which, instead of applying to subgoals, apply to the rules which apply to subgoals. Given that we wish to achieve subgoal *G*, say finding the identity of an organism, there may be as many as 30 rules which could apply. Meta-rules are used to prune and order the list of rules applicable at any one point. These were found to be necessary if the extra domain knowledge was to be applied efficiently and effectively.

Here is a sample pruning rule for MYCIN, taken from Buchanan and Shortliffe (1984, Chapter 28):

METARULE001
IF   1) the culture was not obtained from a sterile source, and
      2) there are rules which mention in their premise a previous organism, which may be the same as the current organism
THEN   it is definite (1.0) that each of them is not going to be useful.

It states that when trying to identify organisms from a non-sterile site, rules which base their identification on other organisms found at that site are not going to be very useful.

Other meta-rules are there to reorder relevant domain rules, and they encode strategic knowledge of the kind 'try this before trying that'. For example:

METARULE002
IF   1) the infection is a pelvic abscess, and
      2) there are rules which mention in their premise entero-bacteriaceae, and
      3) there are rules which mention in their premise gram-positive rods,
THEN   there is suggestive evidence (0.4) that the former should be done before the latter.

Note that meta-rules also admit uncertainty, since their conclusions may be qualified by a certainty factor that is less than 1.

Finally, here is an example of a very general meta-rule, of the kind that might be termed 'domain-free', since it refers to general problem solving strategy, rather than domain-specific medical knowledge.

METARULE003
IF   1) there are rules which do not mention the current goal in their premise, and
      2) there are rules which mention the current goal in their premise
THEN   it is definite (1.0) that the former should be done before the latter.

There are also some antecedent-style rules to perform forward reasoning, i.e. rules which are triggered when their conditions match data, instead of when their conclusions match current goals. These are used when a conclusion has been drawn which allows other common sense inferences to be made. They exist solely in the interests of efficiency, and do not significantly alter MYCIN's fundamental style of reasoning backward from its main goal.

An example of an antecedent rule would be one which enabled the system to infer that male patients are unlikely to be pregnant, along the lines of

IF   sex of patient is male
THEN pregnancy of patient is no.

The point of such a rule is to stop the program from asking stupid questions which would both waste time and decrease the user's confidence in the system. Antecedent rules are often used in conjunction with the PREVIEW mechanism, which checks all the clauses in the premise of a rule to see if any are known to be false before starting to backward chain on the first clause. Thus, if the rule interpreter is considering the application of a rule which contains a test for pregnancy anywhere in the premise, the combination of antecedent rules and PREVIEW will prevent any other clauses in the rule being pursued unnecessarily for male patients.

Certainty factors

Each rule has an associated 'certainty factor' (CF) in the range $[-1, +1]$. This reflects a degree of confidence in the conclusion drawn, given the evidence of the premises. A positive CF indicates a degree of belief, while a negative CF suggests a degree of disbelief.

In fact, MYCIN collects evidence both for and against hypotheses. Evidence for a hypothesis increases the measure of belief (MB) associated with it, while evidence against increases the measure of disbelief (MD), rather than decreasing the measure of belief. The certainty factor itself is calculated by taking the difference between the measure of belief and the measure of disbelief, thus:

$$CF(h,e) = MB(h,e) - MD(h,e)$$

where $MB(h,e)$ is the measure of increased belief in hypothesis, h, based on evidence e, while $MD(h,e)$ is the measure of increased disbelief in hypothesis, h, based on evidence, e.

MB and MD both range between 0 and 1, and so CF will necessarily have an upper bound of 1, in the case where h is certainly known to be true, and a lower bound of -1, in the case where h is certainly known to be false. In the case where $CF(h,e) = 0$, the evidence neither confirms nor disconfirms the hypothesis. Obviously, this is either because there is no evidence either way, i.e. $MB = MD = 0$, or because the conflicting evidence is finely balanced with $MB = MD \neq 0$.

A more complete discussion of inexact reasoning can be found in Chapter 15. Suffice it to say that the use of certainty factors in MYCIN has aroused some controversy. Their principal function is to allow the interpreter to rank hypotheses. They should not be confused with probabilities, in that there is no requirement for the certainty factors associated with a space of alternatives to sum to 1. There are occasions in which ranking by certainty factors does not result in the same ordering as ranking by conditional probability.

6.3 The explanation system

This part of the program is automatically invoked at the end of a consultation, and may also be accessed during the consultation itself. It allows the user to interrogate the system about the consultation, as well as ask more general questions.

MYCIN's question-answering facility is based upon its ability to:

- display the rule being invoked at any point in the consultation;
- record rule invocations and associate them with specific events, such as questions asked and conclusions drawn;
- use the rule indexing to retrieve particular rules in answer to queries.

As mentioned earlier, the consultation involves a search through a tree of goals. Consequently, inquiries during a consultation fall into two types: those that ask WHY a particular question was put, and those that ask HOW a particular conclusion was reached, or can be reached. To answer a WHY question, one must look up the tree to see what higher goals the system is trying to achieve. To answer a HOW question, one must look down the tree to see what subgoals have to be satisfied to achieve the current goal. Thus the explanation process can be considered as a kind of tree traversal, and is thereby reduced to a search problem.

6.3.1 Questions about the consultation

As mentioned above, MYCIN maintains a record of the decisions it makes. It uses this record to explain and justify its decisions in response to questions like 'What made you think that ORGANISM-1 might be a *Proteus*?'. In reply, MYCIN cites the rules that it applied, its degree of certainty in that decision, and the last question asked.

Informational questions merely request the current value of some clinical parameter from the dynamic database, e.g. 'What is the final decision regarding the identity of ORGANISM-1?'.

Explanatory questions ask the system to explain why a particular question was asked at a particular time. The system replies by saying which clinical parameter it was trying to find a value for, and which rule it was trying to execute.

6.3.2 General questions

These reference the rules without considering the state of the dynamic database. They inquire about the general medical knowledge encoded in the rules, rather than about how that knowledge has been applied to a particular patient. An example might be, 'what do you prescribe for *Pseudomonas* infections?'. The reply might be to cite the therapy rule listed in the previous section.

However, the user cannot access the static knowledge contained in simple lists and knowledge tables. Also the mechanisms for creating the therapy lists and choosing the preferred drug are complex LISP functions which the user cannot inspect, and probably would not understand if he could. Finally, the order in which rules are considered for application, and the order in which the conditions of premises are considered are not aspects of the system which the user is able to question.

We shall return to the issue of explanation at a later stage, when we consider more recent developments associated with MYCIN. For now, it is sufficient to note that WHY and HOW questions provide a neat and intuitively satisfying basis for finding out how a rule-based consultation program works. However, one must bear in mind that this approach does not cover every aspect of system function, and that a number of problems remain with regard to making explicit and accessible certain design decisions associated with the organization of knowledge in the actual implementation of the program.

6.4   The rule acquisition system

The 1976 version of MYCIN allows an expert to enter a new decision rule or change an existing rule. The user can enter the rules in the English format used for display purposes, and the program will translate them into the corresponding LISP representation. The internal book-keeping required by the static knowledge structures representing clinical parameters is also done by the program. So the number referencing a new rule will be added to the LOOKAHEAD list for all parameters mentioned in the premise. Similarly this number will be added to the UPDATED-BY list for all parameters mentioned in the action.

In his book, Shortliffe also discussed plans to provide more sophisticated facilities for checking the effects of adding a new rule to an existing rule set. For example, a new rule may introduce a contradiction into the set, or may subsume an existing rule, rendering it redundant, or be subsumed by an existing rule, thereby being redundant itself. When a knowledge base contains hundreds of rules, it is not easy for the expert to anticipate the effects of adding one or more new rules.

These plans were largely realized in a system called TEIRESIAS, developed by Randall Davis, which is designed to help an expert debug and fill out the rule set of an existing expert system like MYCIN (see Davis and Lenat, 1980). It also uses generalizations about the structure of existing rules to generate expectations about what clinical parameters should be referenced by a particular kind of rule, and what the typical values for those parameters might be. TEIRESIAS is described in more detail in the next chapter.

6.5   Evaluation of MYCIN

As early as 1974, an initial study using the current version of MYCIN produced encouraging results. A panel of five experts in the diagnosis of infectious diseases approved 72% of MYCIN's recommendations on 15 real cases of bacteremia. The main problem was not the accuracy of the diagnosis, but a lack of rules for judging the severity of the illness.

In 1979, more formal studies of an improved system showed that MYCIN's performance compared favourably with that of experts on patients with bacteremia and meningitis. The program's final conclusions on ten real cases were compared with those of Stanford physicians, including the actual therapy administered. Eight other experts were then asked to rate the ten therapy recommendations on each of the cases and award a mark out of 80 for each set of recommendations, without knowing which, if any, came from a computer. The results are shown in Figure 6.2.

Ratings by 8 experts on 10 cases.
Perfect score = 80.

MYCIN	52	Actual therapy	46
Faculty-1	50	Faculty-4	44
Faculty-2	48	Resident	36
Inf dis fellow	48	Faculty-5	34
Faculty-3	46	Student	24

Unacceptable therapy = 0.
Equivalent or acceptable therapy = 1.

Figure 6.2   MYCIN's performance compared with human experts.

The differences between MYCIN's score and those of Stanford experts was not significant, but its score is as good as the experts and better than the non-expert physicians.

However, MYCIN is not currently used in wards for a number of reasons, including:

- its knowledge base is incomplete, since it does not cover anything like the full spectrum of infectious diseases;
- running it would require more computing power than most hospitals can afford.

Its running time is acceptable on large machines like DEC-10s and DEC-20s: a consultation might take a quarter of an hour at the terminal. In any case, the interactive nature of the program makes it largely input/output bound. Nevertheless, the language it is written in, INTERLISP, is slow and heavy on memory compared with conventional programming languages, and system performance could be expected to degrade quite rapidly as a function of the number of users in a timesharing environment.

Consequently, it is not really feasible to attempt an evaluation of the cost of a MYCIN consultation in the field. On the other hand, the cost of computing power is falling all the time, and powerful single-user machines are now available. If MYCIN is ever to find its way onto the wards, reimplementation on such a machine seems to be the main option.

Chapter 7 MYCIN Derivatives: EMYCIN, TEIRESIAS and NEOMYCIN

Work on, or related to, MYCIN has continued since the publication of Shortliffe's thesis. The system itself has acquired more rules and some additional features, and validation studies appear to vindicate the general approach. Its success attracted the attention of other researchers, who have tried to abstract general principles from the system for application to other domains, as well as attempting to improve various aspects of the original design.

In this section, we consider a number of new programs, all of which are related to MYCIN, or derived from it in some way. This study will serve to distinguish between those aspects of MYCIN's architecture which are in some sense 'essential' and those which are dispensible or more arbitrarily motivated, e.g. for reasons of efficiency or convenience. Also, proposed extensions to MYCIN, some of which have been implemented, provide a useful guide to the directions that expert systems research is taking in the 1980s.

7.1 EMYCIN as architecture and abstraction

Systems that help an expert develop a brand-new knowledge base are often called expert system 'shells', the idea being that the shell already provides facilities for defining data types and writing rules according to some set of conventions, and 'all' the user has to do is provide the particular data types and rules that codify the knowledge of his domain.

EMYCIN is a domain-independent framework for constructing and running consultation programs. It is 'Empty' MYCIN, or 'Essential' MYCIN, since it can be thought of as the MYCIN system minus its domain-specific medical knowledge. However, it is more than a mere abstraction of MYCIN, since it offers a number of software tools to help expert system architects build and debug large performance programs.

One innovation is an abbreviated rule language (ARL), which is neither LISP nor the subset of English (Doctorese) used by MYCIN, but an ALGOL-like notation which is easier to read than LISP and more concise than the English subset used by MYCIN.

An example of a rule from the SACON (structural analysis) system is given below:

IF   composition = (list of metals) and
        error < 5 and
        nd-stress > .5 and
        cycles > 10000
THEN   ss-stress = fatigue.

Like MYCIN, EMYCIN is basically a backward-chaining production system. However, it supports the antecedent rules of later versions of MYCIN, although it should be noted that these never cause questions to be asked, contexts to be created, or consequent rules to be applied. They are only chained forward when they conclude the value of a parameter with certainty.

There are three main facilities for monitoring the behaviour of the rule set:

1. EXPLAIN. After each consultation, a terse explanation is provided which tells the user how the conclusion was reached. Each rule that was activated is printed along with the cumulative certainty factor of its conclusion, the number of the last question asked, and the value of TALLY when the rule succeeded.

2. TEST. In this mode, the expert can compare the results of the current run of the program with stored correct results and explore the discrepancies. The question/answer facility can be used to ask why new values were concluded, and why correct ones weren't concluded.

3. REVIEW. The expert can review system conclusions about a stored library of cases. This helps him monitor the effects of alterations in the rule set, since the debugging effort may well introduce new bugs.

Batch runs between debugging sessions can be used to see if alterations to improve performance on some cases degrade performance on others. However, it should be stressed that there is no well-understood methodology for incrementally extending knowledge bases in this way, other than attempting to maintain a certain consistency among the way in which rules refer to particular parameters. In the next section, we consider some of the problems of knowledge acquisition and knowledge base development in the context of the TEIRESIAS system.

7.2 Knowledge acquisition in TEIRESIAS

TEIRESIAS (Davis, 1976) is a system devised to help with the development and maintenance of large knowledge bases.

It is clear that developing an expert system along the lines of MYCIN to cover the full spectrum of infectious diseases would require the addition of many hundreds of rules. The task of extending and improving such rule sets would be non-trivial, and so it is not surprising that researchers are now attempting to develop software tools for that purpose.

Maintenance, on the other hand, means responding to problems as they arise, or actively seeking them during tests. Typical bugs might be:

- gaps in the rule set, where possible combinations of conditions are not covered;
- overlapping rules which generate inconsistency or redundancy;
- rules which become outdated, due to new discoveries.

An intelligent system for this task should be able to apply both syntactic knowledge about the rule formalism and semantic knowledge about the domain of application to assign blame to particular rules and suggest modifications.

7.2.1 The transfer of expertise

An expert knows more about his field than he realizes, or can put into words. It is not very helpful to ask him general, open-ended questions like 'what do you know about blood infections?' in an attempt to uncover this knowledge. A better approach, adopted by TEIRESIAS, is to let him bring his expertise to bear upon some problem that will elicit the required knowledge.

An expert can use TEIRESIAS to communicate with an expert system like MYCIN, to find out what the performance program is doing and why. Given that the program is incomplete, and prone to error, one can then ask him the question 'What do you know that the program doesn't know?'. Faced with a specific problem to solve, he can focus his attention upon assigning credit or blame to individual rules, debugging old rules and adding new ones.

There are two main kinds of error that a consultation program can make:

- drawing a false conclusion, e.g. about the identity of a bacterium during diagnosis;
- asking an irrelevant question, e.g. one that has no bearing upon the diagnosis in hand.

Using TEIRESIAS, an expert can stop the program when an error is detected, and trace back through the program's steps of reasoning, using the HOW and WHY facilities described in the last section. At some point it should become apparent that there has been a faulty rule application: perhaps there is an error in one of the rules, such as a condition in the premise which is too general, or perhaps a perfectly sound rule was wrongly invoked because of the absence of a more appropriate rule. The expert can then alter a rule, or add a new rule, before running the program again.

7.2.2 Monitoring changes with rule models

Rule models are generalizations about the kinds of rules that are found in the performance program, and they can be used to monitor additions or alterations to the rule set.

For example, MYCIN's ORGRULES attempt to establish the identity of an organism; the clinical parameter IDENT appears in their action parts. Such rules almost invariably have conditions in their premises which mention the parameters for culture site and infection type. So, if the expert wishes to add a new ORGRULE, it seems reasonable for the system to expect this rule to reference these parameters. If they are not referenced, it can at least point this out to the user, and give him the option of doing something about it.

Another rule model might note that the rules referencing culture site and infection type in their premises also mention the portal of entry of the organism as another of their conditions. Again, the system can prompt the user for this information if it is not provided by the new rule. Further, it can probably deduce which portal of entry is usually associated with the other clinical parameters found in the rule, and fix the bug itself.

Rule models are really a kind of meta-rule, in that they make general statements about rules, instead of statements about objects in the domain of application. In particular, TEIRESIAS has meta-rules which refer to the attributes of object-level rules, instead of referring to other rules directly. Such rules might suggest that, under certain circumstances, it is better to investigate certain parameters before trying to trace others.

Facilities also exist for helping an expert add a new instance of a data type. Errors that commonly occur with this task are giving the new instance the wrong structure, and not integrating the new instance properly into the system. For example, if one wishes to introduce a new clinical parameter to MYCIN, that parameter should inherit the structure of attributes associated with other parameters of that context type, and values for those attributes should fall within the allowed ranges.

A data abstraction used to guide the creation of instances is called a 'schema'. Schemata (or schemas) are descriptions of data types, just as data types are generalizations about data. As such, they can be organized into a hierarchy, where each schema inherits the attributes associated with its superordinate, and has additional attributes of its own.

Creating a new instance then involves tracing a path from the root of the schema hierarchy to the schema representing the appropriate data type. At each level, there will be attributes which need to be instantiated, until the instance is completely described. Relations between schemata will indicate updating tasks that the system might need to perform.

For example, creating a new instance of 'dog' in an 'animal' hierarchy would involve first instantiating those attributes shared by all animals, then those shared by all mammals, and finally those shared by all dogs.

TEIRESIAS therefore distinguishes between three levels of generality:

- domain-specific knowledge about data objects;
- representation-specific knowledge about data types;
- representation-independent knowledge about declarations.

7.2.3 Transparency in TEIRESIAS

The 'transparency' of an expert system is, loosely speaking, the degree to which its behaviour can be understood by the typical user. This does not necessarily mean that the user needs to know all about the particular algorithms that the program follows, or the data structures that the program uses. Rather it means that the user should be able to follow the reasoning of the program and realize why a particular sequence of steps led to a particular result.

Transparency is a virtue for two reasons:

1. It contributes to the acceptance of the system by users.

2. It makes the system easier to extend, modify and debug.

One way of achieving transparency is to provide explanations of program behaviour. The techniques for doing this in TEIRESIAS are inherited from MYCIN and are based upon the assumption that a recapitulation of program actions is sufficient, so long as there is some framework for viewing these actions that will make them comprehensible.

- The level of description for the recapitulation must be carefully chosen; some criteria are suggested below.

- The amount of detail must be sufficient for understanding, but should not include inessential aspects of the implementation.

One way of suppressing irrelevant detail is to select an appropriate conceptual level, e.g. talking about patients and their properties, not nodes and pointers. Nevertheless, the account should be complete, even if some aspects are covered in greater depth than others.

The existence of a shared framework presupposes that the concepts, relations and steps of reasoning employed by the program are comprehensible to the user. The program need not constitute a 'psychological model' of a human expert for this kind of understanding to be possible. Whether or not production rules encapsulate some fundamental truth about human thought processes, their mode of operation is not too hard for users to follow. By contrast, the behaviour of a purely statistical program, which proceeds by calculating conditional probabilities between patterns of data and diagnostic outcomes, is more difficult to explain. This is because the application of, for example, Bayes' theorem, is not so easily construed as a method of reasoning which has something in common with everyday thought. Such programs make no attempt to understand the problem, their knowledge is not accessible to the user, and the steps they follow do not correspond to ordinary methods of collecting evidence and drawing conclusions.

7.3 From MYCIN to GUIDON to NEOMYCIN

Clancey (1983) presents a powerful critique of the use of unstructured sets of production rules in expert systems, largely based upon his experience in attempting to adapt MYCIN for teaching purposes in the GUIDON project. His main argument is that the uniform 'if...then' syntax of production rules hides the fact that such rules often perform very different functions and are correspondingly constructed in different ways. Certain structural and strategic decisions about the representation of domain knowledge are therefore implicit in the rules, but not available to explanation mechanisms. Clancey seeks to remedy this situation by providing an analysis of the different kinds of meta-knowledge that guide the construction and subsequent execution of domain-specific rules. The idea is that such rules are tacitly embedded in an epistemological framework that needs to be made explicit; this approach forms the basic design principle of NEOMYCIN, a reconfiguration of the original MYCIN program.

7.3.1 The ordering of rule concepts

We have already seen that production rules of the general form

$$\text{if } P_1 \ \& \ ... \ \& \ P_n, \text{ then } Q$$

have an informal reading along the lines of 'if P_1 and ... and P_n are true, then perform Q'. The order of the P_i is immaterial with respect to this declarative reading, since $P \ \& \ Q$ is equivalent to $Q \ \& \ P$ in any standard logic.

However, the order of the P_i is material to the procedural interpretation of such rules. Different orderings of conjuncts will produce quite different search spaces which will be traversed in different ways, giving rise to different explanations. Furthermore, the criteria for this clause ordering can be different for different kinds of rule.

Similarly, the order in which rules for a goal are tried will affect the order in which subgoals are generated. So the hand-ordering of rules in the set, like the hand-ordering of conjuncts in premises, will affect the construction and traversal of the search space. For example, making sure that the most 'likely' rules are tried first might save search effort in the majority of cases.

The problem is that the criteria for rule- and clause-ordering are concealed from the explanation facility and hence from the user. Knowledge about which rules to try first and the best order for considering conjuncts is really meta-knowledge, i.e. knowledge about how to apply knowledge. There is little doubt that such knowledge is a crucial aspect of expertise that is difficult to capture and codify.

7.3.2 Structural, strategic and support knowledge

Clancey argues that rule-based systems require an epistemological framework which somehow makes sense of the domain-specific knowledge one is seeking to represent. In other words, inference rules relevant to some problem domain are often implicitly embedded knowledge of a more abstract kind. The best way to explain this is to use Clancey's own example; look at the rule shown in Figure 7.1.

IF   1) The infection is meningitis,
          2) Only circumstantial evidence is available,
          3) The type of infection is bacterial,
          4) The patient is receiving corticosteroids,

THEN There is evidence that the organisms involved are *E.coli* (.4)
            Klebsiella pneumoniae (.2) or *Pseudomonas aeruginosa* (.1).

Figure 7.1   A simplified version of MYCIN rule 543.

The ordering of the conjuncts in this rule is extremely significant. Obviously one needs to establish a hypothesis concerning the nature of the infection (1) before one can decide whether or not the evidence for it is circumstantial (2). Bacterial meningitis is a subclass distinct from viral meningitis, and so (3) can be seen as a refinement of (1). Finally, the decision to delay the test at (4) is probably a strategic one. Making this the first clause would alter the shape of the search space, perhaps causing subsequent tests to be pruned if this one failed.

Similarly, the ordering of goals in the conclusion is significant. The decision to pursue the hypothesis that *E.coli* is the culprit before pursuing any of the others is an example of strategic knowledge embedded in the rules. The explanation system does not have access to such knowledge, and is therefore unable to draw the user's attention to this simple heuristic when trying to account for the behaviour of the program.

Clancey offers a rather attractive analysis of the different kinds of knowledge that make up the epistemological framework of a rule-based system. The main components are described as structural knowledge, strategic knowledge and support knowledge. It is worth considering each of these in turn.

Structural knowledge consists of the different levels of abstraction through which one can view the knowledge domain. Taxonomy is perhaps the most obvious example of a source of knowledge which is not normally represented explicitly in production rules. The knowledge that meningitis is an infection which can be either acute or chronic, bacterial or viral etc., is implicit in many of the premises.

Strategic knowledge is knowledge about how to approach a problem by choosing an ordering on methods and subgoals which minimizes effort in the search for a solution. For example, the rule of thumb that compromised hosts (e.g. alcoholics) are likely to have an unusual aetiology can lead the expert to focus upon less common causes of infection first. Such knowledge typically interacts with structural knowledge, in that such a heuristic is linked to bacterial meningitis, rather than viral.

Support knowledge is typically knowledge involving a causal model of the domain of discourse which explains why certain contingencies typically hold. Thus, the MYCIN rule which links steroid use with gram-negative rod organisms causing bacterial meningitis has as its rationale the fact that steroids impair the immuno-response system. Again, such knowledge makes contact with structural knowledge concerning the classification of diseases and the classification of organisms.

7.3.3 Lessons of GUIDON and NEOMYCIN

In the present context, we are less concerned with how GUIDON and NEOMYCIN work than with the implications of their theoretical foundation for the design of future systems. A number of desiderata emerge from this work, with regard to both the overall architecture of diagnostic expert systems and the kinds of explanation facility that they should provide. Clancey's contribution was to show that these two issues are inextricably linked, and that improvement in the explanation facility of an expert system for pedagogical purposes was ultimately limited by the choice of a particular representational scheme, in this case an unstructured set of production rules.

It is also interesting to note that NEOMYCIN is claimed to be a psychological model of diagnostic behaviour, while no such claims were ever made for MYCIN. Consequently, it exhibits a behaviour quite different from the exhaustive backward chaining from a top-level goal as seen in Shortliffe's original program, e.g. forward reasoning from data, associations which trigger new hypotheses, and a 'working memory' of alternative hypotheses that it explores according to a 'group and differentiate' strategy.

In contrast with MYCIN's use of domain-specific meta-rules, NEOMYCIN embodies a domain-independent strategy for doing diagnosis. This approach is very much in keeping with the tradition of 'standing back' from some working program to look at it from a higher level of abstraction, in order to see what has actually been learned from its implementation, and then performing a rational reconstruction which both extends the power of the original program and achieves its ends in a more principled way. There is much to be said for this as a research strategy in expert systems and artificial intelligence generally.

Chapter 8 INTERNIST: Representation of Knowledge by Structured Objects

MYCIN and its derivatives are typical examples of the use of production rules in expert systems. The rule base is relatively unstructured, so that individual rules can be considered as independent entities whose results are later combined. The flow of control is determined at run-time by the backward-chaining control regime, the context tree and the pattern of rule activations.

In this chapter, we consider in detail a system which is based upon structured objects. In such systems, the modules of knowledge are grouped or connected in some way, and their pattern of activation is guided by this organization as well as the overall control regime. The INTERNIST system is chosen because it is something of a success story, and because it is large and complex enough to have had to address most of the problems associated with processing such representations.

Unlike MYCIN, INTERNIST is a program which sets out to model the actual steps of diagnostic reasoning performed by human clinicians. Typically, a pattern of symptoms will evoke one or more hypotheses about what could be wrong with the patient, and these in turn give rise to expectations concerning the presence or absence of other symptoms. Further observations may lead to some hypotheses being discarded or confirmed, or they may lead to new hypotheses being entertained. The initial setting up of hypotheses is 'data driven', in the sense that a particular manifestation will 'trigger' a number of conjectures. The subsequent gathering of new data in an attempt to support or refute a hypothesis is 'model driven', in the sense that it is based upon stereotypical or schematic ideas about the way in which different diseases manifest themselves.

This chapter begins by describing the theoretical framework within which this work was originally conceived. Then practical details of the implementation of the program are discussed. Finally, some attempt is made to assess the implications of this work for future large-scale expert system endeavours.

8.1 Background in abductive logic

It was Pople's (1973) paper on abductive reasoning which laid much of the theoretical foundation for the development of the INTERNIST system. His point of departure was that the exclusive use of deduction as a mode of inference was often inadequate to the task of solving problems of realistic complexity. In many reasoning tasks, including medical diagnosis, one cannot always reason directly towards one's goal (whether in a forward or a backward direction). This is because the clinician often begins with insufficient information to even formulate the problem properly. For example, he may not have enough information to delineate the space of possible diseases, or the signs and symptoms may point in more than one direction (after all, people are quite capable of suffering from more than one disease).

In a system like MYCIN, which deals with only a fraction of a small branch of medicine (the blood infections), exhaustive depth-first search may be an acceptable way for a machine to approach the problem of checking out alternatives. But Pople was interested in the whole of internal medicine, and in the way in which clinicians are able to arrive at multiple diagnoses. The number of distinct diseases that a clinician is likely to encounter is not huge (estimates vary between two and ten thousand diagnostic categories). However, it is not unknown for a patient to be suffering from ten or more concurrent disease processes. This means that, in the worst case, an exhaustive backward-chaining program would need to consider about 10^{40} diagnostic categories!

What are the alternatives to deduction? There is a tendency for us to forget that there are other modes of inference that humans use as a matter of routine (whether or not they are trained in logic). One is induction: the process whereby we move from the observation that the individuals a, b and c of type T have some property to the generalization that all things of type T have that property. The other is abduction: the process whereby we move from the knowledge that Q follows from P, and the observation that Q, to the conclusion that P. Deduction, by contrast, is moving from the knowledge that Q follows from P, and the observation that P, to the conclusion that Q.

This is easier to understand if we view these three modes of inference as alternative forms of argument in terms of the following schema:

$$(x)(Fx \rightarrow Gx)$$
$$\underline{Fa}$$
$$Ga$$

where $(x)(Fx \rightarrow Gx)$ is the major premise or 'rule', Fa is the minor premise or 'case', and Ga is the 'fact' drawn as a conclusion. In deduction, we move from a rule and a particular case (to which the rule applies) towards a particular fact. In induction, we move from pairs of observations – Fa, Ga, Fb, Gb, etc. – towards the hypothesis that 'all Fs are Gs'. In abduction, we are given the observation Ga, together with the rule that 'F-ness' can cause, lead to, or otherwise generally explain 'G-ness', and we entertain Fa as a hypothesis.

Note, however, that whereas the deduction step is guaranteed to be sound, regardless of the circumstances, the induction and abduction steps are not. In the case of induction, there may yet exist some pair of observations, such as $(Fc, \sim Gc)$, that would refute the hypothesis. In the case of abduction, there may exist an alternative rule, such as $(x)(Hx \rightarrow Gx)$, to account for Ga via the hitherto unremarked observation Ha.

On the other hand, it is also worth noting that induction and abduction are in a sense more 'creative' than deduction. The deduction step merely teases out some item of information which is implicit in the conjunction of case and rule; in other words, it is fundamentally 'analytic'. Induction, on the other hand, is akin to rule formation, while abduction corresponds to something like theory formation; both are 'synthetic' operations of the mind.

The American philosopher Pierce described abduction as one of the bases of scientific thought. Pople saw that abduction was an essential part of the reasoning processes of actual clinicians, and set about its mechanization. His description of abductive inference is worth quoting in full:

> 'The essence of abductive inference is the generation of hypotheses, which, if true, would explain some collection of observed facts.' (1973, page 147.)

The task that Pople set himself was to show that an abductive logic could be mechanized by embedding deductive procedures within a framework of iterative hypothesis and test. The problem is not so much how to generate hypotheses, but how to do so selectively, and in a controlled manner. Unrestricted hypothesizing would lead to combinatorial explosion, from the point of view of the program, and a spate of unrelated and seemingly irrelevant questions, from the point of view of anyone running the program.

The principle that Pople adopted to help cope with this task of the selective generation of hypotheses is known as 'Occam's Razor'. It demands that the simplest possible explanation of the facts should always be preferred. Thinkers obviously have some latitude in how they apply Occam's Razor; for example, they have to make up their own minds what constitutes simplicity. Roughly speaking, simplicity means not importing extraneous ideas or constructing complex causal paths when a smaller set of concepts and a more direct chain of events will provide an explanation of the phenomena under study. For example, one might reasonably apply Occam's Razor to explanations of ancient artefacts which involve creatures from outer space, however attractive such explanations might be!

Occam's Razor is only a 'heuristic criterion of acceptability', as Pople points out, since it doesn't guarantee that the correct hypotheses will always be chosen or generated first. There is no algorithm that will ensure this. All one can do is try to ensure that the final judgement is based upon a synthesis of the available evidence.

Pople formulated and implemented his abductive inference engine in a number of different ways before INTERNIST was finally implemented in INTERLISP, using very much more sophisticated representation and control machinery than was originally envisaged (as is only to be expected). It is both interesting and instructive to follow the development of this system over a period of about ten years. The story of INTERNIST bears out the old AI adage that nothing is ever as difficult as it looks at first sight – it's more difficult.

8.2 Attention-focusing heuristics in INTERNIST

In the simplest case, INTERNIST has to distinguish between a set of mutually exclusive disease hypotheses to arrive at a diagnosis. If a patient is suffering from more than one disease, then the program must find a set of diseases that accounts for some or all of the symptoms. It does this by considering the most likely hypothesis first, noting the symptoms covered, and then proceeding to the next likely hypothesis and so on, until all the symptoms have been accounted for.

An early version of INTERNIST was called DIALOG (Pople *et al.*, 1975): a contraction of 'diagnostic logic'. Its database covered about 50 per cent of the main diseases encountered in internal medicine. It had two main features of interest: its representation of knowledge and the attention-focusing heuristic that it used to generate and test hypotheses.

8.2.1 The representation of knowledge

INTERNIST's medical knowledge is held in the 'disease tree': a hierarchical classification of disease types. The root node in this tree stands for all known diseases, non-terminals stand for 'disease areas', e.g. lung disease, liver disease, while terminals stand for 'disease entities', i.e. actual diseases one can diagnose and treat. This is a static data structure, separate from the main body of the program, rather like MYCIN's knowledge tables. The difference is that they play a far more active role in directing the reasoning of the program. It is interesting to compare the 'rule-based' approach of MYCIN-like systems with the essentially 'model-based' approach described below.

Such a representation of knowledge was indicated by a number of properties of the problem domain:

- The sheer size of the search space made the exploitation of any inherent structure in the knowledge a prime consideration.

- The commitment to abduction as the principal mode of inference meant that relatively straightforward forward- or backward-chaining rules were out of the question – rather one needed to be able to explore a structured space of alternatives, some of which were complementary to one another while others were mutually exclusive.

- The kinds of approximate reasoning required by the task needed to be more sophisticated than the propagation of certainty factors provided in MYCIN, since various factors had to be taken into account, such as the importance of a particular finding, the frequency of association between a finding and a particular diagnostic category, and the cost and risk involved in securing some item of information.

Pople describes the task of diagnosis as the devising of hypotheses which would enable the deduction of signs, symptoms and findings associated with the patient. In order to mechanize this abductive process, special procedures

and data structures were required. The logic of diagnostic inference was described as a four-step judgemental process, along the following lines.

- Clinical observations must be able to suggest candidate diseases capable of causing them.
- These hypothesized candidates should then generate expectations with regard to what other findings might co-occur.
- There needs to be some method for choosing between hypotheses on the basis of available evidence.
- It must be possible to group hypotheses into mutually exclusive subsets, so that the acceptance of one subset means rejection of another, otherwise you would never be able to rule anything out.

The key lies in the bidirectional relationship between diseases and their associated signs and symptoms. INTERNIST considers this link as two separate relations, evocation and manifestation, as follows.

- The EVOKE relation accounts for the way in which a manifestation can suggest the presence of a disease.
- The MANIFEST relation describes the way in which a disease can manifest itself via signs and symptoms.

The INTERNIST knowledge base is constructed in the following way:

1. The basic structure of the hierarchy is determined initially by dividing the 'root' of the disease tree into general areas of internal medicine, such as heart disease, liver disease and so on.
2. At the next level, subcategories are introduced which group together disease areas which are similar with respect to pattern of development (pathogenesis) and mode of clinical presentation (signs, symptoms and so on).
3. Further subdivision of these subcategories goes on until one reaches the level of 'disease entities', that is to say, individual diseases which can be diagnosed as such.
4. Then data are collected concerning the association between disease entities and their manifestations, including
   a) a list of all the manifestations associated with a particular disease,
   b) an estimate of the likelihood that the disease is the cause of the manifestation,
   c) an estimate of the frequency with which patients suffering from the disease will exhibit each manifestation.
5. A list of associated manifestations $(M_1, ..., M_n)$ is attached to the representation of each disease entity, D, along with an evoking facto which estimates the likelihood $L(D, M_i)$ and a frequency factor whic estimates $L(M_i, D)$, both factors being on a scale of 0–5.
6. As well as signs, symptoms and test results associated with some diseas D, there may be other diseases which are themselves manifestations of I

i.e. diseases caused by the original disease, D, and such causal links are also coded in the EVOKE and MANIFEST relationships.

7. Once all this information has been attached to the nodes representing the disease entities (which can be thought of as the 'leaves' or terminal nodes of the disease tree) there is a program which will turn the tree into a generalization hierarchy, that is to say, a tree structure in which non-terminal or 'branch' nodes share only those properties held in common by all of their successors.

8. Finally, data about individual manifestations are entered. The most important properties of manifestations are their TYPE (e.g. sign, symptom, laboratory finding, etc.) and IMPORT (an index on a 1–5 scale of how important a manifestation is).

Steps (1)–(3) create the 'superstructure' of the knowledge base, by determining its basic shape, e.g. the range of categories and the levels of analysis within each category. Steps (4)–(6) correspond to the entry of basic medical knowledge into the database, represented in a manner that is convenient for the consultation program to use. The estimates of likelihood and frequency allow the consultation program to 'weigh the evidence' for and against a particular hypothesis.

At step (7), the program simply computes manifestations for non-terminal nodes representing disease areas by intersecting the manifestations of successor nodes. Consequently, all manifestations associated with a particular non-terminal are also associated with every terminal or non-terminal node directly or indirectly below it in the hierarchy. For example, jaundice is a manifestation associated with particular kinds of liver disease, such as the various forms of hepatitis.

The reasoning behind this generalization procedure is as follows. It was pointed out earlier that the space of diagnostic categories for patients suffering from multiple diseases was extremely large. Because of this, conventional search methods such as depth-first search could not be expected to perform well on realistic cases. What is needed is some way of pruning this search space, or focusing the attention of the program on particular areas of the space, in such a way as to facilitate a speedy diagnosis.

The search problem would not be so acute, even in the case of multiple disease, if there were more direct and reliable associations between diseases and their manifestations, such that the presence of a particular manifestation were sufficient to allow a clinician to conclude the presence of a particular disease. Such relations are termed 'pathognomonic', and they do actually occur. Unfortunately it is rare for a sign or symptom to be pathognomonic in this sense; it is a property more likely to be associated with findings which come from either expensive laboratory techniques or surgical procedures that one would not recommend as a matter of routine.

At higher levels of the disease hierarchy, however, it is possible to establish quite robust associations between common manifestations and whole areas of disease. Thus, jaundice suggests a liver problem, while bloody

sputum suggests a lung problem. INTERNIST uses such associations to 'constrict' the search space, with the intention of homing in on the correct diagnostic category at a certain level of abstraction, before proceeding to the business of arriving at the right diagnosis at the level of disease entities.

The 'constrictors' of a case, in Pople's terminology, are therefore a set of findings which cues the setting up of hypotheses within broad categories of the disease hierarchy. However, constriction is a heuristic device; it is not guaranteed to succeed. At higher levels of the hierarchy, while some manifestations are uniquely associated with disease areas, others are only predominant, i.e. they could be explained by other areas. This situation deteriorates as you go further down the hierarchy, of course.

Hence, step (7) is taken so that the consultation program can begin to make a differential diagnosis at a fairly high level in the hierarchy, using a generalization of the pathognomonic concept. This means that whole classes of diagnoses can be ruled out before going on to make an individual diagnosis. This is one of the mechanisms which make possible the use of the attention-focusing heuristics.

Step (8) elaborates upon the properties of the manifestations themselves, as a further aid to the strategic level of diagnostic reasoning. For example, the TYPE property indicates how expensive it is to test for a manifestation, and how dangerous such a test might be for the patient, so that cheaper and safer manifestations can be followed up first. The IMPORT property indicates whether or not one can afford to ignore a particular manifestation in the context of a particular disease.

8.2.2 Disease models

At the start of a consultation, the user enters a list of manifestations. Each of these evokes one or more nodes in the disease tree. The program creates a 'model' for each such node, consisting of four lists:

1. Observed manifestations not associated with the disease.
2. Observed manifestations consistent with the disease.
3. Manifestations not yet observed but which are always associated with the disease.
4. Manifestations not yet observed but which are consistent with the disease.

Disease models receive positive scores for manifestations they explain and negative scores for ones they fail to explain. Both kinds of score are weighted by IMPORT, and a model gets a bonus if it is causally related to a disease that has already been confirmed. The disease models are then divided into two sets, depending upon how they relate to the most highly rated model. One partition contains the top-ranked model and all those diseases which are mutually exclusive to it, i.e. its evoked 'sibling' nodes in the tree. The other contains all those diseases which are complementary to it, i.e. evoked nodes in other disease areas.

Partitioning involves the concept of 'dominance' in the following sense. Disease model D_1 dominates model D_2 if the observed manifestations not explained by D_1 (or any part-diagnosis done so far) are a subset of those not explained by D_2. Given a top-ranked model, D_0, each member D_i of the evoked models list is compared with D_0. If D_0 either dominates it, or is dominated by it, then D_i is grouped with D_0 on the 'considered' list. Otherwise its consideration is deferred for the moment.

The rationale behind this kind of partitioning is that the set of models being considered at any one time can be treated as mutually exclusive alternatives. This is because, for any D_i, D_j in the set, the diagnosis D_i & D_j would add little or nothing to the explanatory power of either D_i or D_j on their own. Deferred models will be processed in similar fashion once the current problem of deciding between the models associated with D_0 has been resolved; partitioning will begin again with a new D_0, the model of best fit from among the deferred models.

After the initial input, some nodes will have been evoked and others not. The problem for the program is to transform the tree from this starting state to a solution state. A solution state consists of a tree with evoked terminal nodes which account for all of the symptoms.

Having partitioned the disease models, the program uses a number of alternative strategies, depending upon how many hypotheses it is entertaining.

- If there are more than four hypotheses, it adopts a refutation strategy (RULEOUT mode), and tries to eliminate as many as possible, asking questions about symptoms that strongly indicate the presence of candidate diseases.

- If there are between two and four possibilities, it adopts a differentiation strategy (DISCRIMINATE mode), asking questions that will help decide between candidate diseases.

- If there is only one candidate, it adopts a verification strategy (PURSUING mode), asking questions that will confirm the presence of the disease.

This whole process is iterative. Responses to queries asked in any of these modes are processed in much the same way as the original input of manifestations by the user. Thus new nodes are evoked, old nodes are updated, models are ranked and partitioned, and a (possibly new) mode is selected resulting in further questions being asked.

8.3   Concurrent problem formulation in INTERNIST-II

A 'problem' is defined, in the domain of INTERNIST, as a collection of mutually exclusive disease entities, one and only one of which can be said to account for some subset of all the manifestations associated with a particular case. INTERNIST-I's main feature of interest was not so much its problem solving abilities, although its performance was encouraging, as its ability to formulate the problem in the first place, by focusing its attention successively upon a number of hypotheses in its attempts to account for all the data. Recall that the possibility that a patient might be suffering from more than one disease made it essential to be able to partition the set of disease entities in such a way as to formulate more than one 'problem', in the sense defined above.

In fact, in cases where more than one disease appeared to be present, INTERNIST-I still had trouble with the initial focusing of the program's attention upon the right disease area. In other words, it began by considering quite inappropriate problems and, although it generally 'got there in the end', this tended to prolong the consultation unnecessarily. This indicated a lack of clinical meta-knowledge on the part of the program, in exploiting interrelationships between disease areas, as well as a lack of object-level knowledge about degrees of relevance and remoteness in the association between disease areas and manifestations (over and above that derived by generalization over disease entities).

The biggest single obstacle to remedying this situation was the fact that problems were formulated sequentially, considering one complementary model at a time. Ideally, a program for performing multiple diagnoses would be able to bear more than one problem in mind when dealing with a case. If this were possible, then the program could employ additional heuristics. For example, it might decide to focus upon the problem that looked easiest to solve first of all, rather than beginning with the one that best fitted the data; these need not necessarily be the same problem, given the different costs and risks associated with different tests. Also, instead of having an 'absolute' scoring procedure, which considers disease models in isolation from other models similarly evoked, the scoring procedure could be 'relativized' to take concurrent models into account. As Pople (1977) pointed out, INTERNIST-I would give a disease model credit for explaining some manifestation regardless of how remote the association actually was. A better idea is to distribute manifestations to models on the basis of relevance, so that if two disease models, D_1 and D_2, both explain some manifestation, M, then the credit for explaining M should go to the model with the strongest association with M.

Instead of just partitioning the models, INTERNIST-II partitions the disease tree into a forest of subtrees capable of accounting for all of the manifestations. The problem then reduces to one of finding which terminal nodes in this data structure give the best account. The constrictors described in the previous section are used to draw up this conjunction of disease areas, which is collectively known as the 'root structure'.

The root structure is the product of a multi-problem generator which constructs a set of category hypotheses based on two indices:

- the 'constrictor certitude' – i.e. the degree of strictness in the relationship between a manifestation and a disease area;

- the score assigned to each area, bearing in mind the modified scoring algorithm, whereby relevance is taken into account in the attribution of manifestations to diseases.

As before, the search for a complete diagnosis is an iterative and heuristic process. The pool of unexplained manifestations is gradually reduced, and the generator terminates when all the findings have been covered. Because of the heuristic nature of the search, the generator may be called upon to construct an alternative root structure at any time.

The main differences between INTERNIST-I and INTERNIST-II are therefore the following.

- There is no guarantee that 'root-level' hypotheses will be 'problems' in the sense defined for INTERNIST-I. This is because there may be more than one disease entity present within a single disease category, given the multi-problem generation. This is not an uncommon situation; patients may suffer from more than one brand of liver disease, for example.

- Root-level hypotheses need to be refined. So the multi-problem generator needs to be called recursively upon hypotheses to form sub-conjectures in a 'hypothesis reduction' process.

- The context-sensitive scoring procedure improves the ranking of alternatives. Manifestations are deemed relevant to disease categories on the basis of either high evoking strength or high frequency of occurrence. However, this procedure is considerably more complicated than that used by INTERNIST-I; concurrent problem formulation with attribution of manifestations means that straightforward inheritance of manifestations no longer holds, since as more information becomes available the attribution may be altered during hypothesis reduction.

Thus, what began as a relatively simple idea (the application of abduction to diagnosis) and proceeded to an intuitively comprehensible implementation (DIALOG and INTERNIST-I) became considerably more complex, particularly in the area of control, when realistic levels of performance were required. It is hardly an exaggeration to say that this pattern repeats itself throughout the AI literature in fields as diverse as planning, theorem proving and natural language processing. The trick would appear to be not to lose sight of one's original goals and to retain one's vision as the problems pile up, while at the same time recognizing those points at which successive implementations break down and effecting the repairs in a principled way (which is very much easier said than done).

8.4 The implementation of INTERNIST and its current state

Like so many successful expert systems applications, the INTERNIST programs were coded in INTERLISP. The programming environment is very supportive of large scale AI efforts, while special control structures associated with the LISP stack allow the kind of flexible scheduling that INTERNIST relies upon.

Execution times for complex cases ranged from three to seven minutes of CPU in INTERNIST-I, while problem formation in INTERNIST-II took between 20 seconds and two minutes, depending upon the complexity of the case.

The current version of INTERNIST is called CADUCEUS. CADUCEUS displays expert performance on about 85% of internal medicine, with a very large knowledge base consisting of over 500 diseases. It is expected that the system will eventually be in clinical use.

Chapter 9   R1: Recognition as a Problem Solving Strategy

R1 is arguably one of the success stories of expert systems in recent years. It is a program that configures VAX computer systems by first checking that the order is complete and then determining the spatial arrangement of components.

The task is not trivial. Such systems typically consist of 50–150 components, the main ones being the central processor, memory control units, unibus and massbus interfaces, all connected to a synchronous backplane. The buses can support a wide range of peripheral devices – e.g. tape drives, disk drives, printers – giving rise to a wide variety of different system configurations.

Deciding whether or not a configuration is complete is complex, because it requires knowledge of individual components and their relationships. Deciding on a spatial arrangement is difficult, because there are many constraints that need to be taken into account. For example, assigning unibus modules to the backplanes involves taking into account features such as the amperage available on the backplane and the interrupt priority of the modules.

To date, R1 has processed more than 80 000 orders. It is also a large system, containing over 3000 rules, with knowledge of over 5000 different components. Its progress has been well documented over the last 4 years (McDermott, 1980, 1981, 1982, 1984).

In addition to its practical significance, the design and implementation of R1 has also raised a number of theoretical issues. R1 is also interesting because it gives us some insight into the way in which an expert system grows, and how that growth can be managed. However, we shall begin by taking a brief look at its technical foundations: the underlying production rule language that allows such a large rule set to run in a reasonable time.

9.1   The computational background: OPS5

We met OPS5 in Chapter 3, whilst on the subject of production systems. There we considered a simple program for sorting bricks, and saw how the pattern matcher could be used to satisfy non-trivial conditions involving negated elements and the use of comparison operators. Here we look at pattern matching in a bit more detail, and consider the cost of doing computation in this way.

Some form of pattern matching is essential to the operation of pattern-directed inference systems, be they production systems, frame systems or logic interpreters. There are many different kinds of pattern matching, but they all require that a program be capable of recognizing that one expression, E, say (Peter likes LISP) is somehow an 'instance' of another, F, say (Peter likes X). We can look at this from two different levels, the syntactic (to do with the form of expressions) and the semantic (to do with their meaning). Syntactically, E is the same as F, if we perform the substitution of LISP for X in F. Semantically, Peter's liking for LISP is an example of Peter liking something, so E 'matches' F, since the X stands for anything that Peter likes. In this example, E is the 'object' and F the 'pattern', since it is F that contains the variable. The match wouldn't work with F as object and E as pattern.

Consider the following production rule:

IF   Peter likes X &
        X is a programming language
THEN   Peter uses X.

Given that Peter likes LISP, and that LISP is a programming language, we are entitled to infer that Peter uses LISP. However, in order to draw this inference, a program must discover that the conditions (Peter likes X) and (X is a programming language) are satisfied, for some value of X. So it must refer to some store of expressions for candidates that are likely to match the conditions and then painstakingly assure itself that the candidates really do match, while remembering the substitution needed to turn one expression into the other.

9.1.1 The trouble with patterns

The problem with pattern matching is that it is computationally quite expensive. The amount of list processing involved in deciding that one arbitrary list is an instance of another is a function of the length and embeddedness of the two lists, and the number of variables in the pattern, since each time you match a constant against a variable you must assure yourself that the new binding is consistent with an earlier one. In production systems, you are dealing, not with two lists, but with two collections of lists, e.g. a collection of working memory elements and a collection of production rule left-hand sides, and attempting to identify left-hand sides which are satisfied by the contents of working memory. This is called many-pattern/many-object matching, for obvious reasons.

There are several possible sources of inefficiency here.

- The interpreter might simply iterate through working memory, checking all the list structures therein against each of the rules in turn.
- The interpreter might only examine some subset of working memory for each rule, retrieving for match only elements indexed as likely to match that rule, but it would still make N passes through working memory for N rules.

- During successive recognize-act cycles, the same objects might get matched against the same patterns over and over again, incurring the same list processing overhead each time.

Many of the early production systems spend over 90 per cent of their time doing matching of this kind. Even when various forms of indexing were used to hash working memory elements into the set of productions, there remained the within- and between-cycle iteration on working memory. As the saying goes, there had to be a better way.

9.1.2 The Rete match algorithm

There was, and it emerged as the Rete match algorithm (see Forgy, 1982), which went on to serve as the basic pattern matching mechanism of the OPS interpreters. It is based on two fundamental insights.

- The left-hand sides of productions in working memory often share conditions, and naïve approaches will tend to match these conditions against working memory N times for N occurrences. This is an example of within-cycle iteration.
- Working memory is only modified a little each time, yet naïve approaches tend to match all the patterns against all the working memory elements for each cycle. This is an example of between-cycle iteration.

The algorithm reduces the overhead of within-cycle iteration on productions by using a tree-structured sorting network. The patterns in the left-hand sides of the productions are compiled into this network, and the match algorithm computes the conflict set for a given cycle by processing this network. The between-cycle iteration on working memory is eliminated by processing a set of tokens that indicate which patterns match which working memory elements, and then simply updating this set when working memory changes.

To give you a (simplified) idea of how this might work, consider the following OPS5 rule fragment, taken from Forgy (1982):

```
(P PlusOx
   (Goal ^Type Simplify ^Object <N>)
   (Expression ^Name <N> ^Arg1 0 ^Op + ^Arg2 <X>)
   --> ...)
```

If the pattern matcher is to determine whether or not the left-hand side of this rule is matched, it needs to analyse both intra-element and inter-element features of items in working memory. Thus in considering the first pattern, (Goal ...), any candidate for match must have Goal as its class, with Simplify as the value of the Type attribute, together with some value for the Object attribute. These are the intra-element features. But, when proceeding to match the second pattern, (Expression ...), there is an inter-element relationship: the value of the Name attribute in the second pattern must be the same as the value of the Object attribute in the first pattern.

The patterns which occur in the left-hand side of rules are therefore compiled into a network consisting of nodes which test working memory elements for the requisite features in the following way.

The intra-element features are considered first, and the result is a linear sequence of nodes, each of which tests for the presence of one particular feature.

Then the inter-element features are taken into account. Each of the nodes representing an inter-element feature has two inputs, e.g. the node that tests whether or not the Object and Name fields mentioned above are the same needs an input from the part of the network that codes for the first pattern, and an input from the part which codes for the second pattern. So there is a network 'join' at that point.

Following these two-input nodes, there is a node that stands for the whole production, and this is a terminal node of the network. The idea is that if you have succeeded in traversing the network and getting to this node without any of the intra- or inter-element tests failing, then the production represented by the terminal node should be added to the conflict set.

However, that isn't the whole story. It is often the case that the left-hand sides of two different rules can share the same nodes, instead of having duplicate nodes. Consider the left-hand side shown below:

```
(P TimeOx
   (Goal ^Type Simplify ^Object <N>)
   (Expression ^Name <N> ^Arg1 0 ^Op * ^Arg2 <X>)
   --> ...)
```

It is obvious that PlusOx and TimeOx share both intra- and inter-element features. Consequently, it makes sense for them to share both one- and two-input nodes in the network. The network for these two rules would therefore have two terminal nodes; each node, if it is reached, adds the corresponding production rule to the conflict set.

The way that Forgy describes the matcher is as a 'black box', i.e. as a self-contained unit which has an input and an output. The output of the box is the conflict set, the set of all productions that are able to fire. More precisely, the conflict set contains ordered pairs of the form

```
<production, matched LHS elements>
```

called 'instantiations', since we are interested not merely in which rules can fire, but in the values that are bound to their pattern variables by virtue of the working memory elements they matched with.

What, then, is the input to the black box? Not working memory, since this would involve the between-cycle iteration we would like to avoid. The input is a set of tokens which describe working memory changes.

A token is a pair consisting of a tag and list of data elements. Thus

```
<+ (Expression ^Name <N> ^Arg1 0 ^Op * ^Arg2 <X>)>
```

would result in (Expression ...) being notionally added to working memory, while <- (Expression ...)> would result in it being deleted. Modifications to elements are accomplished by the corresponding deletions and additions.

Of course, when the production system is loaded, a certain amount of processing is done before it can run. The left-hand side patterns must be compiled into a network, and if the program starts with a non-empty working memory then its elements must first of all be associated with the patterns that they match. But once this is done, the interpreter necd not iterate on working memory again, it just processes the changes and updates the elements associated with patterns.

Finally, there is no real need to compute the conflict set afresh with each recognize-act cycle. You only need to determine which instantiations in the last conflict set are no longer valid, and which new instantiations have been made possible since the previous cycle. Thus the output from the black box is not really a new conflict set, but changes to the last one.

There is an elegance and an ingenuity about the Rete match algorithm that I find very pleasing. The basic ideas are simple (once they have been pointed out to you), but their implications are far-reaching, and their implementation is non-trivial. The algorithm is efficient even with large sets of patterns and objects, simply because it does not iterate over the sets.

9.2   Configurer of VAXes

Although both R1 and MYCIN are production rule programs, they differ substantially in a number of important respects. Perhaps the main difference is that MYCIN takes a 'top-down' approach to problem solving, i.e. it begins with some goal (producing a diagnosis) and then proceeds to generate subgoals, the conjoined solution of which solve the original goal. R1's approach is wholly 'bottom-up'; it begins with a set of components and tries to produce a configuration within the constraints imposed by the properties of these components and relationships between them.

9.2.1   Components and constraints

R1 needs two kinds of knowledge:

- knowledge about components, e.g. voltage, amperage, pinning-type, number of ports etc., as appropriate;
- knowledge about constraints, i.e. rules for forming partial configurations of equipment and then extending them successfully.

Component knowledge is stored in a database, which is separate from both the production memory of the production system and the working memory of transient data elements. The database is therefore a static data structure, while the working memory is dynamic. Unlike the production memory, the database does not consist of pattern-directed modules, but of more conventional record structures which state, for each component, its class and type plus a set of attribute value pairs. Consider the following example, which describes an RK611* disk controller.

```
RK611*
    CLASS: UNIBUS MODULE
    TYPE: DISK DRIVE
    SUPPORTED: YES
    PRIORITY LEVEL: BUFFERED NPR
    TRANSFER RATE: 212 ...
```

There are 15 classes of unit, e.g. cabinet, backplane, cable, and each type has on average 8 attribute-value pairs associated with it. There are about 50 different attributes, a number of which are shared by most of the classes. Some of the components in the database are really bundles, e.g. RK711-EA contains a backplane, the RK611* controller with disk drive, plus cabling and continuity boards.

Constraint knowledge is provided by each of the rules in R1's production memory. The left-hand sides recognize situations in which partial configurations can be extended, while the right-hand sides perform those extensions. The working memory starts off empty and ends containing the configuration. Components are represented in working memory by component tokens implemented as the usual attribute-value vectors. R1 can perform five actions in accessing the component database: it can generate a new token, find a token, find a substitute for a specific token, retrieve the attributes associated with an existing token, and retrieve a template for filling out.

As well as component tokens, the working memory contains elements that represent partial configurations of equipment, the results of various computations, and symbols which indicate what the current task is.

It is frequently the case that more than one R1 rule could fire at any one cycle. The conflict resolution strategy used in R1 is called 'special case' or 'specificity'. If there are two rules in the conflict set, Rule1 and Rule2, and Rule1's conditions are a subset of Rule2's, then Rule2 will be preferred over Rule1. Another way of looking at this is to regard Rule1 as more 'general' than Rule2; it acts as a default which catches cases for which Rule2 is too specific. Rule2 might therefore deal with an exception to Rule1, in which extra factors need to be taken into account.

Figure 9.1 shows an English translation of a sample R1 rule, taken from Forgy (1982). The 'current active context' referred to in the first condition of this rule will form the subject matter of the next section.

DISTRIBUTE-MB-DEVICES-3

IF   the most current active context is distributing massbus devices
        & there is a single port disk drive that has not been assigned
        to a massbus
        & there are no unassigned dual port disk drives
        & the number of devices that each massbus should support is
        known
        & there is a massbus that has been assigned at least one disk
        drive and that should support additional disk drives
        & the type of cable needed to connect the disk drive to the
        previous device on the disk drive is known
THEN   assign the disk drive to the massbus

Figure 9.1 An English translation of an R1 rule.

9.2.2 Using contexts to impose task structure

In addition to information about components and constraints, R1's working memory contains symbol structures which specify the current context of the computation. This helps to break the configuration task down into subtasks. Moreover, these subtasks can be arranged into a hierarchy with temporal relationships between them. In other words, the main task, say 'configure this order for a VAX-11/780' can be analysed into subtasks, like 'check that the order is correct' and 'arrange the components of the (possibly corrected) order'. Performing these two tasks constitutes performing the main task; however, they should obviously be performed in the order stated. It wouldn't make sense to configure the components in the order, and then check that the order was correct afterwards.

If these two principles are applied recursively, so that each subtask at depth D is analysed into subtasks at depth $D + 1$, with temporal interdependencies between them, the result is a task hierarchy. Unanalysed subtasks will form the terminal nodes of this tree. For example, R1 analyses the configuration task into six immediate subtasks, each involving subtasks of their own:

1. Check the order, inserting any omissions and correcting any mistakes.
2. Configure the CPU, arranging components in the CPU and CPU expansion cabinets.
3. Configure the unibus modules, putting boxes into the expansion cabinets and then putting the modules into the boxes.
4. Configure the panelling, assigning panels to cabinets and associating panels with unibus modules and the devices they serve.
5. Generate a floor plan, grouping components that must be closer together and then laying the devices out in the right order.
6. Do the cabling, specifying what cables are to be used to connect devices and then determining the distances between pairs of components.

Such hierarchies can be thought of as being either determinate or indeterminate with respect to the ordering of subtasks. If there is a fixed order within the subtasks at every depth, then we say that the task analysis is determinate, since the sequence of tasks is completely determined. If there is some latitude with respect to the ordering between some subtasks at some levels, then the task analysis is indeterminate.

R1's task analysis is determinate, in that the tasks are always performed in the same order; this is achieved as follows. Some of R1's rules serve mainly to manipulate context symbols: those working memory elements that tell the program where it has got to in the task hierarchy. Some rules recognize when a new subtask needs to be initiated; these add context symbols to working memory. Others recognize when a subtask has been completed; these remove context symbols from working memory. All other rules contain condition elements that are sensitive to context symbols, so that they only fire when their context is 'active', i.e. when the requisite symbols are the 'recent' context symbols in working memory. In order to understand this, it is necessary to understand the conflict resolution strategy employed by R1.

Each context symbol contains a context name, e.g. 'assign-power-supply', a symbol which states whether the context is active or not, and a time tag which indicates how recently the context was made active. The rules that recognize when a new subtask should be set up do this on the basis of the current state of the partial configuration. Rules which have the appropriate context symbol in their conditions will now receive preferential treatment during the recognize-act cycle. It is customary to put patterns which recognize context among the first conditions in the left-hand side of productions, so that the Rete match algorithm fails quickly on rules that lack the right context recognizers. Rules which deactivate contexts are simply rules whose left-hand side is composed solely of context symbols. Such a rule will only fire when all the other rules sensitive to that context have fired or failed. This is the 'special case' strategy referred to earlier, and the way it is used here ensures that R1 does all it can within a particular context before leaving it.

McDermott's justification for this use of contexts is not that it is essential to the task of configuring a computer system, but rather, that it reflects the way in which human experts actually approach the task. It is one of the strengths of the OPS languages that they support this kind of rule partitioning.

9.2.3   Conflict resolution in OPS5

Now that you have seen how useful context-layering can be, you might be interested to know how OPS conflict resolution can be set up to support it. As we saw in Chapter 3, there are two different strategies built into OPS5: LEX and MEA. You select which one you want by inserting (strategy mea) or (strategy lex) at the top of the source file; the default is LEX.

However, it is the MEA conflict resolution strategy that facilitates the use of the first condition element as a context-sensitive pattern. The rules for this strategy are sketched below to illustrate this point; pay special attention to rule (2). Recall that objects in the conflict set are called 'instantiations': an ordered pair of a production name and a list of working memory elements which satisfy that production's left-hand side.

1. Discard from the conflict set instantiations that have already fired. If the set is now empty, conflict resolution fails, and no rule fires.
2. Compare the recencies of the working memory elements that match the first condition elements of the instantiations. Instantiations using the most recent working memory element 'dominate', i.e. are ranked preferentially for firing.
3. Now look at the remaining working memory elements, and order the instantiations on the basis of the recencies of these elements.
4. If no single instantiation now dominates all the others, compare the dominant instantiations on the specificity of the left-hand sides. The rule whose left-hand side involves the most tests on working memory elements dominates.
5. If instantiations are still tied, make an arbitrary selection from among the dominants.

The LEX strategy is like MEA, except that rule (2) is missing, and rule (3) now applies to all working memory elements in the instantiations, and not those working memory elements minus those which matched the first condition. For a fuller treatment of these strategies, the reader is referred to Forgy (1981) and Brownston *et al.* (1985). Whether or not you have fully comprehended these algorithms at a first reading, it should be fairly clear that they serve similar functions.

- They prevent loops by stopping instantiations from executing more than once. (Note that, in the terminology, rules 'fire' and instantiations 'execute'. You can't execute a rule, because a rule does not contain bindings for variables, whereas the instantiation does. Firing a rule means executing an instantiation of it.) However, this doesn't mean that OPS programs never loop. A rule might fire repeatedly, cycle after cycle, with a different instantiation each time. The conflict resolution strategies will not detect such loops, and it's rather unreasonable to expect that they should.
- They give preferential treatment to the most recent working memory elements. This is very congenial to a 'bottom-up' or 'forward reasoning' search strategy, where you want to be all the time building on your most recent results. Without such conflict resolution strategies, the program might wander from task to task, firing rules just because they are applicable, but regardless of whether they are relevant to the current task.
- They give preference to productions with more specific left-hand sides. This facility is very useful in a wide range of applications, where you wish to deal with exceptions and defaults in a fairly natural way. We have already seen how this strategy has been applied in R1.

In conclusion of our discussion of contexts, it is perhaps worth pointing out that R1 has no real knowledge of the properties of the contexts it deals with. McDermott admits that context names are just symbols, unlike components, say, which have all kinds of attributes and values associated with them. Consequently, R1 cannot reason about contexts in the same way that it can reason about components or constraints; it simply recognizes when a new context is needed and when it has done all it can in a particular context. This seems to be all that the task requires. However, one could perhaps conceive of other artificial intelligence applications in which reasoning about context was important, e.g. a dialogue-understanding program which tries to discern whether a particular series of statements is meant to be serious or intended as a joke; or a tactical decision program which tries to decide whether a particular manoeuvre on the part of an enemy's forces is a bluff, an exercise or a genuine attack.

9.2.4   Reasoning with constraints: the Match method

To illustrate the use of constraints by R1, let us consider subtask (3) in Section 9.2.2: the configuration of the unibus modules in their boxes and cabinets.

The main trouble with 'bin packing' problems of this kind is that there is usually no way of pruning the search space, because there is no suitable evaluation function for partial configurations. In other words, there is no formula that you can apply which will allow you to say that partial configuration C is better than some other partial solution D. A system of functional and spatial relationships is a complex whole, and it succeeds or fails as such. It is not possible to tell in advance, by looking at some solution fragment, whether or not it will lead to a complete and acceptable solution, unless there are regularities in the system, e.g. various kinds of symmetry, which introduce redundancy.

In the context of subtask (3), there are certain constraints that can be used to inform the search for a solution:

- Each unibus module requires a backplane slot of the right pinning type.
- Each backplane in a box must be positioned so that its modules draw power from only one set of regulators.
- Regulators can only supply a certain amount of power, regardless of the number of slots available on the backplane.
- If a module needs panel space, the space must be in the cabinet that contains the module.
- Some modules may require supporting modules, either in the same backplane or in the same box.
- There is an optimal sequence for modules on the unibus, in terms of their interrupt priority and transfer rate, and so modules should be positioned as close to that sequence as possible.

Obviously there is a limited amount of box space. As a result, you can't tell whether or not a module's configuration is acceptable until all the modules are on the unibuses. Sometimes R1 has to generate more than one candidate solution before an acceptable one is found.

Although R1 may have several attempts at a particular task, as in the above example, it never backtracks. In other words, it never makes a decision which it later has to go back and undo. At any point in the problem solving process, it has enough knowledge to recognize what to do – this cuts down on trial and error search. Backtracking is computationally expensive, especially in terms of run-time storage, as well as making the behaviour of programs hard to understand.

The basic problem solving method used by R1 is called, rather confusingly, 'Match'. All pattern-directed inference systems use matching to some extent, of course, but Match with a big 'M' is more than this. A program using Match 'recognizes' what to at any given point in its execution, rather than generating candidate solutions and then trying them out as in the 'generate and test' paradigm used by expert systems like DENDRAL.

We don't usually think of matching as being search; pattern-matching is normally a process whereby search is initiated, continued or terminated. For example, matching often determines whether or not an operator is applicable, or whether a solution has be found. However, Match can be considered as a search technique in which you look for an exemplar which instantiates some 'form', a form being a symbolic expression containing variables. An example of a form would be the left-hand side of a production rule: a symbol structure made up of one or more patterns which may share variables. The search space for Match is then 'the space of all instantiations of the variables in a form' (McDermott, 1982, page 54), with each state in the space a partially instantiated form.

It is the form that embodies the domain-specific knowledge about constraint satisfaction, and it is the Match method which applies this knowledge to particular problems. However, McDermott lists two conditions which must be satisfied if this rather 'weaker' notion of search is to be successful in finding the solution to some problem:

1. The correspondance condition. It must be possible to determine the value that a variable can take on 'locally', i.e. using only such information as is ready to hand at the point of correspondance when you compare the exemplar with the pattern. In the case of R1, 'ready to hand' information is that information which is available from the current context. Decisions must not depend upon information that will only become available in 'daughter' and 'sister' contexts elsewhere in the hierarchy. This is not to say that contexts should be independent; merely that subsequent matches do not affect what has already been matched.

2. The propagation condition. When an operator is applied, this should only affect aspects of the solution which have not yet been determined. In other words, there should be no 'retroactive' effects of decisions;

decisions must be partially ordered. This condition is so called because the consequences of our decisions should propagate in one direction only: from a particular context to its 'daughter' and (as yet unvisited) 'sister' contexts, and not to its ancestors (or 'aunties').

McDermott divides R1's rules into three categories, depending upon the role they play in the Match method.

1. Operator rules create and extend partial configurations.
2. Sequencing rules determine the order in which decisions are made, mostly by manipulating contexts.
3. Information-gathering rules access the database of components or perform various computations for the benefit of the other rules.

It was noted earlier that the use of contexts in configuration had a certain psychological justification, in that human experts tended to approach the problem in this way. No attempt was made to justify contexts by saying that they were somehow 'necessary' from a formal or computational point of view. With regard to Match, the situation is somewhat reversed. Humans frequently depart from the Match method, in that they tend to use a form of heuristic search that involves some backtracking. However, the computational advantages of Match are considerable, and there are formal, or at least semi-formal, reasons for supposing that heuristic search is not a good method for programming a solution to this problem. These reasons include the paucity of adequate evaluation functions and the inherent inefficiency of backtracking mentioned earlier.

9.2.5   Some interesting facts and figures about R1

The initial version of R1 was handed over to DEC (Digital Equipment Corporation) in January of 1980. The rule set consisted of about 750 productions, and these were adequate for configuring the VAX-11/780. By 1984, the rule set had grown to around 3300 productions, and the range of systems configured included several other members of the VAX-11 and PDP-11 range.

The average number of patterns in a production's left-hand side is about 6, while the average number of actions in the right-hand side is 3. R1's component database currently contains about 5500 entries. Despite the size of the program, run-time statistics show that an average consultation takes less than two CPU minutes running on a VAX-11/780. This is an unqualified testimony to the power of the OPS concept and the efficiency of the Rete match algorithm. About 50% of the knowledge in the production memory is frequently used, so one is not running a tiny subset of the system at any one time.

About 10% of R1's solutions exhibit problems of one kind or another. If you redo the calculations so as to consider only distinct problems, hence not counting different manifestations of the same problem more than once, the figure drops to around 3%. Many of these problems relate to missing or incorrect part descriptions, and are therefore corrigible; a smaller proportion involve incorrect rules.

9.3   R1 and OPS: summary and conclusions

One of the things that renders R1 a serious object of study is that it gives us some insight into the way in which a large and non-trivial knowledge-based program can develop over a period of years. There are two main issues involved here: evaluation and extension. Evaluation is concerned with determining how well an expert system does the job it sets out to do, while extension is concerned with adding new knowledge to the knowledge base.

9.3.1   Evaluation of an expert system

Evaluation is a difficult issue to address; it is even difficult to discuss. Expectations regarding expert system performance are often hazy. The program must run in a reasonable time and be able to deal with a collection of 'typical' cases, perhaps those cases used to elicit the knowledge from the domain expert. However, it is wishful thinking to suppose that one can devise some test or series of tests that will tell you when an expert system has reached some imaginary peak of performance. In realistic domains that lack the structure of formal systems like mathematics and logic, it is unlikely that you will ever be able to 'prove' that your expert system is indeed an expert in any rational sense. The evidence must be empirical, and yet the range of possible situations that your program might encounter will be vast in any non-trivial application. Even though R1 has to date processed 80 000 orders, it has only seen a small fraction of the space of possible orders it might receive.

In the early days of R1, McDermott reports that it was predicted that the program would have to be 90% correct in its configurations before it began to be useful. R1 took 3 years to reach this goal, but experience shows that the prediction was in érror. The program was able to assist with configuration before it reached this criterion, because it did no worse than its human predecessors. The configuration task is such that no single individual is entrusted to perform it alone; individuals typically lack both the knowledge and the time to take total responsibility for an order. So there was already sufficient redundancy in the system for R1 to usefully contribute its two cents' worth.

Is comparison with a human expert the criterion? This is more difficult than it sounds. In addition to the problem of finding a suitable set of test cases, there is the problem of making the right comparison. The configuration task is usually performed by technical editors; however, R1 does the job at a lower level of detail than this human expert, taking in aspects of the role of the technician who physically assembles the system. So should we compare R1 with the technical editor plus the technician? Well, it's not really that simple either: R1 doesn't really assemble the system, of course, so it's operating rather differently from the man who actually manipulates the components, and is therefore able to experiment with them directly. Surely this isn't comparing like with like?

Given that we can't prove that a system is expert, using the apparatus of either mathematical logic or psychological experiment, what does that leave? It leaves us with the much weaker notions of adequacy, parsimony and elegance. A system is adequate to a task if it succeeds on test cases, or fails in such a way as can readily be put right. A system is parsimonious if it doesn't use a sledgehammer to crack a nut; in other words, it shouldn't use more conceptual and computational devices than it needs. Elegance is more difficult to define, but it may nonetheless be important. A system is elegant if it exhibits a requisite variety in its methods, but no more; it does the same kinds of things in the same way, and there are clean interfaces between different modules. I have seen many programs which are both adequate and (sometimes too) parsimonious, but which lack elegance. There is no symmetry, no uniformity and hence no clarity and no easy extensibility – which leads us to the next section.

9.3.2 Knowledge elicitation and extensibility

I shall consider elicitation along with extensibility, because decisions taken during the initial knowledge elicitation stage may have profound effects upon the extensibility of the resulting system.

In the case of R1, McDermott (1982) has a number of interesting observations to make.

- Human experts have a clear idea of the regular decomposition of the main task into subtasks, and the temporal relationships between these subtasks.
- Within subtasks, however, their behaviour is more driven by exceptions than regularities, e.g. 'when performing subtask x, do y, unless z'.
- Humans are not very good at recalling these exceptional circumstances on demand, i.e. they are driven by events.

It can readily be seen that this regularity of relations between tasks but irregularity within tasks is dealt with in a peculiarly satisfying way in OPS5 by the use of contexts and special cases. Refinement of rules and contexts provides a modular way of correcting erroneous behaviour during the initial stages of program development. In addition to adding new knowledge for the purpose of debugging old knowledge, there are three other reasons for extending a knowledge base:

- to add new knowledge about a wider class of data, e.g. configuring new types of machine;
- to add new knowledge and introduce new subtasks which 'flesh out' the main task, e.g. being more sophisticated about the placement of panels;

- to extend the definition of the main task, e.g. asking R1 to configure multiple CPU orders.

When is the extensibility task complete? Judging from the experience with R1, the answer may be – never. The domain of computer systems is constantly changing; this means new components with new properties capable of entering into new relationships with each other, and so both the database and the production memory will be in a more or less constant state of flux. 'Hang on,' I hear you say, 'if you're all the time extending the system, it will never be wholly bug-free.' That is correct. Furthermore, the system will always present the evaluation process with a moving target, making an already difficult task even more difficult.

It would be pleasant to be able to counterbalance all this with some good news, but there isn't any. There is a tendency to talk about incremental program development as if tossing a new rule into the knowledge base were a trivial matter, so that after a certain point in the program's working life, extension could be left to personnel less experienced in knowledge engineering than the program's creator. The literature offers little or no evidence of this as a general principle, although there are probably some classes of domain which present less of a problem than others. The experience with R1 is that incremental development leads naturally to redundancy and *ad hoc* solutions; in other words, unless vigorously opposed, the amount of disorder in the program will always increase. Rebuilding a system from scratch is expensive in terms of time, money and effort; so it seems likely that the only alternative is occasional surgery to combat the more malignant manifestations of universal entropy.

9.3.3 What has been learned from building R1?

It might be felt that R1 is just a commercial success story which hasn't really advanced our state of knowledge. I think that this is untrue for two reasons: we have learned a lot about the development process, as indicated above, and we have learned something about the power of production systems using the Match method. Thus, for certain classes of problem, Match has been shown to be a more natural solution than the backward chaining of rules in MYCIN. Given the advent of PROLOG, this is perhaps a timely warning, since the tendency of naïve practitioners in the UK is to use PROLOG's depth-first search with automatic backtracking to implement a backward-chaining 'production system', whether or not this method really suits the problem or the nature of the underlying search space. There are several powerful reasons for not doing this:

- PROLOG-based production systems are unlikely to be as efficient as OPS, since they lack any equivalent of the Rete match algorithm.
- Depth-first search is inherently costly and it is also incomplete (since it may never terminate).

- There are domains with enough structure to allow programs to make hard and fast decisions based on situational cues.

Needless to say, this is not an attack on PROLOG, but a cautionary note to the effect that the 'obvious' and 'easy' ways of doing things don't always work – a phenomenon well known to artificial intelligence programmers. An example of a sensible application of PROLOG to expert-level problem solving can be found in Chapter 11. But next we turn to another success story: the rational reconstruction of PUFF as the CENTAUR system.

Chapter 10 CENTAUR: A Combination of Frames and Rules

CENTAUR is an expert system which combines the frame-like structure of systems like CADUCEUS with the rule-based approach of MYCIN and its derivatives. The system was originally used to reimplement PUFF (a consultation program for pulmonary disease originally constructed in EMYCIN), but the basic approach shows signs of being applicable outside the medical domain. Aikins' (1983) account of CENTAUR is particularly clear, and the comparisons drawn between her program and earlier systems are very instructive.

10.1 Knowledge representation in CENTAUR

In Chapter 4, a 'frame' was defined as a very flexible kind of record, capable of representing information about 'typical' objects and situations. One suspects that a great deal of our general knowledge about the world has this fundamental character. For example, a typical car has four wheels and a typical gun fires bullets, even though there are such things as three-wheeled cars and flame-throwers.

Trying to represent this kind of information using either rules or logic poses difficult problems. To handle exceptions using rules alone, one would have to cover all special cases in the premises: a clumsy and unacceptable solution if applied on a grand scale. To handle exceptions using logic, one engages in non-monotonic reasoning, i.e. one must be prepared to retract 'old' propositions as well as assert 'new' ones. This complicates matters considerably, and neither the formal nor the computational ramifications of having to resolve such conflicts is well understood.

Aikins argues that using more than one knowledge representation structure has two main advantages.

1. It is not necessary to force all that is known about the domain into a single codification scheme.

2. Different types of knowledge can be separated in the formalism.

Unlike some expert systems theorists, Aikins does not argue for a particular kind of knowledge structure; rather she is concerned that the chosen scheme or schemes should be expressive enough to represent different kinds of knowledge and render them explicit so that they can be manipulated by the program. This might include knowledge about the function or purpose of knowledge units, and the context in which particular knowledge units should be applied. Such information could be useful in guiding and regulating the activation of the large number of pattern-directed modules typically required to solve non-trivial problems by symbolic computation.

Aikins defines 'context' as 'the set of facts or preconditions which when taken together describe the situation in which the knowledge is applicable'. In production systems of the kind discussed so far, it is clear that the sole contextual mechanism is the working memory, insofar as it is the matching of the trigger patterns of rules against tokens representing goals or data in the working memory which decides which rules are entitled to fire. Conflict resolution, where provided, suffers from two main faults from the present point of view.

1. The mechanism is coded into the interpreter, and therefore difficult to modify, although options are often supplied (as in OPS5).

2. The strategic knowledge implicit in the conflict resolution algorithm is nowhere represented explicitly, and therefore cannot be reasoned about by other parts of the program.

One of the arguments for the use of frames is that they allow one to augment domain knowledge with knowledge about the context in which such knowledge is applied. For example, experts have knowledge about the inherent reliability of data that has been gathered in different ways. They also have expectations about patterns in the data, and can detect obvious inconsistencies and inaccuracies.

The original implementation of PUFF in EMYCIN performed satisfactorily, in terms of solving the problems posed to it, but the knowledge representation was found to be deficient in a number of respects.

- It was difficult to represent typical patterns of data or typical classes of patient.

- Adding or modifying rules to encode additional knowledge or refine existing knowledge frequently had unexpected effects.

- Changing the order in which information was requested from the user proved to be difficult, since the requests were automatically generated as the interpreter fired the rules.

- Generating clear explanations presented problems, since little more than a trace of rule activations was available.

Aikins argued, as Clancey had done, that the very modularity and uniformity of production rules, which had been cited as positive features, had their negative aspect. Most rule sets contain implicit groupings, either using various kinds of indexing concealed in the interpreter (e.g. the ORGRULES and PATRULES of MYCIN), or having conditions and actions that manipulated goal tokens in working memory (e.g. the context symbols of R1). Many of the problems cited above can be traced to the failure to differentiate between the different kinds of knowledge, which may need to be represented and applied in different ways.

10.1.1 The structure of prototypes

In order to explain how CENTAUR works, it will help if I first summarize the domain of application. PUFF's task is to interpret measurements gained from certain tests of pulmonary function (i.e. the working of the lungs). Typical measurements are the amount of gas in the lungs, and the rates of flow of gases into and out of the lungs. The purpose of the tests is to determine if the patient shows signs of lung disease, and gauge the severity of his or her condition. The program was developed by Stanford University in conjunction with the Pacific Medical Center in San Francisco.

The basic idea in CENTAUR is that frame-like structures provide an explicit representation of the context in which production rules do their reasoning. This allows one to separate strategic knowledge about how to control the reasoning from situational knowledge about what can be inferred from what set of facts. In theory, this allows inferential knowledge to be put to different uses in different contexts, with gains in both economy and coherence for the knowledge representation.

Thus production rules can be conceived as simply one kind of value for a particular kind of slot in a frame. Associating rules with slots in frames provides one mechanism for organizing rules into what appear to be natural groupings. The other slots in a given frame provide the explicit context in which its rules are applied. The frame-like structures used in CENTAUR are prototypes, components and facts.

Of the 24 prototypes, 21 represent disease patterns in pulmonary function, thus representing domain-specific knowledge rather in the manner of INTERNIST's disease areas, one represents knowledge common to all such diseases, while the other two represent relatively domain-free knowledge about how to run a consultation and how to review the evidence. Thus knowledge is organized around the diagnostic categories themselves, as in INTERNIST, rather than this organization being only implicit in a set of uniform and unstructured rules.

Prototypes in CENTAUR contain both object- and meta-level knowledge. They are arranged in a network, a portion of which is reproduced in Figure 10.1. At the top of the hierarchy is the CONSULTATION prototype, which effectively controls the way in which the consultation develops through various stages, such as initial data entry and the triggering of hypotheses. Then there is a layer of prototypes which represent different pathological states, such as RESTRICTIVE LUNG DISEASE and OBSTRUCTIVE AIRWAYS DISEASE. Finally, diseases are specialized according to their subtype and degree of severity. Thus OBSTRUCTIVE AIRWAYS DISEASE can be categorized as MILD, MODERATE, MODERATELY SEVERE or SEVERE, while its subtypes are ASTHMA, BRONCHITIS and EMPHYSEMA.

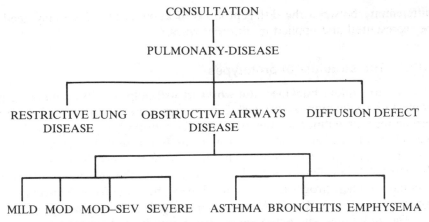

Figure 10.1   Prototypes representing lung pathology.

Each prototype has slots for a number of components, which point to subframes of knowledge at the object level. Thus, associated with each pulmonary disease prototype, there are slots which represent lung tests, each of which is a frame-like structure in its own right, with its own internal structure. For example, the OAD (Obstructive Airways Disease) frame has 13 components, each with its associated name, range of plausible values, and importance measure. In addition, a component frame often contains a special slot, called 'inference rules', which holds a set of production rules for inferring a value for that component. If no such rule set is provided, or if the rule set fails to return a value, then the system questions the user. This provision of a rule set is rather like procedural attachment: the main differences are the stylized syntax in which rules are written and the gain in modularity over the use of general procedures. Conventional procedural attachment can involve arbitrarily complex pieces of LISP code which are hard to understand and modify.

The facts that the program works with are frames with six slots, containing information about the name of the parameter, its value, the degree of certainty, its source, classification and justification.

As well as domain-specific knowledge, prototypes contain control slots, meta-level knowledge about how to reason with these knowledge structures. The slots hold LISP clauses for:

- instantiating a prototype, by specifying a set of components for which values should be determined;
- reacting to its confirmation or disconfirmation, by specifying the set of prototypes to be explored next;
- printing statements that summarize the final conclusion.

Each control slot can be considered as the consequent part of a rule whose condition is that the situation must match that described by the prototype.

Aikins characterizes the general approach being used in CENTAUR as 'hypothesize and match', i.e. the basic problem solving paradigm involves seeing how well some (possibly idealized) representation of a hypothetical situation actually fits the facts. CENTAUR's prototypes therefore represent hypothetical diagnoses, and the task is to find a diagnostic category that is supported by the data. This is done by attempting to instantiate prototypes in order to determine the goodness of the match, and it may involve obtaining more information from the user.

10.1.2 Rules embedded in prototypes

The reader will remember that it is the prototype components which represent the majority of the domain-specific object-level knowledge, since it is these structures which contain information about the tests which can be used to diagnose a particular pulmonary disease. These components are the values of slots in the disease prototypes, but they have their own internal structure and are therefore prototypes in their own right. Thus, in addition to having production rules embedded in prototypes, it is true to say that there are also prototypes embedded in other prototypes. This introduces another dimension of organization in the arrangement of prototypes in addition to the hierarchical one explicitly represented in terms of types and subtypes of disease. Data structures which can be embedded in themselves in this way are often called 'recursive'.

There are five different kinds of rules used by CENTAUR:

1. Inference rules. These are associated with components representing clinical parameters, and specify ways in which their values might be determined.

2. Triggering rules. These are antecedent rules associated with clinical parameters which serve to advance prototypes as hypotheses with some degree of certainty.

3. Fact-residual rules. After a conclusion has been reached, in the form of a set of confirmed prototypes, these rules attempt to account for any case data that has been left out.

4. Refinement rules. These suggest further tests, and their execution returns a final set of prototypes with an indication of which ones account for which facts.

5. Summary rules. These have actions which cause the information in prototypes to be translated into English and printed.

Other slots include those for general book-keeping, e.g. name of the author, source of the information, and those which record the circumstances under which the prototype was evoked for explanatory purposes.

CENTAUR's rules are therefore classified according to their function. In the EMYCIN implementation of PUFF, all rules are classified as inference rules, even though many of them do other things, e.g. summarizing evidence and setting default values. Also, since CENTAUR rules are the values of slots, their context of application is made explicit. For example, in the EMYCIN implementation of PUFF, rules for inferring the values of clinical parameters are indexed according to which parameter features in the conclusion, or action, side of the rules, as is the case in the original MYCIN program. In CENTAUR, rules for inferring a particular parameter are stored in a slot value in the prototype component representing that parameter, and only applied within in the context of that prototype, i.e. when that prototype is active.

Another way of looking at this is to say that EMYCIN's rule invocation is guided globally and extrinsically by the context tree, whereas rule invocation in CENTAUR is controlled locally and intrinsically by prototype activation. Aikins' argument is that her reimplementation of PUFF is both conceptually cleaner and computationally more intelligible, although the actual performance of the problem solving program is not significantly improved. In other words, one of the interesting things about CENTAUR, and the reason for including a chapter on the system in this book, is that it raises issues with regard to the design and implementation of expert systems generally, and constitutes a convincing demonstration of the fact that there is always more than one way of applying the techniques of knowledge-based programming to the solution of some problem.

10.2 CENTAUR's control structure: hypothesize and match

A run of the CENTAUR consultation program consists of an interpreter executing an agenda of tasks. Each task is an action, specified by a call to a LISP function. New tasks are added to the agenda by prototype control slots and by other tasks (of which they are the subtasks).

A primary use for the agenda is to provide an explanation of why the system behaved as it did in the course of the consultation. Consequently, each task entry contains information about both the source of the task and the reason that the task was scheduled. The source of the task will be a prototype or another task, since tasks are added to the agenda either by prototype control slots or in the course of executing tasks already on the agenda. The reasons are generated from the name of the prototype and the name of the control slot responsible for setting up the task. However, there are some general tasks which are not specific to any one prototype, such as 'order the hypothesis list', and these have text strings associated with them which give reasons for their use.

During program execution, a prototype is always in one of three states:

- inactive, i.e. not being considered as a hypothesis;
- potentially relevant, i.e. suggested by data values;
- active, i.e. selected from the above and placed on the hypothesis list.

The reader will remember that disease prototypes represent hypotheses, rather as do disease models in INTERNIST. The hypothesis list is simply a list of prototypes paired with their certainty factors, ordered in decreasing order of certainty. Two other lists keep track of confirmed and disconfirmed prototypes.

The key stages in a CENTAUR consultation are:

- entering the initial data;
- triggering the prototypes using antecedent rules;
- scoring the prototypes and selecting one to be 'current';
- using known facts to fill in the current prototype;
- testing the match between the facts and the expected values;
- accounting for data left over by the initial diagnosis;
- refining the diagnosis accordingly;
- summarizing and printing the results.

Thus the consultation proceeds in stages, rather as a normal consultation might. However, it is important to stress that there is nothing in the LISP code which explicitly represents these stages, in the way that tasks are represented, say. Rather, the stages fall out of the program behaviour, generating a chain of events that we recognize as being typical of clinical diagnosis.

Figure 10.2, taken from Aikins (1983), shows the initial stage of a CENTAUR consultation. Lines beginning with two asterisks indicate responses typed by the user. Everything else is output by the system, with tracing information shown in brackets.

```
18-Nov-79 23:22:24 [consultation of 23-Feb-77 11:55AM]

*CENTAUR*

Tracing level (0-3)
** 2
Agenda printing?
** No
Consultation strategy:
** ?

Please select from among CONFIRMATION, ELIMINATION,
FIXED-ORDER
Consultation strategy:
** CONFIRMATION
```

Figure 10.2   Starting a CENTAUR consultation.

To begin with, the CONSULTATION prototype is selected as the current prototype, and the empty agenda is given two tasks: to 'fill-in' and then 'confirm' the current prototype, courtesy of the TO-FILL-IN and IF-CONFIRMED control slots in the CONSULTATION prototype. The TO-FILL-IN slot of the prototype actually contains three tasks, each of which sets a variable for the consultation:

- TRACING-LEVEL. This variable can take a value from 0 to 3 and governs the amount of detail in the trace left behind by program execution.
- AGENDA-PRINTING. This variable specifies whether tasks will be printed out as they are added to the agenda and executed.

```
CONSULTATION
------------
NAME: CONSULTATION
HYPOTHESIS: A consultation is desired
EXPLANATION: Consultation
AUTHOR: AIKINS
DATE: 27-OCT-77 15:58:45
MORESPECIFIC (DOMAIN PULMONARY-DISEASE)


TO-FILL-IN:
 Ask for the TRACING-LEVEL for the CONSULTATION
 Ask for the AGENDA-PRINTING for the CONSULTATION
 Ask for the STRATEGY for the CONSULTATION


IF-CONFIRMED:
 Set the confirmation threshold to 0
 Set the percentage of filled-in slots necessary to confirm
 the prototype to .75
 Set the default procedure for filling in slots to fill
 in slots in decreasing order of their importance measures
 Determine the domain of the consultation
 Select the current best prototype
 Fill in the prototype
 Apply tasks in the if-confirmed slot
 Mark facts that are accounted for by the prototype
 Apply the refinement rules associated with the confirmed
 prototypes
 Apply the summary rules associated with the confirmed prototypes
 Execute actions associated with the confirmed prototypes
```

Figure 10.3   Unfolding of tasks in CENTAUR.

- STRATEGY. This variable determines which of the three different strategies the system will use for selecting the current best prototype on the hypothesis list.

There are three different strategies available for selecting the best current prototype: confirmation (select the best match and attempt to confirm it), elimination (select the worst match and attempt to eliminate it), and fixed-order (use a predetermined order of evaluation).

This use of prototypes can be contrasted with the use of meta-rules in EMYCIN on two counts.

1. Meta-rules select object-level rules on the basis of their content, and not the context in which the selection is made.
2. Meta-rules typically satisfy system goals; they do not usually set them.

The first three tasks in the IF-CONFIRMED slot set other variables which control the consultation, such as setting the percentage of a prototype's slots that have to be filled in before that prototype can be considered confirmed. This allows the knowledge engineer to experiment with variations on the basic control regime, and possibly tune the system for different domains. The rest of the IF-CONFIRMED tasks control the stages of the consultation, as can be seen from the listing of the CONSULTATION prototype reproduced in Figure 10.3.

Once the domain of the consultation has been determined (in the present context this is pulmonary function) PULMONARY-DISEASE becomes the next current prototype. As you can see from the network fragment given in Figure 10.3, it is the only successor to the CONSULTATION prototype. It is the PULMONARY-DISEASE prototype which elicits the initial data from the user, by asking a series of questions, as shown in Figure 10.4.

It can be seen from this transcript that data values trigger prototypes even as they are being entered. Thus, the FEV1/FVC ratio of 40 activates the OAD prototype with a certainty measure of 900. (FEV1 stands for the Forced Expiratory Volume in one second, i.e. the volume of air expelled in one second during a forced breathing out, starting with the lungs full of air, while FVC stands for Forced Vital Capacity, i.e. the volume of air expired during a rapid forced breathing out, starting with the lungs full of air and ending with whatever residual volume of air is left in the lungs after full expiration.)

Certainty measures range from -1000 to 1000, and indicate how sure the system is that the prototype cited matches the data for a particular case. In other words, it is a measure of how well the actual values provided by the user fit into the prototypical or expected values stored in the slots of a prototype, and it is used to select the current best hypothesis. These measures are similar to the certainty factors found in MYCIN and EMYCIN, and the algorithm for combining more than one measure is the same in each case.

After the initial data has been elicited, a summary of the triggered prototypes is printed out for inspection, as shown in Figure 10.5.

```
————————PATIENT-7————————
1) Patient's identifying number:
** 7446
2) referral diagnosis:
** ASTHMA
   [Trigger for ASTHMA and CM900]
3) RV/RV-predicted:
** 261
4) TLC (body box) observed/predicted:
** 139
5) FVC/FVC-predicted:
** 81
   [Trigger for NORMAL and CM500]
6) FEV1/FVC ratio:
** 40
   [Trigger for OAD and CM900]
7) the DLCO/DLCO-predicted:
** 117
   [Trigger for NORMAL and CM700]
8) Change in FEV1 (after dilation)
** 31
9) MMF/MMF-predicted:
** 12
   [Trigger for OAD and CM900]
10) The slope F5025:
** 9
   [Trigger for OAD and CM900]
```

Figure 10.4   Questions and triggers in CENTAUR.

```
Hypothesis: ASTHMA, CM: 900, Reason: RDX was ASTHMA
Hypothesis: NORMAL, CM: 500, Reason: FVC was 81
Hypothesis: OAD, CM: 900, Reason: FEV1/FVC was 40
Hypothesis: NORMAL, CM: 700, Reason: DLCO was 117
Hypothesis: OAD, CM: 900, Reason: MMF was 12
Hypothesis: OAD, CM: 900, Reason: F5025 was 9


More specific hypotheses chosen: NORMAL, OAD
 [New prototypes being filled in... NORMAL, OAD]
```

Figure 10.5   Summary of triggered prototypes.

NORMAL and OAD will be considered next, since these are immediate successors of the PULMONARY-DISEASE prototype. Consideration of the ASTHMA hypothesis will be deferred, because asthma is a subtype of OAD.

The reader will have noticed that not all of the data values entered were responsible for triggering a prototype, and also that more than one prototype has been triggered. In other words, some data values did not suggest any initial hypotheses, while some values suggested OAD, and others suggested normality. As the new prototypes for NORMAL and OAD are filled in, data values such as TLC (Total Lung Capacity), which did not activate any prototypes, will be considered in the context of active hypotheses, and may cause their certainty measures to be altered. Thus, the TLC value of 139 casts doubt upon the hypothesis of normality, as shown in Figure 10.6. Data values which fall outside the range of expected values stored in the slots of a prototype will tend to lower the certainty measure associated with that prototype.

```
!Surprise value! 261 for RV in NORMAL, CM: 700
!Surprise value! 139 for TLC in NORMAL, CM: 400
!Surprise value! 40 for FEV1/FVC in NORMAL, CM: -166
!Surprise value! 12 for MMF in NORMAL, CM: -499
!Surprise value! 9 for F5025 in NORMAL, CM: -699
```

Figure 10.6   CENTAUR reporting unexpected data values.

Figure 10.6 shows that, although NORMAL was suggested as a hypothesis by two of the original test results, five other test results militate against this hypothesis being correct, and its certainty measure is reduced accordingly. (Data values which fall within the ranges specified in a prototype's slots raise its certainty measure, but this is not shown in the printout.) The hypothesis list is then constructed and ordered, with OAD as the current best prototype:

```
Hypothesis List: (OAD 999) (NORMAL -699)
I am testing the hypothesis that there is Obstructive
Airways Disease.
```

Eventually, the system will confirm the hypothesis that the patient is indeed suffering from OAD, that the degree of OAD is severe, and that the subtype of OAD is asthma. The consultation now moves into the refinement stage, which causes further questions to be asked, such as the degree of dyspnoea (shortness of breath). This stage is instigated by the application of refinement rules, which are stored with the relevant prototypes (see Figure 10.7).

```
[Refinement rules being applied...]
20) The number of pack-years of smoking:
** 17
21) The number of years ago that the patient stopped
smoking:
** 0
22) The degree of dyspnea:
** NONE
```

Figure 10.7 The application of refinement rules.

Now summary rules associated with the confirmed prototypes are executed, as shown in Figure 10.8. These merely summarize the information that has been gained in the process of filling in the prototype, and require no

```
[Actions slot of OAD being executed...]

Conclusions: the findings about the diagnosis of
obstructive airways disease are as follows:
  Elevated lung volumes indicate overinflation.
  The RV/TLC ratio is increased, suggesting a severe degree
of air trapping.
  Forced Vital Capacity is normal but the FEV1/FVC ratio
is reduced, suggesting airway obstruction of a severe
degree.
  Low mid-expiratory flow is consistent with severe
airway obstruction.
  Obstruction is indicated by curvature of the flow-volume
loop which is of a severe degree.
  Following bronchodilation, expired flow shows
excellent improvement as indicated by the change in the
FEV1.
  Following bronchodilation, expired flow shows
excellent improvement as indicated by the change in the
MMF.
  Reversibility of airway  obstruction is confirmed
by improvement in airway resistance following
bronchodilation.
```

Figure 10.8 Applying the summary rules.

further interaction with the user. The actual printing out of findings is done by the `actions` slot of the prototype in question.

```
[Actions slot of PULMONARY-DISEASE being executed...]
    ———Prototype Summary———
    ———Obstructive Airways Disease———
Obstructive Airways Disease was suggested by the
following findings
  The fev1/fvc ratio of PATIENT-7: 40
  The mmf/mmf-predicted ratio of PATIENT-7: 12
  The f5025 of PATIENT-7: 9
In addition, Obstructive Airways Disease is consistent with
  The tlc/tlc-predicted ratio of PATIENT-7: 139
  The rv/rv-predicted ratio of PATIENT-7: 261
  The f25 of PATIENT-7: 45
  The severity of coughing of PATIENT-7: NONE
  The degree of sputum production of PATIENT-7: NONE
The Obstructive Airways Disease accounts for the
following findings:
  The referral diagnosis of PATIENT-7
  The fev1/fvc ratio of PATIENT-7
  The f25 of PATIENT-7
  The severity of coughing of PATIENT-7
  The degree of sputum production of PATIENT-7

All facts have been accounted for by the confirmed
prototypes.

Conclusions:
  Smoking probably exacerbates the severity of the
patient's airway obstruction.
  Discontinuation of smoking should help relieve the
symptoms.
  Good response to bronchodilators is consistent with
an asthmatic condition, and their continued use is
indicated.
  The high diffusing capacity is consistent with asthma.
Pulmonary Function Diagnosis:
  Severe Obstructive Airways Disease
  Asthmatic type.
Consultation finished.
```

Figure 10.9 CENTAUR's final conclusions.

The printing of the final conclusions is performed by the `actions` slot of the PULMONARY-DISEASE prototype, as in Figure 10.9.

The stage-dependent behaviour of the program makes the program's output particularly easy to understand. At every stage of the process, it is clear what CENTAUR is trying to achieve, and which prototypes are active. This makes both debugging the program and understanding its conclusions easier than would be the case without the additional structure provided by the hierarchical frame system.

The next section goes into the explanations aspect in more detail.

10.3   Explanation and knowledge acquisition in CENTAUR

In order to understand a consultation, in terms of both the direction that it takes and the results that it returns, a user must be able to understand:

- the questions being asked;
- the reasons for asking them;
- the justification for intermediate conclusions.

There are four principal shortcomings associated with the kinds of explanation generated by EMYCIN:

1. The user needs to be able to follow the backward chaining of rules, and one suspects that this mode of reasoning is not typically employed by humans.
2. The knowledge in the rules may not be complete, or may not be specified at a level of detail that makes rule applications easy to follow.
3. Knowledge about context and control is not distinguished from knowledge about the content of the domain, i.e. there is no clear demarcation between meta- and object-level.
4. Each rule application only explains the most recent question, with no broader context being supplied.

10.3.1   Asking and answering questions

CENTAUR asks questions of the user if it fails to deduce some piece of information it needs from its rules, or if it needs a value for a parameter that is explicitly labelled 'ask-first'.

Questions asked of the system by the user include the HOW and WHY of EMYCIN, but with a stage-dependent interpretation. Thus, a WHY question asked in the context of a particular prototype during the diagnostic stage will be interpreted as 'why are you considering this prototype?'. In the review stage, however, such a question would be interpreted as 'why was this prototype confirmed?'. CENTAUR always displays the current prototype, so that the context of the question and answer are clear.

In addition to HOW and WHY, there are the CONTROL and ? keywords. The CONTROL command prints a translation of the current control task from the system agenda, while ? elicits a restatement of the question and the list of responses expected by the current prototype. However, CENTAUR does not have EMYCIN's 'general question' facility, although there is no reason why one could not be implemented.

As we have seen, the final interpretation consists of a list of confirmed prototypes, accompanied by a good deal of additional information, including:

- findings that suggest each prototype (the trigger values);
- findings consistent with each prototype (the plausible values);
- findings inconsistent with each prototype (error or surprise values);
- findings not accounted for by any prototype (residual facts).

Any test results not accounted for by any prototype on the confirmed list are listed, together with any other prototypes that might account for them. This helps to track down both possible errors in the tests and possible bugs in the knowledge base. Finally, a statement of conclusions and final diagnosis is presented along with a list of those prototypes which were disconfirmed during the consultation.

10.3.2   Creating new prototypes

CENTAUR has a LISP function called PROTOTYPEMAKER for adding prototypes to the knowledge base, but it is meant to be used by the knowledge engineer and not the domain expert. This function works by filling out a template derived from the prototype record declaration; prototypes are represented internally as LISP record structures. Modification to existing prototypes is achieved simply by using the INTERLISP record editor.

10.4   Summary of CENTAUR

Aikins states that it was relatively easy to represent knowledge about pulmonary function in terms of prototypes. Many medical texts present diseases by discussing typical cases. The notion of a frame is very general; the whole idea is that they should be capable of being used to capture knowledge about a very wide class of situations.

Another advantage of prototypes from the programming point of view is that they provide a way of controlling interactions between modular units of knowledge. Although the premise-action rules of production systems are supposed to be logically independent of each other, adding new rules to a system can have unforeseen effects. Relationships between prototypes are specified explicitly in the slots, and so the programmer can exercise a certain amount of choice over this.

However, it should be pointed out that CENTAUR contains fewer than 30 prototypes, and it is not altogether clear what would happen as the number of prototypes increased. The potential for complexity in terms of both relationships between prototypes and competition between them for a place on the hypothesis list could conceivably lead to the kind of scheduling and focusing problems that arose with earlier versions of INTERNIST. Having an agenda could obviously help here, as a means of imposing some kind of order from above, yet in principle one may not want to introduce another degree of complexity by overriding control decisions made by the prototypes. After all, the ability to take such decisions locally is part of the attraction of frame systems. It could be that there is some aspect of a consultation which is smaller than the 'stages' represented by higher-level prototypes and yet larger than the 'context' supplied by prototypes at the object level. Also, in certain domains, entertaining one prototype as a hypothesis might commit one to ruling certain others out; it should be possible to specify relations like mutual exclusion between prototypes by using special slots.

It might be supposed that the success of CENTAUR means that objections to frames, such as those noted at the end of Chapter 4, are irrelevant in practical applications. However, this would probably be the wrong conclusion to draw. The issues at stake are a bit more complicated than that.

Firstly, frames were conceived as a mechanism for storing general knowledge about the world, rather than specialized knowledge about a narrow domain. Encoding expertise of this kind is a rather different enterprise than trying to capture less well-defined ideas about everyday life. Thus Aikins does not employ many of the more adventurous aspects of frames, which attempt to deal with the fuzziness of natural categories and multiple perspectives upon objects and events.

Secondly, I think it is fair to say that Aikins did not set out to address any of the epistemological problems noted in Chapter 4, such as the difficult distinction between essential and accidental properties. Rather, frames are used as a structural device, for packaging knowledge and making it easier to apply. Her use of frames is therefore neutral with respect to many of the issues raised by Brachman (1985).

It is often the case in artificial intelligence that techniques developed with rather grand designs in mind eventually get scaled down and used for something less grand. Thus Quillian's work on semantic nets, which was intended to result in a 'teachable language comprehender', inspired structures which saw action in a more modest capacity, as ways of encoding static systems of concepts. In a rather similar fashion, 'frame theory' as originally promulgated by Minsky (1975) is somehow less central than the techniques which it has spawned. This is hardly a criticism of the pioneering work of either of these researchers, since a man's vision ought to exceed his grasp. I also doubt that this phenomenon is confined to the field of artificial intelligence, although critics of AI often speak as if it were!

Chapter 11 Meta-level Inference and Common Sense Reasoning in MECHO

MECHO is a program written in PROLOG which solves a wide range of problems in Newtonian mechanics (Bundy, 1978; Bundy *et al.*, 1979). It uses the technique of meta-level inference to guide search over a range of different tasks, such as common sense reasoning, model building, and the manipulation of algebraic expressions for equation solving. In order to understand some of the problems posed by this domain, it helps to look at earlier programs and the difficulties they faced.

11.1 Envisionment in NEWTON

De Kleer's (1979) work on knowledge representation for expert problem solving was extremely influential in that it encouraged researchers to use multiple representations and apply different reasoning techniques to each of these different views of the problem. The principal distinction drawn in physics problem solving was between qualitative and quantitative knowledge. A qualitative representation of a scene involving pulleys, strings, masses, and so on, would code for gross and relative features of objects and their relationships to one another. Thus, object *A* can be known to be above object *B*, or bigger than object *C* without the specification of exact positions, or precise measurements of size. A quantitative representation would be a set of equations which precisely specified the position, volume etc. of the objects involved, and described their movements and collisions within some spatial-temporal framework.

Reasoning with qualitative representations is very much like everyday reasoning. For example, we know that unsupported objects fall to the ground, and that a roller-coaster released at the top of a steep slope will gather enough momentum to climb a gentler slope once it reaches the bottom. Reasoning with quantitative representations will more closely resemble calculation: the symbolic manipulation of equations and numerical quantities.

De Kleer implemented an expert physics problem solving program called NEWTON, which deals with the mechanics of objects moving on surfaces; he made the following claims for it.

- It uses qualitative reasoning whenever possible, and only resorts to equations if necessary.

- It recognizes nonsensical problems by using common sense reasoning.
- It is not confused or made inefficient by irrelevant facts, objects or equations.

The fundamental qualitative process in NEWTON is called 'envisionment'. This can be thought of as a succession of 'snapshots' which describe an object's changes in position over time, and attribute causality to changes in velocity, direction and so on. These snapshots are organized into a tree-like data structure, which stands for an entire event. Qualitative ambiguities correspond to forks in the tree, with descendant nodes describing possible futures based on incomplete information. Some problems can be solved by envisionment alone, while others can be shown to be insoluble.

Quantitative knowledge is represented in NEWTON by grouping equations together into packages with the cumbersome title of Restricted Access Local Consequent Methods (RALCMs). For example, the equations which represent the relationships between the angles and sides of a triangle form one such group. The idea is that the process of envisionment should steer the program towards the right packet of equations, without having to decide for every equation known to the system, 'Is this relevant or not?'.

The role played by envisionment in NEWTON is rather similar to that played by plan generators in earlier programs and by meta-level inference in later programs; indeed, it provides the link between them. A recognition of the qualitative ambiguities to be resolved on the way to a goal results in a primitive plan. It also constitutes a way of reasoning about what you know, and what you still need to know in order to solve a problem.

The advantages of this kind of dual representation are, therefore:

- simple problems can be solved by simple techniques;
- even where qualitative analyses fail, they set up plans which can simplify subsequent quantitative analyses;
- qualitative analyses can handle indeterminacy and incompleteness in problem specification.

It is obvious that expert-level problem solving requires both domain knowledge and strategies for applying that knowledge. However, it is all too easy to forget that most applications also require the ability to do common sense reasoning using general knowledge about the world. In other words, the practice of even the most esoteric skills often takes place within situations which obey the normal laws of time and space which govern ordinary objects and events. It is arguable that human beings 'know' a great deal about these mundane spatial, temporal and causal relationships between everyday entities, and that many of our more specialized activites rely upon this epistemological base.

As mentioned in Chapter 1, a good deal of early AI research involved reasoning about 'micro' or 'toy' worlds, consisting of simple objects, such as a child's building blocks, and the rather straightforward relationships between them, e.g. Block1 is on top of Block2, and so on. However, there is a sense in which there are no micro worlds, but only perspectives on the real world, in which the knowledge that we have acquired simply by 'being in the world' applies. One suspects that the majority of this knowledge has never been formally described, partly because it contains certain basic assumptions without which we could not proceed.

This is extremely bad news for expert systems designers, because it forces them to make certain difficult decisions concerning:

- the amount of general knowledge one needs as a precondition to applying the more specialized domain knowledge;
- the depth of understanding of the real world 'setting' of the domain that the program must achieve;
- the degree to which convenient idealizations and simplifying assumptions can be incorporated into the program's model of the domain.

The MECHO program, to which we now turn, is worth studying because it addresses some of these issues in an interesting and creative manner.

11.2   MECHO as an essay in computational logic

The MECHO project was a large-scale affair with many facets, including natural language understanding, physics problem solving, and algebraic manipulation (see Chapter 14 of Bundy, 1983 for an overview). Figure 11.1 is intended to give you some idea of its main components and the relationships between them. Our main interest is in the mechanisms associated with the problem solving and database control modules.

Quantitative aspects of physics problem solving are handled by an equation-solving program called PRESS. This uses some of the same principles of meta-level inference as the main MECHO program to guide search, and is therefore more than a mere 'number crunching' package. The syntax and

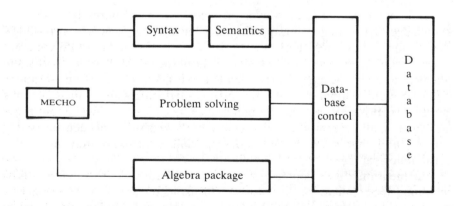

Figure 11.1   Overview of MECHO.

semantics modules address the problem of natural language understanding in this domain.

MECHO follows de Kleer into the world of Newtonian mechanics, and adopts much of his outlook on qualitative and quantitative representations, but employs radically different methods for controlling the search for a solution. This account will concentrate almost exclusively upon the question of how one controls deductions involving logic-based representations. However, the control issue cannot be considered in isolation from some of the knowledge representation problems that the researchers faced. Accordingly, we shall begin with a detailed examination of the techniques employed, particularly those dealing with time and motion.

11.2.1   Knowledge representation in MECHO

The MECHO interpreter, called MBASE, is written in PROLOG, a programming language which is essentially a theorem prover for a subset of predicate logic. Thus MECHO itself is not implemented directly in PROLOG, and its inference engine does not conform to the standard procedural interpretation of the Horn clause subset. Creating one's own language in this way is fairly common in artificial intelligence applications, since it gives one precise control over the way in which programs execute, as well as the flexibility to experiment with different data structures and methods of procedure invocation.

In order to give substance to this discussion, I shall draw my examples from the 'roller-coaster' problems (see Figure 11.2) described by de Kleer (1979) and cited in Bundy (1978).

1. The sliding block. At time t, the block starts from rest at point a. Will it reach point d?

2. The loop the loop. At time t, the block starts from rest at point a. How small can h be, such that the block will still loop the loop?

3. The great dome. The block is given a nudge from rest. At what point does it take off from the surface of the dome?

It can readily be seen that the above problems are not easy to understand without the aid of a diagram. The behaviour of particles on complex paths is something that we tend to visualize in a rather intuitive way at the level of qualitative analysis. The MECHO project adopted de Kleer's method of symbolic notation, which involved describing paths in terms of their first and second derivatives of slope and concavity. Thus a path such as S, shown in Figure 11.3, can be partitioned into subpaths of invariant slope and concavity. The diagram is reproduced from Bundy (1978).

What follows is a somewhat simplified view of the syntax and semantics of MECHO's knowledge representation. The examples of MECHO code are all taken from publications of the MECHO group, but they have in some cases been altered by me to make them more readable and easier to understand. These changes are all cosmetic (e.g. using longer and more mnemonic variable names) and therefore should not detract from the fundamental issues.

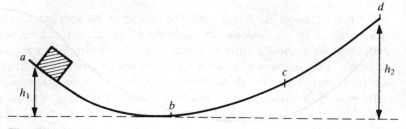

1. The sliding block.

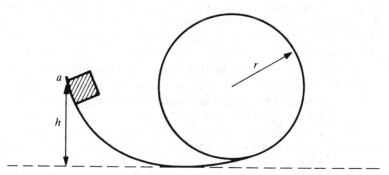

2. The loop the loop.

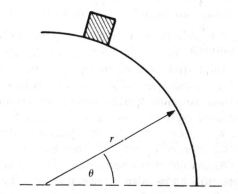

3. The great dome.

Figure 11.2 Roller-coaster problems.

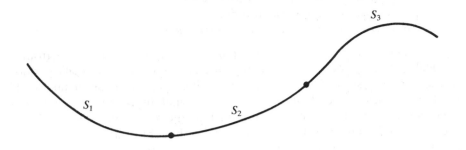

Path	Slope	Concavity
S_1	Down	Concave
S_2	Up	Concave
S_3	Up	Convex

Figure 11.3   Representing slope.

A knowledge base for MECHO is a set of clauses of the general form

$$P \leftarrow Q_1, \ldots, Q_n.$$

where P is the conclusion that we wish to draw, and the Q_i are the conditions that must first be satisfied. As in PROLOG, a query that unifies with P can be construed as a procedure invocation, and the unifier can be considered as a mechanism for passing actual parameters to the Q_i, which constitute the body of the procedure. In the case where there are no conditions, the arrow can be dropped, and P usually denotes a fact.

Facts are ground literals such as:

isa(m, moment).
isa(p, period).
initial(p, m).

which collectively assert that **m** is some interval, called a **moment**, which is the first moment in some larger interval, **p**, which is a **period**. All symbolic descriptions dependent on time have an argument that codes for particular moments or periods, for example

at(block, position, moment).

Qualitative inference rules are procedures, such as the following, in which expressions with an initial capital letter are variables.

motion(Part, Path, Start, Side, Per)
← get_Started(Part, Path, Start, Side, Per),
 no_StoPPing(Part, Path, Start, Side, Per),

11.2.3 The use of schemata and meta-rules

In order to explain the way in which MECHO attempts to control deduction in the course of searching for a solution, it seems sensible to take a specific example, and give a sketch of the mechanisms needed to solve it. I have chosen a pulley problem from an examination paper, cited in Bundy *et al.* (1979).

The statement of the problem in English is as follows:

'Two particles of mass b and c are connected by a light string passing over a smooth pulley. Find the acceleration of the particle of mass b.'

Such a problem statement would be input to the program and processed by the natural language routines in the syntax and semantics modules. The internal workings of these modules do not concern us here. Their output is a predicate calculus representation of the problem in terms of a set of assertions, e.g. information about the different kinds of entity, such as physical objects and periods of time;

> **isa(period, period1)**
> **isa(particle, p1)**
> **isa(particle, p2)**
> **isa(string, s1)**
> **isa(pulley, pull)**

information about the subparts of an object, such as a string, which will have two ends and a mid-point;

> **end(s1, end1, right)**
> **end(s1, end2, left)**
> **mid-point(s1, mid-point1)**

information about relationships between objects, such as the string, the particles and the pulley at a particular point in time;

> **fixed-contact(end1, p1, period1)**
> **fixed-contact(end2, p2, period1)**
> **fixed-contact(mid-point1, pull, period1)**

information about the properties of objects;

> **mass(p1, mass1, period1)**
> **mass(p2, mass2, period1)**
> **mass(s1, zero, period1)**
>
> **coeff(pull, zero)**
>
> **accel(p1, a1, 270, period1)**
> **accel(p2, a2, 90, period1)**
>
> **measure(mass1, b)**
> **measure(mass2, c)**

and information about which quantities are given and which are sought;

given(mass1)
given(mass2)

sought(a1).

A great deal of additional information is required to solve problems of this kind. In addition to knowledge of Newton's laws of motion, one needs knowledge about both pulley systems and the kind of assumptions that one is allowed to make in solving such problems. The former is general knowledge about a common form of mechanical device, whereas the latter is meta-knowledge about the 'rules of the game' when answering examination questions. For example, one is allowed to assume that the acceleration is constant, although the question doesn't explicitly say that this is the case. Without such simplifying assumptions, the problem would be too difficult for students.

MECHO uses various structures to represent these different kinds of everyday knowledge. A common method is to use 'schemata', i.e. data structures like frames which store knowledge about typical objects or assemblies, as in CENTAUR's use of prototypes. Consider the code for the following pulley schema:

sysinfo(pullsys,
       [Pull, Str, P1, P2],
       [pulley, string, solid, solid],
       [supports(Pull, Str),
        attached(Str, P1),
        attached(Str, P2)]).

Let's look at this schema one line at a time. Taken that way, it's really very straightforward. **sysinfo** is simply a predicate which takes four arguments. The first argument, **pullsys**, says that this schema is meant to describe a typical pulley system. The second argument is simply a list of the components of the pulley system, i.e. there is a typical pulley, **Pull**, a typical string, **Str**, and two objects, **P1** and **P2**. The third argument contains type information about the entities in the second argument, i.e. **Pull** is a pulley, **Str** is a string, and **P1** and **P2** are solid bodies. The fourth argument contains a list of the relationships that hold between these entities in a typical pulley system, i.e. the pulley supports the string, while the string has an object attached at each end.

The information contained in schemata such as these often seem (to us) to be very trivial and obvious. However, there is no way in which a computer program can be made aware of such details unless they are supplied as data. Many MECHO schemata are concerned with such matters as the components of composite objects, in terms of both their type and the relationships that hold between them.

The following example shows a schema which is concerned with kinds of assumptions that one is entitled to make in the context of such problems.

As another example of a meta-rule, consider the following:

solve(U, Expr1, Ans)
← occ(U, Expr1, 2),
    collect(U, Expr1, Expr2),
    isolate(U, Expr2, Ans).

In other words, **Ans** is an equation that solves for **U** in **Expr1** if

- **Expr1** contains two occurrences of **U**;
- **Expr2** is **Expr1** with these two collected together;
- **Ans** is **Expr2** with **U** isolated on the left-hand side.

Thus, an alternative to chunking is to use high-level strategies which decide, at any given point in the computation, which inference rules should be applied. If this decision is taken at each step in the search, the number of candidate rules being considered at any one time can be kept comparatively small. This approach can obviously be combined with the hand ordering of inference rules in the database, and the control exercised over the depth of call during the deductive process.

11.3 Computational logic and natural reasoning

The MECHO work has implications beyond the domain of physics problem solving. In my opinion, it stands alone as an exploration of the strengths and weaknesses of logic-based methods for large-scale artificial intelligence applications. It is particularly useful because many of the papers produced by people associated with the project make explicit the kinds of design decisions that were made during the implementation of the program. The wisdom of these decisions can therefore be weighed by readers, who can draw their own conclusions on the basis of the information provided. Also, these papers discuss wider issues to do with the syntax and semantics of logic as a representation language.

MECHO exhibits a number of explicit departures from both the syntax of the first-order predicate calculus and its procedural interpretation in standard PROLOG. The architects' avowed intention was to work towards an alternative computational logic for natural reasoning which contained control primitives that would specify the way in which rules would be used. Of particular importance are 'meta-predicates', such as **method**, which manipulate formulae as if they were objects and affect the way in which they are called. Also, the schema cueing plays a crucial role in dynamically generating contextual information necessary to the computation. One can see how this mechanism is analogous to the use of frames in introducing certain assumptions about typical objects and events.

Some of the syntactic and semantic departures are fairly common in today's logic-based systems, for example:

1. Functions and equality are deliberately avoided, although some predicates have function properties, as described above. Intermediate unknowns are represented by specially generated constant symbols, rather than functions. The equality axioms are combinatorially explosive and computationally intractable.

2. Objects are assumed to have unique names. Along with the banishment of function symbols, this helps side-step the whole problem of deciding whether or not two entities are distinct. For example, the north end of one path might be the south end of another, but they would have the same internal name in MECHO.

3. The program is assumed to have complete information, i.e. all the objects are known as are all the relationships between them. Thus, if some proposition, P, cannot be proven, it is assumed to be false. This avoids some of the difficulties of dealing with negation, which are particularly pronounced in resolution refutation with Horn clauses.

The representational restrictions in (1) and (2) do not appear to handicap MECHO's ability to solve problems in the domain of Newtonian physics. However, it is not altogether clear that the conventions adopted provide a general solution to the problems engendered by functions and equality in all or any domain. (The MECHO group makes no such claims.) The assumption of complete information, while entirely justifiable in the context of physics examinations, is less acceptable in the more general field of expert systems applications, although there may be problem solving contexts where the assumption holds as a special case. For a treatment of reasoning with incomplete knowledge, the reader is referred to Levesque (1984).

Both Bundy (1978) and Bundy *et al.* (1979) contain interesting self-criticisms by the authors of the MECHO system regarding the way in which the meta-level is implemented. Because PROLOG only has one level of syntactic structure, PROLOG variables are used to range over both individuals at the object-level of the domain (e.g. strings, pulleys and particles) and units of knowledge at the meta-level (e.g. facts and formulae). The mixture of object- and meta-level assertions in MECHO's code is conceptually confusing, and could well make the system hard to adapt or extend.

Another criticism that could be made of the implementation concerns the embedding of control information in the rules, using annotations such as DBC and CC, in addition to the extant 'cut' and 'fail' of PROLOG. Such extra-logical features must surely detract from the legibility of the clauses and the declarative nature of the knowledge base, both of which are cited as benefits of applying logic programming to expert systems. However, there is no doubt that the functionality of such features is required; the question arises as to whether this is the best way to express this information. Alternatives might include: making the interpreter more intelligent, so that it 'knows' when to call to what depth; attempting to represent this knowledge explicitly in meta-rules; or writing a compiler that takes declarative rule specifications and inserts the necessary control annotations. The latter option might be a way of preserving the efficiency of the present implementation.

Finally, the issue of 'chunking' versus meta-rules raised earlier seems to me to be unresolved. On the side of chunking, it has to be said that there is a certain naturalness in storing like with like, so that all the relevant information about a particular topic can be accessed easily and directly applied without more ado. On the side of meta-rules, it is clear that they give the programmer even greater flexibility than that afforded by most frame systems, since meta-rules can be used to exert complete control over the storage and retrieval of knowledge. Such flexibility in frame systems requires multiple inheritance and powerful facilities for combining methods. However, the computational cost of meta-level reasoning can be high, since one is doing extra theorem proving.

Nevertheless, MECHO is one of the few logic-based problem-solving programs relevant to expert systems research which has confronted the key issues of knowledge representation and control. It has pushed hard enough at these problems to reveal the potential strengths and weaknesses of logic programming as a fundamental technique. The main lesson to be learned is that raw PROLOG, like raw LISP, is unsuitable as a knowledge representation language, but can be used quite successfully to implement an interpreter for such a language. Most other applications of logic programming to expert systems have been content to inherit the syntax and semantics of PROLOG whole and entire. However, such applications have been, for the most part, trivial in comparison to what MECHO attempted to do; some involve little more than database query.

Chapter 12   **Tools for Building Expert Systems**

In a number of previous chapters we have already broached the topic of software tools for building expert systems. It seemed sensible to discuss EMYCIN while MYCIN was still fresh in our minds, and deal with OPS5 and R1 together. In this chapter, we will take a rather more systematic look at the scene by considering a number of exemplars. However, it is important to stress that this survey is not meant to be either a comprehensive, up-to-the-minute consumer guide or a detailed discussion of all the deep, theoretical issues involved in designing expert systems architectures. The intention is rather to give the reader some technical insights into the functionality of typical tools, and convey the flavour of the current debate regarding what the tools of the future should be like.

The majority of the tools currently available seem to fall into three classes:

- expert systems shells, i.e. abstractions over an applications program, or a class of such programs, as EMYCIN was over MYCIN;

- high-level programming languages, i.e. languages which to some extent conceal their implementation details from the programmer, freeing him from worries about low-level efficiency, e.g. OPS5;

- mixed programming environments, i.e. a set of software modules which allow the programmer to mix programming paradigms, in the way that CENTAUR, say, mixed rule- and frame-based formalisms.

These categories need not be mutually exclusive, but they tend to be. Shells allow non-programmers to take advantage of the efforts of programmers who have solved a problem similar to their own; users of shells who find themselves having to program generally feel let down in some way. High-level programming languages are for people who have some background in programming but would rather not spend their time on the details; what a higher-level language gives them is fast prototyping, so that ideas can be explored and evaluated with a minimum of fuss. Further development may continue in this language or not, depending upon a number of issues, including the hardware and software environment that the applications program will eventually run in and the ability of the high-level language to support the necessary extensions and complications involved in turning a prototype into the real thing. Mixed programming environments are really for skilled programmers, regardless of what their purveyors may say to the contrary. Programming in more than one style using more than one language is more trouble than it's worth unless you know exactly what you're doing.

There are lots of ways in which one could lay out this chapter, but I thought I would begin by considering some of the limitations that shells impose upon their users, so that the reader will understand why there is so much interest in the other options.

12.1   Experiences with EMYCIN in the US and the UK

One of the major applications of EMYCIN in the US was PUFF (Kunz *et al.*, 1978): an expert system for diagnosing pulmonary disease. It was this system which Aikins reimplemented as a mix of rules and frames in CENTAUR. PUFF in EMYCIN is just EMYCIN's rule interpreter, explanation and acquisition modules, plus a pulmonary disease knowledge base.

12.1.1   The PUFF experience

Although the EMYCIN version of PUFF performed well as a diagnostic problem solver, a number of shortcomings were noted on the knowledge representation side (Aikins, 1983).

- The production rule formalism employed by EMYCIN made it difficult to distinguish between different kinds of knowledge, e.g. heuristic knowledge, control knowledge, knowledge about expected values for medical parameters.

- The relatively unstructured rule set employed by EMYCIN made difficult the acquisition of new knowledge, since adding a rule to the set involved making changes elsewhere in the system, e.g. to the knowledge tables containing information about medical parameters.

- The exhaustive backward chaining employed by EMYCIN as its major mode of inference, involving both object- and meta-level rules, made the generation of comprehensible explanations quite difficult, since programming decisions about the order and number of clauses in a rule could have profound effects upon the nature of the explanatory trace.

Other criticisms voiced by Aikins concerned not only the particular implementation of PUFF in EMYCIN but the functionality of rule-based systems generally. A good deal of expertise consists of knowledge about typical patterns of data; typical in the sense of either frequently occurring or idealized. Experts can recognize familiar patterns with ease, and are capable of classifying (possibly noisy and incomplete) patterns in terms of the prototypical ideal. They also have valuable intuitions about what constitutes a relevant, interesting or surprising data value, and they use such clues to decide what to do next. None of this is very easy to represent using condition-action rules, unless one allows these rules to become arbitrarily complex.

A further problem is that human experts are many-faceted beings. They often play rather different roles during different stages of their work: data gatherer, sympathetic listener, incisive questioner, hypothesizer and critic. It is very hard to capture this context-dependent aspect or expertise by running a set of rules under a uniform control regime.

12.1.2 Experiences in cancer research

The research group at the Imperial Cancer Research Fund (ICRF) in London is one of the leaders in the application of expert systems technology to non-trivial tasks in the UK. One of their recent projects involved trying to build a system that would advise doctors in the management of terminal patients (Alvey, 1983). The fundamental design problems that they experienced in the creation of a 200-rule prototype caused them to look in the direction of PROLOG for their second-generation system.

Alvey summarized the problems that he had under the following headings:

1. Problems with the knowledge format. EMYCIN provides only rules or simple lists for the representation of knowledge. The rules represent inferential knowledge, while lists represent simple facts. However, there are pharmacological facts that need to be qualified, e.g. the potency of drugs as a function of route of administration, and the knowledge engineer has little choice but to put these in the rules.

2. The role of variables in the rules. The fact that you don't have the full power of quantification, as in first order logic, makes it impossible to represent rules such as 'don't recommend a drug if the patient is already taking it'. Yet this seems like a perfectly natural rule for a knowledge engineer to want to express, since it reflects the way in which clinicians actually reason.

3. Trouble with the explanation system. Although EMYCIN is capable of providing a trace of rule activations, such a trace is often quite verbose. In general there appears to be an adverse trade-off between writing 'powerful' rules with many clauses which execute in an efficient and well-controlled manner, and writing a greater quantity of smaller 'weaker' rules with fewer clauses which are probably less efficient, but which generate more comprehensible explanations.

4. Incremental development of the knowledge base. Adding new rules often causes unpredictable effects upon a running program, even if the declarative reading of the new rule is innocuous. This is because different kinds of rules which refer to different classes of entity, like patients and drugs, are treated differently by the interpreter.

The significance of these criticisms is two-fold. Firstly, it is difficult to express certain kinds of declarative knowledge using the production rule formalism provided by EMYCIN, as suggested by points (1) and (2). Secondly, just because you succeed in expressing a piece of declarative knowledge as a production rule, this doesn't mean that its procedural interpretation will have the effect that you intended. Alvey concluded that guidance was needed on methods for designing such rules, but that such guidance was not easy to obtain. This wry observation reminded me of my first forays into OPS5, when I found that an ill-considered addition to the rule set could have quite unpredictable effects upon a working program if I had not thought carefully enough about conflict resolution.

The practical conclusion drawn from the experiences of Alvey and his colleagues at ICRF was that it was worth exploring PROLOG as a basis for an expert systems architecture. The reasons for the choice of PROLOG as an alternative are not explicitly stated in the referenced paper, but the general feeling was that PROLOG would give them more flexibility in designing the architecture of their choice. However, I feel this should not be taken as a straightforward comparison between EMYCIN and PROLOG, since one is, after all, no more than a shell, while the other is a full-blooded programming language.

Further criticisms of EMYCIN from ICRF by Myers *et al.* (1983) are also instructive and grouped under two headings:

1. The run-time interface. Consultations are always system-initiated, and the question/answer dialogue is rather rigid, permitting no intervention on the part of the user. The explanation system describes rather than justifies patterns of reasoning, as Clancey pointed out in the course of his work on NEOMYCIN.

2. The build-time interface. Access to the knowledge base is limited. The knowledge engineer can only access a single rule or a single parameter at a time using the edit facilities provided, while there are obviously intimate connections between medical parameters and the rules that reference them.

They also found that the sharp division between 'running' and 'building' modes was quite inconvenient in practice. Ideally, one would like to be able to run the inference engine while building, or access the knowledge base at run-time, for the purposes of experiment and debugging. (Most modern LISP environments provide such facilities, and once you've used them, you're hooked for life.)

To summarize, EMYCIN certainly has shortcomings from the knowledge engineering point of view, but then it was the first of its kind. Whether PROLOG is the answer to all or any of these problems is an empirical issue which remains to be resolved. There is no doubt that the Horn clause subset of logic has greater expressive power than the production rule formalism provided by EMYCIN, hence satisfying criticisms (1) and (2) of Alvey. However, I suspect that raw PROLOG will pose its own problems of control under the headings of (3) and (4). The solution to these problems (e.g. along MECHO-like lines perhaps) will require skilled programming, whereas the whole point of having an expert systems shell is surely to avoid such an effort.

The layout of the rest of this chapter is as follows. Next, there is a critical look at two tools based on structured objects: AL/X and LOOPS. The first is a shell abstracted, like EMYCIN, over an applications program, while the second is a high-level programming language embedded in INTERLISP. Then two PROLOG-based tools are examined: a shell called APES and a sophisticated programming environment called MANDALA. An attempt is made to determine what they have to offer over and above first-generation shells like EMYCIN or LISP-based tools like LOOPS.

12.2   Structured objects in AL/X and LOOPS

The AL/X expert systems shell is derived from PROSPECTOR: a rule-based system which uses a partitioned semantic network to represent the premises and actions of its rules. This architecture provides an interesting contrast to MYCIN and EMYCIN, insofar as it shows how a different underlying representation can be used to similar effect. Although PROSPECTOR's control structure is essentially the backward chaining one familiar from MYCIN, an inference network is used to structure the rule set, and provide connections between evidence and hypotheses.

12.2.1   The partitioned network in PROSPECTOR

PROSPECTOR is a consultation system to assist geologists in 'hard rock' mineral exploration. However, a clear separation is maintained between the geological knowledge base and the mechanisms which apply this knowledge. The main function of these mechanisms is to match incoming data supplied by the user against geological models which describe disjoint classes of sites. The models are therefore formal descriptions of ore deposits, while the data are surface observations. The latter are assumed to be incomplete, and so the user is interested in the degree of the match, which indicates the probability of certain ores being present.

A consultation consists of the user giving the system information about the prospect, such as rock types. This helps the system to identify a set of possible or candidate models for consideration. Once the initial data has been volunteered, the system displays the candidate models and their associated certainty factors, and the user is given the opportunity to rule some of them out. The remaining models are then explored, starting with the hypothesis which has the highest certainty factor or simply the highest number of connections between it and the data. The system proceeds to ask questions of the user in an attempt to confirm the current model.

As we noted earlier, production rules work best when knowledge can be expressed as independent 'recognize-act' pairs. They are less suitable for taxonomic relationships such as 'element of' and 'subset of'; such hierarchies are best modelled by tree structures, as in CADUCEUS. PROSPECTOR combines semantic nets and production rules in an attempt to get the best of both worlds: the modularity of the rule-based approach together with the structural-descriptive power of network formalisms, in much the same way that CENTAUR did (in fact, PROSPECTOR did it first).

In the partitioned nets used by PROSPECTOR, the equivalents of MYCIN's clauses are represented by 'spaces', i.e. constellations of nodes and links in which attributes or relations are connected to their arguments. Spaces can, in turn, be treated as if they were just complex nodes, and so linked to form new spaces. Thus clauses which are conditions can be connected to form a premise, and the resulting space can be linked to an action clause to make a rule.

Furthermore, relations between rules can be made explicit using links. An obvious example is where the conclusion of one rule constitutes evidence for another, i.e. its consequent matches one of the other rule's antecedents. Rules can also be linked implicitly by the element or subset relations of their constituents: e.g. a rule about lead sulphides should be sensitive to the detection of galena, since galena is a lead sulphide.

The organization of the inference network is such that the nodes are spaces representing assertions, and the links are inference rules. This structure mediates the explicit links between antecedents and consequents. There is also a taxonomic network which classifies minerals in much the way that you would expect, e.g. a biotite is a mica, a mica is a silicate and so on. This structure mediates the implicit links provided by set-theoretic relationships.

Together, these structures fill the gap in MYCIN and EMYCIN mentioned earlier, when it was noted that facts in the static database were not sufficiently organized, and that the lack of proper quantification made the statement of general rules like 'don't prescribe a drug the patient is already getting' impossible. The semantic network formalism used in PROSPECTOR has the full power of the predicate calculus. The inference network also takes over some of the functions of meta-rules, since it controls the order in which rules are invoked and applied.

12.2.2 Propagating degrees of belief in AL/X

As in PROSPECTOR, AL/X provides facilities for associating degrees of belief with spaces in the network, and propagating these 'certainty factors' through the network as evidence accumulates. Each space has three sections:

- the text section, which describes the content of the space, and stores text for explanations and other purposes;
- the inference section, which specifies both the prior degree of belief in the space and its links with other spaces in the network;
- the control section, which supplies such information as whether or not the contents of the space are 'askable', or whether the space can be treated as a goal.

Let's concentrate for a moment upon the inference section. The prior degree of belief represents degree of belief in the space as hypothesis before any evidence is gathered. This is the starting point for the current degree of belief, which may alter as evidence accumulates.

The degree of belief, D, in some hypothesis, H, is usually given by the following formula:

$$D(H) = 10 \log[P(H)/(1 - P(H))],$$

where $P(H)$ is the probability of H, and the logarithm is to the base 10. $P(H)/(1 - P(H))$ will be familiar to fans of horse-racing as the 'odds' on H. (The logarithm is taken to compress the range, and ensure that interpolation is not biased towards confirmation of the hypothesis.)

The inference section also specifies the logical and Bayesian links with other spaces. The logical operators supplied are 'and', 'or' and 'not'. As an example of how these might be used, consider the following example.

```
space H
        text description
            ...
        inference
            prior 0
            logical definition
                and (I J K)
    ...
```

The 'logical definition' slot says that the degree of belief in H is a function of the degree of belief associated with spaces I, J and K. The function associated with 'and' is the 'min' function, familiar from MYCIN and other applications of 'fuzzy' logic in AI. Thus $D(H) = \min[D(I), D(J), D(K)]$. The function for 'or' is 'max', while the function for 'not' is 'inverse', i.e. $D(\text{not } (H)) = - D(H)$.

Bayesian links deal with conditional probabilities, i.e. the case where one space implies, or is implied by, another. Positive and negative weights are employed to propagate the effect of truth or falsity of evidence upon the degree of belief in the space as hypothesis. To see how this works, let's look at our schematic example again:

```
space H
        text description
            ...
        inference
            prior 0
            logical definition
                and (I J K)
            rules antecedents
                (A pw 10 nw -5)
    ...
```

If A is true, then this will increase $D(H)$ by 10; if A is false, then this will decrease $D(H)$ by 5. However, if $D(A)$ does not equal 100 (certainly true) or -100 (certainly false), then only a certain proportion of the appropriate weight will be used to update $D(H)$. The antecedents tag specifies the directionality of the dependency, i.e. that $D(A)$ affects $D(H)$ and not vice versa.

Jones (1984) did a comparative study of AL/X and OPS5, in the course of which he implemented a first-aid advisor in both systems. The AL/X version contained about 100 spaces, and was therefore of sufficient size and complexity to provide an adequate test of the system's main features. His comments and criticisms are extremely instructive, and they centre upon the propagation of values through the inference network using the mechanisms outlined above.

A major irritant encountered in the implementation of spaces concerned with diagnosis was that every new piece of evidence automatically updates the current degree of belief in all the spaces with which it has Bayesian links. Such a propagation mechanism is really too powerful, and it makes the generation of questions difficult to control. Jones gives the following example.

The first-aid advisor would only ask questions whose answers supply antecedents for the 'dislocation' space when the site of injury was known to be a joint. The relevant antecedents were 'swelling', 'inpain', 'deformed' and 'bruising', which are all spaces in their own right. Unfortunately, these spaces are also antecedents of 'fracture', and so D(fracture) is duly updated by the propagation mechanism, along with D(dislocation). Yet we already know that the site of the injury is 'joint', and so fracture can be ruled out. Thus a space which does not represent a candidate diagnosis can become more likely in a wholly serendipitous way.

The control section of a space cannot prevent this from happening, as the propagation is entirely automatic. You can prevent 'fracture' from being asked about if the site of injury is 'joint', but you can't stop it being updated. This is an all-too-common example of a shell feature which can work against you in a particular domain, although it may be entirely acceptable in other applications. In other words, the formal machinery for performing some function can have a sensible informal reading in one domain and a nonsensical one in another. This business of getting a good match between the properties of a domain and the formal machinery (logical, mathematical, etc.) made available by various expert systems tools is not very well understood at the present time.

Jones was forced to take a number of rather counter-intuitive steps to solve this particular problem. All diagnostic spaces were given a negative prior degree of belief. This was so that, even in the case where all the evidence except site pointed to a particular diagnosis, the current degree of belief of a space would not rise above zero, the reporting level. The value of the negative weight associated with site in antecedent rule slots in diagnostic spaces was increased, and the positive weight was also increased, to ensure that goals of appropriate site did reach reporting level, even though they began with a negative degree of belief. Eventually, the system began to behave in the desired manner, i.e. all spaces remained with a current degree of belief over -100 (below which they are not supposed to fall, such a value being technically illegal), each space eligible for consideration on the basis of site was reported with at least degree 0, and no other space was reported, regardless of how much non-site evidence was turned up on its behalf. The point is that a certain amount of rather arbitrary juggling with values was required to make this work.

OPS5 came out of this comparison quite well, although as with the EMYCIN versus PROLOG comparison hinted at in Alvey (1983), one is not really comparing like with like, as Jones acknowledges. AL/X is no more than a shell, whereas OPS5 is as much a programming language as PROLOG. The verdict was that although AL/X was easier to learn, OPS was easier to use once you had learned it. Using OPS5, one could implement one's own machinery for propagating inferences in precisely the manner required by the particular domain. Anyone with previous experience of AI programming can learn OPS5 in a weekend, although it takes longer to become really proficient, of course.

12.2.3 Doing your own thing in LOOPS and KEE

The moral of the previous sections on EMYCIN and AL/X is that although the knowledge engineer may benefit from exploring the kinds of facilities that shells provide, sooner or later he is likely to succumb to the temptations of doing his own programming. Structured objects can, in theory, provide a relatively painless way of indulging this particular vice (anything as addictive, time-consuming and mind-bending as AI programming has to be a vice). In this section, we explore a new generation of intriguing programming paradigms of which LOOPS is an exemplar.

In the beginning, there was LISP, a programming language based on a mathematical system known as the lambda calculus. A LISP program was no more than a suite of functions, defined in terms of each other, or (recursively) in terms of themselves. The basic data structure was not the array or the record but the list, and LISP programs themselves were nothing but (somewhat embedded) lists. Other data structures were quickly provided, but they grew and multiplied in a rather unprincipled fashion, and were often employed in a rather undisciplined way. Eventually, it was realized that notions of structured programming and abstract data types could and should be applied to LISP, and that, far from cramping anyone's style, this would make AI programming less hazardous to mental health.

The main effect of this fortuitous attack of sanity was 'defstruct': a facility for defining arbitrary data types, creating and destroying instances of them, and specifying how these fundamentally abstract entities would be implemented, e.g. as pointer structures, arrays, vectors etc. Different dialects of LISP had their own versions of this, of course, but they became the principal way of implementing frame-like structures. As such, their slots were often filled by procedures, which meant that they were far more than passive data structures; for example, when activated, they could make decisions about control, as we saw in CENTAUR. Nevertheless, their moment in the spotlight was more often decided globally by an interpreter.

It was left to the message-passing paradigm of programming (Hewitt, 1977) to liberate these structured objects from conventional control structures. Objects are allowed to communicate directly with each other, as long as they do so using prescribed communication protocols. They now have the appearance of autonomous agents, armed with their own data (values of local variables) and their own methods (private procedures). The outcome of this revolution is an even higher degree of modularity than that provided by purely procedural paradigms, and far more control options. For example, you can represent a hypothesis as an object with its own internal values and its own procedures for verifying itself which use those values, and keep it on an agenda while you explore other alternatives.

LOOPS combines four programming paradigms, of which message-passing forms an integral part.

1. Procedure oriented programming. The basic LISP paradigm in which procedures are (for the most part) active and data are (for the most part) passive, even though procedures are, in fact, data objects in themselves. Procedures can side-effect data objects, i.e. permanently change their public value.

2. Rule oriented programming. Like the above, except that condition-action rules play the role of procedures. Rule sets are themselves objects.

3. Object oriented programming. Structured objects have the characteristics of both program and data, and side-effects are normally local to objects, and only allowed through the 'proper channels' of the right protocol.

4. Data oriented programming. In some sense the inverse of the above. Data access and update trigger procedures, so that things happen as a side-effect of patterns in the data and the actions of other procedures on data.

LOOPS grew out of experiments with a representation language called LORE, but it has an acknowledged debt to a large number of earlier systems, including FLAVORS on the Lisp Machine, KRL (Bobrow and Winograd, 1977), and UNITS (Stefik, 1979). Earlier experiments, like UNITS, had proved difficult for non-*aficionados* to use, partly because the user interface was not well engineered, and partly because one still had to do a fair amount of LISP programming to produce one's own procedures. Initial attempts to provide a 'rules language' left quite a lot to be desired (Rawlings and Fox, 1983), since one was given little more than a conventional programming language with GOTOs, assignment, iteration, and so forth. Further, the generalization hierarchy within which units were embedded provided only a small number of semantic links, and this was felt to be unduly restrictive. These and other restrictions both forbade multiple inheritance and made it impossible to have more than one perspective on the same knowledge, such as classifying diseases in different ways, e.g. by site, by pathogenesis, by geographical distribution, etc.

However, it seems that KEE (which is essentially 'Son of UNITS') surmounts most of these problems. Message-passing replaces procedure-writing and the rules language provided more closely resembles the syntax and semantics of productions. Multiple inheritance of properties is now supported and, like LOOPS, the package is embedded in a congenial programming environment. Both KEE and LOOPS are relatively new at the time of writing, and so it seems premature to judge how far non-LISP programmers find them useful. The object-oriented paradigm can be conducive to the writing of clean and effective code, but it is hard to tell how the average practitioner will get on until there is a significant user base. Stefik *et al.* (1983) suggest that it is possible to learn enough LOOPS in three days to program a small knowledge-based system, but their report is too anecdotal for this claim to be evaluated.

There is a grain of truth in a recent jibe from Japan which describes LOOPS as the PL/1 of knowledge-based programming (Furukawa *et al.*, 1984). The implication is that it is possible to take a more unifying view of multiple programming paradigms in the context of logic programming. On the other hand, Bobrow (1984) argues that multiple paradigms are necessary, because no single paradigm, including logic programming, is powerful enough. There is much to be said on both sides of this debate; more than can be covered here. However, we shall come back to this topic later in the chapter, when we consider the implementation of objects in the MANDALA system.

In their critique of UNITS, Rawlings and Fox also made a point of comparison with PROLOG. It would seem that there is a growing tendency for expert systems theorists and practitioners to compare the functionality of new tools with the basic facilities that PROLOG either provides now or might provide in the near future. Thus it is to PROLOG that we now turn, to discuss both these basic facilities and the kinds of superstructures that they can be used to build.

12.3 Logic for expert systems: APES and MANDALA

In the beginning, there was PROLOG, based not upon lambda calculus but a subset of predicate calculus. This subset, known as the Horn clause subset, has the nice property of completeness mentioned in Chapter 5. Completeness, you recall, means that if any proposition, P, does in fact follow from some set of propositions, S, then you can prove that $S \rightarrow P$ using only legitimate rules of inference. Many alternative methods of representing knowledge either do not have this property or are so informally specified that it simply isn't clear what their logical properties are. Generally speaking, this is a Bad Thing.

On the practical side, PROLOG gives you several useful things for free:

- an indexed database containing clauses which can be used to represent either procedures or data;
- pattern-matching in the form of 'most general unification' which, omitting the gory details, allows both the datum and the pattern to contain variables and returns a substitution which would render them identical;

- a built-in control strategy (depth-first search) with a top-down search rule (clauses nearer the 'top' of the database are accessed first) and a left-right computation rule (subgoals are processed in the left-to-right order in which they are listed).

On the strength of these facilities, Rawlings and Fox are not alone in suggesting that one could implement frames and the like in PROLOG in a relatively straightforward manner. Both particular facts and 'type' information could be coded as unit clauses, for example

> **fact(eb-virus, sequence, [C, A, G, ..., T, A, T]).**
>
> **isa(eb-virus, herpes-virus).**

while inheritance mechanisms could be implemented by PROLOG procedures.

There are a number of problems with this view, none of them fatal, but none of them trivial either. This is a large topic, and we can only consider some of the aspects here. Let us restrict ourselves to looking at a couple of immediate issues to do with representation and control.

One of the things that current implementations of PROLOG don't provide is conventional data structures such as arrays or records, or pointers for creating arbitrarily complex networks. These things can all be simulated using complex terms or embedded lists, but the accessing and updating of these structures using pattern-matching is, for the most part, very much less efficient than 'lower-level' representations which give you uniform access to indices and fields by name, instead of by position. There are some smart programming tricks that you can use to ameliorate the situation, but then you're into 'real programming', rather than the high-level stuff that the knowledge engineer is after all paid to do. Also, the database indexing as provided probably isn't clever enough to support efficient access to a large collection of frame-like clauses; this is something else that your 'real programmer' must do, so don't think you're going to be able to replace him by using PROLOG.

The built-in control structure, which I dishonestly listed as a 'plus' above, can be something of a liability in non-trivial applications. One cannot imagine a frame-based system like CADUCEUS functioning adequately (or even at all) under a depth-first search regime. Again your real programmer will have to be resurrected, and put to work writing an interpreter in PROLOG which implements the control strategy you need.

None of the above constitutes an argument against the principle of somehow combining logic programming with object oriented programming. This seems to me to be a Good Thing, although the details of how best to bring this about are still some way from being worked out. Concurrent PROLOG may provide at least part of the answer (see Shapiro and Takeuchi, 1983).

The moral of this story is (the not very surprising one) that PROLOG is a programming language, just as LISP is. It is not a knowledge representation language, any more than LISP is, because it doesn't have built-in facilities for the flexible access and application of knowledge, although you can create such facilities if you are a real programmer, as you can in LISP. One might argue that the inclusion of a pattern-matcher and a keyed database make PROLOG a slightly higher-level language than LISP (to the tune of about two pages of pretty-printed LISP code), but more than that may be claiming too much. The idea that PROLOG is somehow easy to program in is a little misleading, and based upon an impression of the ease with which database entries and database queries can be constructed. This is not to be confused with real programming in PROLOG, as your real programmer will tell you.

The ideal would be to find some way of combining relational and functional programming in a way that does violence to neither yet significantly extends the functionality of either one in isolation. We shall return to this subject when we consider the MANDALA system, which makes a serious attempt to marry aspects of the object-oriented and logic programming paradigms. First, however, we shall consider APES, an expert system shell written in PROLOG, which might go some of the way towards satisfying the desiderata laid down by practitioners such as those at ICRF.

12.3.1 APES: Horn clause logic as a rule-based language

The rationale for using PROLOG as a vehicle for expert systems development is that ground unit clauses can be considered as representing the facts or data of a domain, while non-ground, non-unit clauses represent general rules.

There is a tendency to call such a construal of a logic database a 'production system', but I think this usage should at least be qualified in the following ways:

- it blurs the traditional distinction between the temporary working memory and the permanent production memory;
- there is no PROLOG equivalent of the Rete match algorithm for either efficient conflict resolution or efficient 'working memory' update;
- a little programming is required if you want to run your 'production system' forward instead of the normal backward-chaining mode.

Having said that, there is no doubt that Horn clauses do provide a rule-based language, and that unification is more powerful (though typically less efficient) than the pattern matching facilities provides by production rule interpreters like OPS5.

The APES shell (Hammond and Sergot, 1983) runs a collection of Horn clauses as a rule-based program, just as PROLOG does, with three embellishments:

- 'Negation as failure'. This is the convention whereby failure to prove a goal leads to the assumption that the proposition concerned is in fact false.
- An explanation system. An explanation is simply an edited form of the proof constructed by the program; raw PROLOG does not supply proofs,

as proofs are not produced without cost, and PROLOG is intended to be a programming language not a theorem-prover.

- 'Query the user'. This is where the system asks the user for information at failed tip nodes in the proof tree, if the predicate concerned is tagged 'askable'.

It can readily be shown that 'negation as failure' suffers from both theoretical and technical defects (Shepherdson, 1984). It is also rather unsatisfying from an epistemological point of view, since it assumes that the expert is omniscient. On the other hand, since PROLOG does not supply classical negation, and negative information is often an important factor in problem solving, some surrogate has to be supplied. It is worth pointing out in passing that PROLOG is not alone in this regard. OPS5 uses 'negated' condition elements which are only satisfied if there is no matching pattern in the working memory, and there are some restrictions as to where in the left-hand side such conditions can appear.

The explanations provided in APES are simply proofs, analogous to traces of rule activity in EMYCIN. Consequently, this facility does not answer the calls of Clancey and others for a justification of the reasoning, rather than just a description of it. For an approach to explanations that attempts to meet this criterion, the reader is referred to the work of Swartout (1983), described in Chapter 14.

The ability to query the user at 'dead ends' in the proof is a useful augmentation of PROLOG for expert systems purposes, but this ability is somewhat vitiated by the fact that APES inherits PROLOG's depth-first search strategy whole and entire, so that there is very little flexibility in the order in which questions can be asked. The top-down search rule and the left-right computation rule remain unaltered, with no attempt at query optimization along the lines of, for example, Warren and Pereira (1981). This makes the facility less interesting than it might otherwise have been.

On the positive side, APES has a rather neat front end, which is based around the syntax of Simple PROLOG, and the proofs generated are often more readable than the traces of rule activation provided by EMYCIN and the like. Also, the rules tend to have a declarative reading which is very clear and direct. In cases where problem solving reduces, in some sense, to logical deduction of a comparatively uncomplicated kind, i.e. seeing whether or not a goal follows from a set of axioms, such tools provide an apposite solution.

In other cases, however, where the reasoning involved is causal or abductive, requiring a little scheduling of hypotheses (e.g. CADUCEUS), it is unlikely that such mechanisms will serve as they stand. Hopefully, future developments will provide facilities for dealing with control, at a somewhat higher level than the traditional 'cut' and 'fail'. A good deal of research all over the world is still going into the issue of how the PROLOG interpreter itself may be improved in this regard.

The shortcomings of EMYCIN with regard to the unstructuredness of its rule base are obviously shared by systems like APES, where the logic database is simply an unstructured set of clauses. The whole point of systems like PROSPECTOR and CENTAUR was to try and provide a natural structuring of knowledge that would help with problems of control, as well as provide a well-tempered representation. This leads directly to the next section: an attempt to embed structured objects in PROLOG.

12.3.2 Logic programming meets objects in MANDALA

Furukawa *et al.* (1984) argue that the double reading of Horn clauses, as declarative specifications susceptible of a procedural interpretation, allows you to capture and express the functionality of advanced programming paradigms, such as the object-oriented style, as well as the knowledge base management capability required for expert systems applications. They point out that the four paradigms on offer in LOOPS (rule, object, procedure, and data oriented styles) all require distinct mechanisms for their implementation. This complicates both the structure of these systems and the structure of the representation languages they employ.

The suggestion is that some, if not all, of this seeming variety can be mapped onto logic programming concepts. Thus object oriented programming might correspond to stream programming in Concurrent PROLOG, while the rule oriented paradigms corresponds to clausal programming in ordinary PROLOG. The latter correspondence is familiar to us from our discussion of APES; the former might bear some explanation.

The basic idea is that a prototypical object, or 'unit world' in the terminology of MANDALA, is a named set of axioms, which can be thought of as the methods of a typical object of that class, i.e. its local procedures. An instance of a unit world, however, is not really a data structure at all but a process. Associated with the process is an input stream, which provides messages for the instance. On receiving a message, the instance uses the axioms it has inherited from its unit world to solve the problem posed by that message.

Things are a little more complicated than the above, of course. For a start, the instance must be able to call up the hierarchy of prototypes, so that methods associated with higher-level unit worlds can be applied. Furthermore, as well as availing themselves of different axiom sets, different instances might want to use different inference procedures.

Associated with MANDALA is an experimental programming environment which embodies a multiple window manager. Such windows would be associated with processes representing instances, enabling the programmer to monitor, edit and pass messages to the corresponding instance. The window manager is defined as just another unit world, a stored set of axioms which govern the behaviour of the windows it creates.

There is little doubt that systems such as MANDALA, and also LOOKS (Mizoguchi *et al.*, 1984), derived much of their inspiration from LOOPS and its forerunners. For example, the programming environment in MANDALA is reminiscent of the use of FLAVORS on the Lisp Machine to manage the multiple window facility. However, the claim is that the new generation of such tools based in logic will be more uniform, elegant, and be assured of nice meta-logical properties, such as soundness and completeness.

It is a little too early to attempt an assessment of these claims at the time of writing. Nevertheless, MANDALA's implementation of objects as processes and message-passing as stream programming carries conviction, and has the potential to be very much more efficient than more conventional methods of representing objects in logic (such as embedded lists, nested terms and so on, made legible by infix operators) as described in the LOOKS reference cited above.

12.4   Inconclusive conclusions concerning expert systems tools

The title of this section is not altogether facetious, since I did warn the reader at the outset that our coverage of this topic would be neither broad nor deep. However, I have tried to give useful pointers to relevant literature and raise at least some of the issues. Life in the land of expert systems tools is already quite complicated, and things will undoubtedly get worse before they get better (or worse still).

Having said that, I shall nevertheless stick my neck out and try to make a number of useful generalizations.

Complex systems require that designers and programmers work at many different levels. Someone somewhere, maybe more than one person, has to hold all these levels in his head, if integration is going to be achieved. Anything that makes this task easier is worth trying, even if the programming paradigm that results is less efficient, if there is no other way of achieving such a simplification.

The above applies mostly to the task of system construction, which roughly corresponds to knowledge representation plus implementation of the requisite inference engine(s) plus knowledge base management. However, anything that makes either knowledge elicitation (the preceding phase), knowledge validation (the succeeding phase) or knowledge modification (the iterative phase) easier is also worth trying. It could be that logic has something to offer here, although proponents of this view should not regard its truth as simply obvious. Proving that a large body of knowledge is consistent is entirely problematic, while proving the correctness of large and complex programs isn't exactly trivial either.

The importance of good programming environments simply can't be overestimated. One frequently hears of people lamenting the passage of paper tape and insisting that they wrote better programs back in the 'good old days'. Although one shouldn't expect an environment to come complete with a 'read programmer's mind' facility, there are many modern programming aids – e.g. interactive debuggers, the ability to mix and trace and break both interpreted and compiled code, multiple windows – which make life almost worth living, and which I would be very loath to relinquish. Needless to say, these tools are not a substitute for thought, but they do render the dreadful business of writing and debugging complex programs under pressure of time a reasonably sane activity.

At the time of writing, it is hard to know whether the LISP versus PROLOG debate implicit in all this is healthy competition or ruinous rivalry. I strongly suspect that the latter is the case, at least in the UK (where the situation is further complicated by the persistence of POP and the advent of POPLOG). There is something rather odd about an opposition between the functional and relational styles of programming, when they have so very much in common. It can hardly be said that lambda calculus and predicate logic are in any way incompatible. We seem to be witnessing a social phenomenon, which is something well outside the scope of the present work.

Chapter 13 Knowledge Acquisition

There are two further problems associated with expert systems research which show little sign of going away, although both are active areas of research. One occurs at the very outset of any expert system application, from the knowledge engineer's point of view, namely the elicitation of knowledge from the human expert. The other occurs at the end of every run of an expert system program, from the end user's point of view, namely the quality of explanation that the system can offer. These problems are not wholly unrelated, but I shall treat them in separate chapters for the sake of convenience.

13.1 The problem of knowledge acquisition

Early expert systems applications were either programmed by persons who were themselves domain experts, or else implemented in very close collaboration with such experts. Knowledge acquisition (or elicitation) is almost universally acknowledged to be a time-consuming process, the logistics of which we do not understand very well. It is often referred to as the 'bottleneck' in the business of designing, implementing and applying expert systems to real problems (Buchanan *et al.*, 1970; Hayes-Roth *et al.*, 1983).

As Shortliffe (1976) pointed out, the formulation of decision rules is no simple matter, because experts typically do not structure their decision-making in any formal way, and they may have great difficulty in isolating and describing the steps of reasoning that they take. Indeed, it has often been said that one of the motivations for undertaking any knowledge engineering exercise is to codify and thereby render explicit the valuable knowledge that many experts possess (Sridharan, 1978). Human expertise is a scarce resource and an expensive commodity; expert systems technology appears to offer the possibility of making such knowledge cheaply and more widely available.

Buchanan *et al.* (1983) offer an analysis of knowledge acquisition in terms of a process model of how to construct an expert system (see Figure 13.1). It is worth including a brief summary of these stages here.

1. Identification. Identify the class of problems that the system will be expected to solve, including the data that the system will work with, and the criteria that solutions must meet. Identify the resources available for the project, in terms of expertise, manpower, time constraints, computing facilities and money.

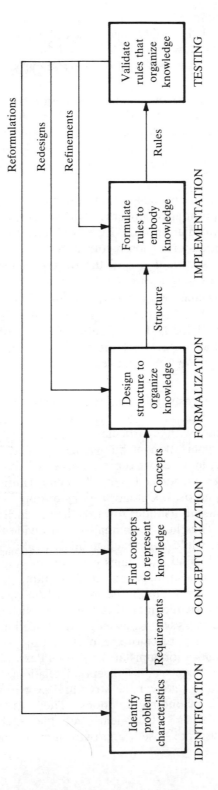

Figure 13.1   Stages of knowledge acquisition.

2. Conceptualization. Uncover the key concepts and the relationships between them. This should include a characterization of the different kinds of data, the flow of information and the underlying structure of the domain, in terms of causal, spatio-temporal, or part-whole relationships, and so on.

3. Formalization. Try to understand the nature of the underlying search space, and the character of the search that will have to be conducted. Important issues include the certainty and completeness of the information, and other constraints upon the logical interpretation of the data, such as time dependency, and the reliability and consistency of difference data sources.

4. Implementation. In turning a formalization of knowledge into a runnable program, one is primarily concerned with the specification of control and the details of information flow. Rules will have to be expressed in some executable form under a chosen control regime, while decisions must be made about data structures and the degree of independence between different modules of the program.

5. Testing. The evaluation of expert systems is far from being an exact science, but it is clear that the task can be made easier if one is able to run the program on a large and representative sample of test cases. Common sources of error are rules which are either missing, incomplete or wholly incorrect, while competition between related rules can cause unexpected bugs.

As Figure 13.1 suggests, the primary consideration in designing an expert system is the class of problems that you want the system to solve. It is a mistake to begin either with a particular conceptual analysis of the domain or with a particular organization of knowledge in mind. This is because one suspects that the way in which we represent concepts to ourselves and the way in which we organize our ideas depends to some significant extent upon our current needs and purposes. Categorizations of objects and their properties tend to depend upon our attitudes towards them, which depend in turn upon our ultimate goals. Thus hungry animals might divide the world into edible and inedible things, while frightened animals might divide the world into things you can hide behind and things you can't.

The distinction drawn between identification, conceptualization and formalization can also be found in the work of Wielinga and Breuker (1984) who distinguish 'knowledge identification', 'knowledge conceptualization' and 'epistemological analysis'. Knowledge identification simply refers to the recording of what one or more experts report on their knowledge; knowledge conceptualization aims at the formal description of knowledge in terms of primitive concepts and conceptual relations; and epistemological analysis is concerned to uncover the structural properties of the conceptual knowledge, such as taxonomic relations. They also identify a level of implementational analysis, which deals with the mechanisms upon which other levels of analysis are based, e.g. pattern-matching, slot-filling, and so on. However, they insert a level of 'logical analysis' between the epistemological and the implementational, which applies to the kind of inferential knowledge that is implicit in many so-called 'inference engines', e.g. the use of *modus ponens* by forward- and backward-chaining production systems. For Wielinga and Breuker, testing is part of the implementation level, which is consistent with Buchanan's diagram in which testing feeds back into implementation.

Various tools can currently be employed to make the actual business of building knowledge-based systems easier, ranging from the text and structure editors supplied with systems like LOOPS and KEE up to the EXPLAIN, TEST and REVIEW facilities provided by EMYCIN. However, the hope for the future is that more programming tools will be endowed with intelligence, in that they will act as aides, advisors or assistants in the whole process of expert system building. This is something of a research issue at the present time, and there are a variety of positions one can adopt with respect to what should be provided, as was noted in Chapter 12. The next section looks in a little more detail at some of the practical problems surrounding current technology, while Section 13.3 looks at machine learning to see how far knowledge acquisition might be automated.

13.2   Using environments for knowledge engineering

In addition to some of the theoretical issues addressed in Chapter 12, there are a number of methodological issues that need to be considered with respect to getting the best out of such tools as are currently available. One problem with new tools like LOOPS and KEE is that we have yet to build up a solid experiential base in their use to solve really difficult problems. This problem manifests itself in rather different ways at different levels of the process of constructing an expert system.

13.2.1   Epistemological problems

At the highest, epistemological, level of analysis, it is often unclear as to what the 'objects' in the object-oriented program should represent. In the early object-oriented languages, where the principal application was the writing of software to perform simulations, this was less of a problem. Computational objects stood for classes or instances of the real objects in whose behaviour one was interested. Thus, simulating the behaviour of a production line would involve creating computational objects that represented the configuration of machines, while messages represented the exchange of information, energy and partly-assembled products. The programmer's task is made relatively easy, because there is a comprehensible mapping from computational objects to objects in the world.

In many expert systems applications, one might need the computational objects to stand for far more abstract entities, if this style of programming is actually to be used to solve the problem. Hence objects might stand for facts and goals, sets of rules or individual hypotheses. It is then much less easy to decide what kinds of messages such entities should exchange, and what the meaning of those messages might be. For example, a fact might send a message to a hypothesis, saying 'I support you!', or a rule might send a message to a goal, saying 'I might be able to derive you'. However, such behaviour must be tightly controlled, if it is to remain focused on the task in hand, and there is a certain unnaturalness in doing things this way.

A lot depends on the level at which this kind of behaviour is going on. If objects are just the low-level implementation vehicle for getting a particular pattern of reasoning, then this need have no epistemological consequences at all. It is simply a feature of the host programming language for your expert system application, and the objects may well remain hidden from view. If, on the other hand, the objects are visible to both the expert during system development and the user during system performance, then the appropriateness of this mapping between abstract and computational objects needs to be established.

Even in genuine simulation applications, the object-oriented style of programming is not without its problems. Many important events occur as (possibly unintended) side-effects of other events which are hard to characterize in terms of message-passing. Klahr *et al.* (1982) cite an example from air battle simulation. Suppose an unauthorized aircraft penetrates airspace monitored by a radar installation. In a simulation program, the easiest way to 'wake up' the computational object representing the radar is to get the intruder to send the radar a message, saying 'I am here!'. However, such behaviour clearly does not correspond to anything that is happening in the real world. Furthermore, even if the intruder was foolish enough to deliberately broadcast his position, such behaviour would require him to know the position of all the in-range radar stations: a piece of knowledge that he would not normally possess. In other words, although the unnatural solution is computationally tractable, it attributes knowledge to computational objects that their real counterparts do not have.

Alternative ways of tackling this problem have problems of their own. One possible solution is to create 'auxilliary objects' which have god-like knowledge of what is going on, and get them to send the appropriate messages. These objects would be experts on non-intentional events, such as triggering radar trackers, and would manage the whole business of their genesis and development. However, in order to do this, they would need to communicate with other, less divine, domain-level objects, and so these objects would still need to be able to send and receive messages that are somehow unnatural. Also, the problem regarding the ontological status of abstract objects noted earlier remains.

Another possible solution to this problem raises the issue of 'grain-size', i.e. what level of detail should we use computational objects to represent? If one was prepared to have objects representing air molecules, one could have molecules of intruded airspace sending messages of protest to radar stations monitoring them. However, such anthropomorphic behaviour seems unnatural in itself, and the computational cost of representing airspace in this way would undoubtedly be prohibitive!

The problem of grain size is not limited to object-oriented systems, of course. It is a general problem for knowledge representation, and there are few theoretical guidelines to aid the knowledge engineer. Most people make case-by-case decisions based on rules of thumb derived from personal experience.

13.2.2 Implementation problems

In more conventional styles of programming, there exist notions of what constitutes good programming practice. Furthermore, whole books have been written which deal with aspects of program design, programming style and efficiency considerations. Even if some of these topics are controversial (e.g. what is good style?), such texts, together with word of mouth from more experienced programmers, help the novice learn his trade.

Such is less routinely the case in the context of AI programming in general, and knowledge engineering in particular. Many LISP primers still contain horrendous programs that would make any 'structured programming' enthusiast shudder with horror. Sample programs are often peppered with non-standard flow of control, cavalier use of dynamic variable binding, and the careless manipulation of data structures such as property lists. This situation has improved dramatically in recent years – compare Winston and Horn (1985) with Winston and Horn (1981), for example. Nevertheless, writing good LISP code is a skill that not many people acquire, and many famous AI programs contain the most appalling examples of bad programming practice.

The fact that it has taken 25 years for something resembling a good LISP programming style to become widespread does not augur well for the new languages, tools and environments that are currently emerging. It is pretty unclear to me as to what constitutes good LOOPS style, for example, and I have seen knowledge engineers who have years of experience in structured languages run amok when faced with a mix of procedural attachment, combined methods and active values! None of this is intended as a serious criticism of LOOPS (which I have unfairly singled out as the target of these comments), rather it is a sad fact of life that powerful tools require equally strong methodologies for their application if they are to serve our purposes. Perhaps we can take comfort from the example of OPS. It has taken only six years for a definitive text to appear telling prospective knowledge-based programmers how to write effective OPS5 code.

Proponents of 'logic for expert systems' have contributed surprisingly little to this debate. Anyone who has ever marked a student exercise knows that it is as easy to commit gross errors of taste in PROLOG as it is in LISP, in terms of impenetrable flow of control and unprincipled side-effects. As Kluzniak and Szpakowicz (1984) point out, it is by no means self-evident that 'programming in logic' results in either better programs or less programming effort. Thus it is not altogether clear why a set of predicate calculus formulae should contain fewer bugs than a set of program statements, or be any easier to debug. The hope that this should be the case seems to be based upon the idea that one can use logic to prove that a particular knowledge-based program does or does not have certain properties, and can therefore guarantee its correctness, or at least discover its limitations, at the outset. I find it hard to believe that this is possible given the complexity of today's programs, where modules of incomplete, uncertain and maybe even inconsistent knowledge compete for the attention of some interpreter, and are applied or not under some heuristic control regime.

In short, it seems that 'heuristic programming' is here for some time to come, in at least two senses: (a) the programs will continue to be guided by the opportunistic application of imperfect knowledge, and (b) the programmers will continue to develop systems by rapid prototyping followed by incremental augmentation of the knowledge base and 'hand-tuning' on a largely experimental basis. This is not altogether good news, but I suspect that it is the truth. The development of a more rigorous methodology is a desirable research goal, but a good deal more homework needs to be done before it becomes a reality.

13.3   Reasoning about reasoning in META-DENDRAL

Given that knowledge engineering itself requires expertise, the question naturally arises as to how far one could replace the knowledge engineer by a program that is capable of acquiring knowledge of a domain from examples, and then encoding that knowledge in an appropriate representation.

In Chapter 1, the problem of knowledge acquisition was mentioned, and its relation to machine learning. There appear to be three alternatives to the 'hand-building' of a knowledge base by a combination of domain expert and knowledge engineer:

1. Interactive programs which elicit knowledge from the expert during the course of a 'conversation' at the terminal.
2. Programs which learn by scanning texts rather as humans read technical books.
3. Programs which learn the concepts of a domain from some set of examples, or 'training instances'.

Attempts at the first two methods are relatively scarce. Designing knowledge elicitation dialogues is not easy, and the problem of natural language understanding plagues both approaches. The third approach, that of automatic theory formation, has been applied with some success (e.g. Buchanan and Mitchell, 1978).

In this section, we review an application of a learning technique known as 'version spaces' (Mitchell, 1978, 1982) to META-DENDRAL: the program discussed in Chapter 2 which helps a chemist to derive new rules for associating spectral processes with the substructural features of molecules. In attempting to derive a general rule of mass spectrometry from a set of examples of how particular molecules fragment, META-DENDRAL is tackling a concept learning problem. Mitchell (1978) defines such problems as follows.

> 'A concept can be conceived of as a pattern which states those properties which are common to instances of the concept. Given (i) a language of patterns for describing concepts, (ii) sets of positive and negative instances of the target concept, and (iii) a way of matching data in the form of training instances against hypothetical descriptions of the concept, the task is to determine concept descriptions in the language that are consistent with the training instances. In other words, given some set of entities for which you know either that they are examples of the concept (positive instances) or that they are not examples of the concept (negative instances), how can you best describe the concept in the language provided? 'Consistency', in this context, means that the description matches all the positive instances but none of the negative ones. Hence we assume that the training data contains no errors, and that the language for describing the concept is capable of generating at least one description that is consistent with the training instances.'

This defines concept learning as a search problem, since the language of permissible concept descriptions can be thought of as generating a space of possible solutions to the problem. The job of a concept learning program is to examine this space, using the constraints supplied by the training instances. The following section describes in more detail the way in which META-DENDRAL's concept learning problem is represented.

13.3.1 META-DENDRAL's pattern language

In order to reason about the rules for mass spectrometry, META-DENDRAL needs a language for representing concepts and relationships in that domain. As suggested above by the definition of concept learning, this will need to be a pattern language, in this case for describing chemical structures. More precisely, a pattern in META-DENDRAL stands for the chemical substructure of a molecule, an atom or a set of bonds which predicts a spectral peak. Given a particular pattern site, the set of allowable patterns will be restricted to contain only those atoms which could be connected to the site by some chain of chemical bonds. Patterns which do not fit this constraint can be ruled out, even if they can be generated by the definition of the language.

The pattern language used by META-DENDRAL is a structural language whose simplest constituents are nodes and links, which can be connected together into a network. The nodes stand for atoms, or configurations of atoms, while the links stand for chemical bonds. In the language, it is possible to place constraints upon the properties that nodes have, such as atom type, number of unsaturated electrons, etc. As a matter of convenience, hydrogen atoms are not explicitly represented by nodes, but are associated with other nodes as 'Hydrogen-Neighbours'. This is because they are so common that they would clutter the representation unnecessarily.

A pattern in this language matches some training instance just in case there is a mapping from the nodes and links of the instance to the nodes and links of the pattern that satisfies all the constraints placed upon the nodes and links of the pattern. Thus, in order to match a pattern of nodes and links representing atoms connected by chemical bonds, the components of an instance must not have properties or relationships which violate the stated constraints. They may, however, exhibit properties or relationships which are not predicted by the pattern so long as the constraints remain intact.

It was mentioned earlier that one can consider concept learning as a search problem. The concept description language outlined above can be thought of as being capable of generating a space of possible concepts that the program might be able to represent to itself and therefore learn. Learning a particular concept involves searching this space for valid descriptions of the concept, i.e. descriptions which satisfy the constraints imposed by the training instances supplied. Once one has reduced some learning problem to a search problem in this way, there are obviously many ways in which one could go about solving it. The next section describes a general method for solving problems of this kind, called 'version spaces'.

13.3.2 Version spaces

In the context of a concept learning problem, a version space is simply a way of representing the space of all concept descriptions consistent with the training instances seen so far. This will obviously be a subspace of the space of all possible concepts that the pattern language is capable of describing. Given that training instances are considered one at a time, it will be necessary to update the version space for a particular problem with each new instance.

It is easy to see that the version space for a particular concept-learning problem after the presentation of the first training instance will simply be the set of all concept descriptions consistent with that instance. However, even at this stage, we need to consider efficient ways of representing the space. For example, the language may be capable of generating an infinite set of concept descriptions, and the version space may be an infinite subset of this set. Thus, representing a version space may mean storing the information required to generate every concept description in the space, rather than storing every description explicitly. The situation is further complicated as new instances are added, since we want to be able to update the space efficiently as well as store it efficiently.

The principal advantage of Mitchell's technique for representing and updating version spaces is that they can be determined instance by instance, without looking back to examine either past training instances or previously rejected concept descriptions. In order to realize the benefits of this, imagine a situation in which, every time a new instance was presented, the program needed to compare it with all the previous instances, and reconsider concept descriptions it had ruled out. Such an approach would produce combinatorial problems of the kind described in Chapter 1. It would also be 'counter-intuitive', in that one would like to think that learning is both incremental and focused. In other words, it ought to get easier as you go on, and the whole process ought to converge on success.

Mitchell found the key to the problems of efficient representation and update by noting that the search space of possible concept descriptions is not without structure, i.e. it contains redundancy. In particular, he observed that a partial order can be defined over the patterns generated by any concept description language of the kind described above. Most important is the relation 'more specific than or equal to', which can be defined as follows:

Pattern P_1 is more specific than or equal to pattern P_2 (written as $P_1 \geq P_2$) if and only if P_1 matches a subset of all the instances that P_2 matches.

Consider the following simple example from Winston's 'blocks world' learning program. The pattern P_1:

standing	supports	lying
brick	$\longrightarrow$	wedge OR brick

is more specific than the pattern P_2:

NOT lying	touches	any orientation
ANY shape	$\longrightarrow$	wedge OR brick

because the constraints imposed by P_1 are only satisfied if the weaker constraints imposed by P_2 are satisfied. Another way of looking at this is to say that if P_1's constraints are satisfied, then so are P_2's, but not conversely.

Note that for a program to appreciate an example of partial ordering such as that shown above, it would need to understand a number of concepts and relationships:

- It would need to know that if B is a brick then B is a shape, i.e. to have some criteria for categorizing the kinds of entities in the domain that are represented by nodes in the structural language.
- It would need to know that if A supports B then A touches B in the blocks world, i.e. to realize that there is redundancy in the domain relations.
- It would need to understand the logical meaning of terms such as NOT, ANY and OR, in terms of the restrictions or permissions that they imply for the matching process.

The program needs to know these things in order to satisfy itself that there is a mapping between P_1's nodes and links and those of P_2 such that each constraint in P_1 is in fact more specific than the corresponding constraint in P_2. Once it can grasp this relationship of specificity, the way is open for a representation of version spaces in terms of their maximally specific and maximally general patterns. This is because the program can then consider the version space as containing:

1. The set of maximally specific patterns.
2. The set of maximally general patterns.
3. All concept descriptions which occur between the boundary sets (1) and (2) in the partial ordering.

This is called the 'boundary sets representation' for version spaces, and it is both compact and easy to update. It is compact because one is not explicitly storing every concept description in the space. It is easy to update, because defining a new space corresponds to moving one or both of the boundaries.

13.3.3 The candidate elimination algorithm

A version space, as described so far, is no more than a data structure for representing a set of concept descriptions. However, the term 'version spaces' is often applied to a learning technique which applies a particular algorithm, known as the 'candidate elimination algorithm', to such data structures. This algorithm works by manipulating the boundary sets that represent a given version space.

The algorithm begins by initializing the version space to the set of all concept descriptions consistent with the first positive training instance. In other words, the set of maximally specific patterns (S) is initialized to the most specific concept descriptions that the pattern language is capable of generating, while the set of maximally general patterns (G) is initialized to the most general concept descriptions available in the language. As each subsequent instance is processed, the sets S and G are modified in order to eliminate from the version space just those concept descriptions which are inconsistent with the current instance.

In the course of learning, the boundaries should move towards each other monotonically, i.e. without back-and-forth movement in which they sometimes move further apart. Moving the S boundary in the direction of greater generality can be considered as a breadth-first search from specific patterns to more general ones. The object of the search is to compute a new boundary set which is just sufficiently general that it does not rule out a newly-encountered positive instance. In other words, S moves when the program encounters a new positive instance which does not match all of the patterns in S. Correspondingly, moving the G boundary in the direction of greater specificity can be considered as a breadth-first search from general patterns to more specific ones. The object of this search is to compute a new boundary set which is just specific enough to rule out a newly-encountered negative instance. Thus G moves when the program encounters a negative training instance which matches some pattern in G.

These searches must be controlled if we are to ensure that patterns in the new boundaries will be consistent with past instances. In moving S, each pattern in the new S must be more specific than some pattern in G. This ensures that every pattern in the new S will be consistent with all past negative instances. Otherwise, one might move S too far and, in attempting to admit the present positive instance, admit a past negative one. In moving G, every pattern in the new G must be more general than some pattern in S. This ensures that every pattern in the new G will be consistent with all past positive instances. Otherwise, one might move G too far and, in attempting to rule out the present negative instance, rule out a past positive one.

It is important to stress that this algorithm does not employ heuristic search, because the constraints are exact and they are guaranteed to cause the problem to converge on a solution. The restrictions on these searches are the key to controlling the combinatorics of the update problem. As hinted earlier, the version spaces technique has a number of pleasing properties, which are worth listing.

- All concept descriptions that are consistent with all of the training instances will be found.
- The version space summarizes the alternative interpretations of the observed data.
- The results are independent of the order in which training instances are presented.
- Each training instance is examined only once.
- One never needs to reconsider discarded hypotheses.

The fact that the version space summarizes the data so far means that it can be used as a basis for generating new training instances, i.e. instances that might bring the boundaries closer together. The fact that you consider each instance only once means that the program doesn't need to store past instances. Thus the time required by the algorithm will be proportional to the number of observed instances, rather than some explosive function of this number. The eschewal of backtracking also contributes to the efficiency and simplicity of the algorithm. Mitchell also reports an extension to the algorithm which finds the set of maximally consistent concept descriptions in the case where no concept description is consistent with every training instance, but that is beyond the scope of this text (see Mitchell, 1978, Chapter 5).

13.3.4   Matching instances to patterns in META-DENDRAL

META-DENDRAL uses the same language to describe training instances as it uses to describe patterns, although only a subset of the pattern language is required to do this. Each training instance is a complete molecule with a particular site in the compound, rather than a constrained description of a molecule.

Matching instances to patterns involves defining a connected mapping from pattern nodes to instance nodes. A mapping, X, is connected if the mapping is one-to-one and injective, and if every pair of instance nodes, $X(p_1)$ and $X(p_2)$, corresponding to pattern nodes p_1 and p_2 share a common link if and only if p_1 and p_2 also share a common link. We also require that the feature values of each instance node of the form $X(p)$ satisfy the feature constraints of the corresponding pattern node, p.

It is now possible to give Mitchell's domain-specific definition of partial order for META-DENDRAL, using the definitions given above. Lower-case letters stand for pattern nodes, while upper-case letters stand for whole patterns. Pattern P_1 is more specific than or equal to pattern P_2 if and only if there is a connected mapping, X, of nodes in P_2 into nodes of P_1 such that for each pair of nodes, p_2, $X(p_2)$, the feature constraints associated with $X(p_2)$ are more specific than or equal to the feature constraints associated with p_2. In trying to understand this definition, and how it applies to the mass spectrometry domain, it is worth looking back to the blocks world example given earlier. In the world of chemical structure elucidation, the analogue of blocks are the atoms and superatoms, while the analogue of spatial relationships such as 'supports' and 'touches' are chemical bonds.

The general-to-specific ordering on patterns defined above can be expressed in terms of a general-to-specific ordering on the constraints that apply to nodes. For example, consider the constraints that can be placed on the number of 'non-hydrogen neighbours' that an atom can have, i.e. the number of non-hydrogen atoms that bond with it. Thus having zero or more non-hydrogen neighbours is obviously a more general constraint than having one or more, or having two or more.

13.3.5 Domain knowledge and heuristics in RULEGEN

As outlined earlier, META-DENDRAL is designed to help a chemist correlate spectral processes and structural features. Chemist and program co-operate in deciding which data points are interesting and then look for processes that might explain them. These explanatory rules are production rules of the kind described in Chapter 2, which attempt to predict fragmentation pathways and atom migrations.

Knowledge of chemistry can be employed by the candidate elimination algorithm in two ways.

1. The representation language for chemical substructures allows forms which are syntactically distinct but semantically equivalent patterns, i.e. it can generate expressions which are different in form but have the same meaning. Knowledge of the meaning of these patterns can therefore be used to delete redundant patterns from the version space boundaries. This has no effect upon the completeness of the version space approach.

2. Version space boundaries grow quite large for some problems. It is therefore useful to apply various rules of thumb to prune these boundaries. However, if heuristic methods are used, one can no longer be sure that the program will determine all of the concept descriptions that are consistent with the training instances.

As an example of the former, consider the interdependencies that exist between node features, i.e. the features associated with an atom or superatom. In some cases, values for some subset of the features of a node will completely determine the value of another feature, due to knowledge about the valencies of particular atoms, say. Thus, a pattern representing a carbon atom with only three non-hydrogen neighbours and no unsaturated electrons can only be matched by an instance which has one hydrogen neighbour, since carbon has valency 4. A semantically equivalent pattern would be one representing a carbon atom with only one hydrogen neighbour and no unsaturated electrons. Inspection of the two sets of constraints given below should convince you that these two patterns will match exactly the same class of instance nodes.

P_1
Atom-Type = C
Non-Hydrogen-Neighbours = 3
Hydrogen-Neighbours = any
Unsaturated-Electrons = 0

P_2
Atom-Type = C
Non-Hydrogen-Neighbours = any
Hydrogen-Neighbours = 1
Unsaturated-Electrons = 0

Allowing variants of this kind would simply multiply the size of the boundary sets with no corresponding gain in information. To prevent this, whenever a new pattern is added to a boundary set, implicit node constraints are made explicit. The two semantically equivalent nodes shown above would then reduce to the following single node:

P_3
Atom-Type = C
Non-Hydrogen-Neighbours = 3
Hydrogen-Neighbours = 1
Unsaturated-Electrons = 0

The following are general heuristics for pruning the boundary sets which affect the completeness of the candidate elimination algorithm.

- Since META-DENDRAL forms rules for whole classes of compounds, one can use simple assumptions about chemical structures to prune boundaries, e.g. assuming that all atoms with a valence of 4 are carbon atoms, which will often be the case for organic molecules.

- The user can select a subset of the node features supplied by the pattern language when updating the boundary, resulting in a reduced rule language.

- The user can limit the number of alternative mappings of patterns to instances considered by the program, which may reduce the size of the boundaries and reduce the time required to compute them.

- The user can simply set an arbitrary ceiling on the size that boundaries are allowed to achieve, and then truncate them. The specific boundary set is pruned by deleting patterns which contain the fewest number of nodes, while the general boundary is pruned by deleting patterns which contain the largest number of nodes. The rationale for this is that in each case these patterns will be furthest from the 'inner' limits of the boundary set.

Mitchell claimed that the version space approach added the following new capabilities to the original META-DENDRAL program.

- Additional training data can modify existing rules without the original data having to be reconsidered.

- The learning process is properly incremental, in that one can determine to what degree each rule has been learned and reliably employ partially learned rules.

- The new rule formation strategy avoids the expensive 'coarse search' of RULEGEN and focuses upon the most 'interesting' training data first.

- The method for considering alternative versions of each rule is more complete than the generalization and specialization operations of RULEMOD.

In summary, the version spaces approach appears to provide an incremental learning methodology that is both principled and efficient. Candidate elimination can be contrasted with depth- and breadth-first search strategies in that it determines every concept description consistent with the training instances, rather than finding a single acceptable concept description (depth-first search), or all maximally specific concept descriptions (breadth-first search). As Mitchell points out, the chief manpower cost involved in applying this kind of technology to real problems is the construction of the set of training instances.

13.4   What is the state of the art?

Knowledge is a mysterious kind of entity, about which we know remarkably little. The term 'knowledge engineering' implies that knowledge-based systems can be built by applying tools to some substantive material, like wood or stone. If this is indeed an appropriate metaphor, which may or may not be the case, a greater understanding of this material would help us fashion better tools and use them more effectively.

Knowledge engineering is still an art, and not a science. The advent of new technology, in the form of personal workstations with powerful programming tools, does nothing to change this, just as a novelist does not become a scientist simply because he is using a word processor. If anything, the situation is complicated by the fact that the knowledge engineer is supplied with little in the way of guidelines as to how to maximize his use of the technology supplied.

It seems that until we know more about the nature of human knowledge, the design of knowledge elicitation methods and tools will remain an empirical exercise, guided by little more than trial and error and common sense. Viewed in this light, appeals to logic appear as wide of the mark as the appeal to technology criticized above. We want expert systems to exhibit the kind of rationality we associate with human beings, rather than the kind that we associate with theorem provers. This statement is not motivated by anthropomorphism, or even a desire to advance our understanding of human psychology. It is quite simply an essential requirement for the mechanization of expertise, and it may mean that future systems will be less, not more, 'logical' than they are now, in that their reasoning may go even further beyond the bounds of the well-known calculi than they do at present.

In attempting to articulate the differences in behaviour between men and machines, Bronowski (1965) once wrote that

'In trying to formalize a rule, we look for truth, but what we find is knowledge, and what we fail to find is certainty.'

Logic is primarily concerned with truth and validity, and its well-understood branches all deal with categorical reasoning. In the realm of expert systems, we deal not with truth, but with knowledge, and the validity of arguments does not establish the certainty of their conclusions. Knowledge is corrigible and therefore subject to change at both the object- and meta-levels. Ideally, knowledge-based programs should be able to learn at both levels, i.e. induce both object- and meta-level rules on the basis of their experience with solving problems. This is probably just as difficult as trying to formalize both our knowledge about the world and the behaviour of the system in some calculus, such that it could be proved, in principle, that the system had certain properties and that its behaviour could be predicted in all cases – but a successful outcome would be more interesting. This is because we would have made progress in the mechanization of creativity, which is probably among our planet's scarcer resources. Readers who are interested in this topic (which is well outside the scope of the present book) should consult Lenat (1982).

Machine learning is an entirely non-trivial branch of AI in which progress has been unsurprisingly slow. Research on this topic can be divided into two camps: the 'cognitivists', who are interested in developing a theory of human learning by writing programs which simulate phenomema observed both inside and outside of the psychologist's laboratory; and the 'automatic programmers', who are interested in mechanizing cognitive skills such as learning by induction for the purpose of getting machines to generate or tune knowledge-based programs, but who are not committed to doing it in an anthropomorphic fashion. This is a caricature of the two camps, of course. Nevertheless, different researchers in this field often have different motivations, and the above division reflects the main approaches.

It is clear that many aspects of machine learning relevant to expert systems are still topics for research, e.g. learning from incomplete and uncertain information, learning from errorful descriptions, and learning general rules with exceptions. However, it seems likely that such research will make a positive contribution in the long run; the pioneering work of Michalski augurs well for future developments (Michalski and Larson, 1978; Michalski and Chilausky, 1980). Bundy *et al.* (1985) provide a good review of research into rule-learning, which will give the general reader some idea of the state of the art.

In the next chapter, we move on the the topic of automatic explanation facilities. This does not mean, however, that we have entirely finished with the topic of knowledge acquisition, since the process by which knowledge passes from man to machine is relevant to the way in which information can subsequently flow in the opposite direction. Progress on each front seems to require a better understanding of the relationship between these two topics.

Chapter 14 Explaining Expert System Behaviour

As we saw in Chapters 7 and 10, there are two compelling reasons for the requirement that expert systems should be able to explain their reasoning and justify their conclusions in a manner that is intelligible to users.

1. The consumers of automatic advice need to be convinced that the reasoning behind a conclusion is substantially correct, and that the solution proposed is appropriate to their particular case.

2. The engineers of an expert system need to be able to satisfy themselves that the mechanisms employed in the derivation of a conclusion are functioning according to specification.

The main difference between the needs of the users that we have called the engineer and the consumer concerns the level at which the explanation should be presented and the degree of understanding which the user is presumed to have with respect to the system's internal workings. In other words, one expects the knowledge engineer to know more about both the problem solving domain and the computational mechanisms by which the system derives solutions. This difference in knowledge also imparts special privileges to the user, in that the interface should allow the engineer to make changes to the system on the basis of his response to the explanation. Thus the engineer may wish to revise certain rules, or remove certain facts from the knowledge base. He may wish to restart the computation, putting on extra levels of trace, and having certain subresults made visible as they are computed.

14.1 Survey of the state of the art

Such progress as has been made in the generation of explanations can be summed up in the following way. The pioneering efforts of Stanford researchers in the 1960s and 1970s provided little more than high-level trace facilities in the first instance, although these were subsequently augmented by a range of debugging tools. More recent efforts have concentrated on making certain issues to do with the control of inference and the underlying architecture more explicit.

As we saw in Chapter 6, early approaches to explanation, e.g. MYCIN (Shortliffe, 1976), combined a declarative reading of production rules with a simple natural language translation system to generate an augmented trace of the system's reasoning. The trace facility was an augmented one, because it was possible to ask 'HOW' and 'WHY' questions during the execution of the program. WHY questions looked up the AND/OR tree representing the search space of production rules activated so far, while HOW questions looked down the tree to applicable rules not yet activated. Such traces were also of use to the knowledge engineer, since they laid out the pattern of rule firings upon which the reasoning was based. However, such traces are extremely verbose and hard to follow, even in the traversal of a relatively shallow search space.

Even producing this rather rudimentary level of explanation required a certain amount of machinery. The system had to be able to display the rule being invoked at any one time; record rule invocations and associate them with specific events, such as questions asked and conclusions drawn; and use the rule indexing to retrieve rules relevant to particular parameters. It also needed to be able to retrieve parameter values in response to simple requests for information.

EMYCIN (Van Melle *et al.*, 1981) developed and elaborated these facilities to some extent. The EXPLAIN, TEST and REVIEW options were provided as debugging aids for the knowledge engineer. The EXPLAIN option gave terse explanations about how the current values for various parameters were derived, while TEST compared the current value of each parameter with the value stored for the particular case being considered. The REVIEW option was provided as an aid to amending the knowledge base if the explanation proved to be unsatisfactory. A global variable called IMPORTANTPARMS could be used to tell the system which parameters these options should examine.

EXPLAIN worked by printing each rule that contributed to the conclusion, together with the certainty factor that resulted from the successful application of the rule, the 'tally' value associated with the evaluation of the premises of the rule, and the last question asked by the system before the conclusion was drawn. In addition, EMYCIN had three levels of trace: one that printed a trace of all the conclusions made at the time that the inferences were drawn; one that printed rule failures as well as rules that fired successfully, and a verbose account of the flow of control. A useful additional tool provided for the knowledge engineer was the batch facility, whereby any changes made to the knowledge base could be tested by running the system in batch mode on a set of stored cases.

The problems associated with understanding, monitoring and correcting the behaviour of an expert system multiply as the knowledge base increases in size (Davis, 1980). For example, it becomes more difficult to ensure that new rules are consistent with old ones, and to understand the flow of control in situations where large numbers of applicable rules may be in competition for the attention of the interpreter. The introduction of meta-rules in MYCIN, which was intended to make some of the control choices explicit, opened the door to reasoning about problem solving strategy, in addition to reasoning at the object level of the domain. It then became feasible to think about meta-level reasoning in the context of explanations, such that explanations of what had been inferred could be augmented by an account of why certain inferences had been drawn in preference to others. The notion of a 'rule model' also emerged in this context, i.e. the idea that certain classes of rules can be identified on the basis of shared goals in their conclusions, or shared parameter tests in their conditions, so that new rules added to these classes should conform more or less closely to the syntactic skeleton associated with old rules already in the class.

Two rational reconstructions of the early Stanford work were attempted towards the end of the 1970s. One was the NEOMYCIN system (see Chapter 7), which represented an attempt to take a more principled approach to medical problem solving, based on epistemological and psychological considerations. The other was the CENTAUR system (see Chapter 10), which experimented with a mixed representation of knowledge, combining frames and production rules in an attempt to be explicit about the context in which domain-specific knowledge was applied.

Each of these efforts had implications for the design and development of expert systems. Clancey argued forcibly for a more psychological approach to expert-level problem solving that involved modelling the diagnostic strategies that clinicians actually use. Aikins' argument for the mix of rules and frames was more at the level of implementation, in that the resultant structuring of information made it easier to locate and modify knowledge in the resultant program.

These efforts also had implications for the design and implementation of explanation facilities. In NEOMYCIN, there was an emphasis on 'strategic explanation', in which one tried to make clear the plans and methods used in attaining a goal, instead of merely citing the rules employed (Hasling *et al.*, 1984). In other words, the program was expected to have some explicit representation of the problem solving process, as well as domain knowledge. In CENTAUR, there was an emphasis on the context in which reasoning was done, and the stage-dependent nature of expert-level problem solving. In order to understand why a particular question was asked, one needed to understand not merely which rule fired but the active hypothesis that was being considered.

14.2   Explanations and automatic programming

Swartout (1983) agrees with Clancey and Aikins that providing traces of rule activations may describe program behaviour, but they cannot be said to justify it. This is because although the justification is part of the knowledge used to design and implement the program, this knowledge is nowhere represented explicitly in the code. In other words, the 'knowing how' of the system, i.e. the principles of reasoning in the domain, is typically confused with the 'knowing that', i.e. the model of the domain that the system reasons with.

14.2.1 Automatic programming in XPLAIN

The idea behind the XPLAIN system is a simple but powerful one which links the two processes of designing an expert system and obtaining coherent explanations from it. One way to design an expert consultation program is to specify the domain model and the domain principles, and then invoke an automatic programmer upon this specification to generate the performance program. The process of integrating the prescriptive and descriptive aspects of the specification into the final system is recorded and used to produce explanations of the system's behaviour.

The domain model contains facts about the domain of application, such as causal paths and taxonomies. This concept corresponds quite closely to what Clancey would call structural knowledge, i.e. the kind of knowledge that underlies situation/action rules of the usual kind. The domain principles include methods and heuristics, which are usually either hard-coded into the interpreter or given to the interpreter as meta-rules. This corresponds quite closely to what Clancey would call 'strategic knowledge'. Swartout argues convincingly, as Clancey does, that separating out these different kinds of knowledge has positive effects upon aspects of system performance other than the explanation facility, such as modifiability.

Swartout collected observational data on the kinds of questions that medical students and fellows asked when they ran the Digitalis Therapy Advisor. Three kinds of question were identified:

1. Questions about the methods employed by the program, e.g. how it calculates values for certain parameters.

2. Justifications of program behaviour, e.g. why are certain adjustments to therapy recommended.

3. Explanation of system questions, when there is some doubt about what kind of answer the system wants or expects.

The first type is the kind of question that most expert systems can answer without difficulty. All that is required is that the program be able to produce an English description of the code that is executed. The second type requires something more: the ability to represent and reference the medical knowledge underlying the code. The third type requires something more again: the ability to represent the user's understanding of the terminology in a question and resolve any conflicts between that understanding and the intended meaning. XPLAIN concentrates upon the second type of question.

The automatic programming approach adopted in the XPLAIN system can be seen as a way of combining both the specification and implementation phases of constructing an expert system. The idea is that the specification of the domain model should be entirely declarative, since the program may want to use the same piece of knowledge in different ways. This is a somewhat stronger notion of declarativeness than the sense in which production rules, say, are declarative. The domain principles are used to refine the goal structure associated with the task in a recursive manner until there are methods associated with each of the bottom-level steps that the program has to perform. Again, the kind of control exercised by domain principles is rather more thorough-going than the related concept of a meta-rule, since the former does more than merely order or prune the application of domain-specific rules.

The integration of the program fragments thus generated is a complex process that need not concern us here. However, as in planning, potential interactions between program actions have to be resolved by splits and joins. There are constraints on the way in which split/joins are refined, and these are themselves derived from the domain model and the domain principles.

14.2.2 Explanations in XPLAIN

The explanation system makes use of the resultant refinement structure, as well as the explicit representations of the domain model and domain principles. The aspect of most interest here is the answer generators, which determine which parts of the knowledge structure to use in response to the user's questions. To do this, three kinds of knowledge are required:

1. Knowledge of the state of program execution.

2. Knowledge of what has already been said.

3. Knowledge of the user's interests.

Swartout draws attention to the problem of 'computer artefacts' in previous explanation systems. These artefacts are aspects of the computation which derive not from the underlying domain model or the domain principles but from the simple fact that parts of the program are nothing more than low-level algorithms which are implemented so that the computer will run the consultation. Such computational artefacts are of no interest to physicians, and users are unlikely to understand either how they work or why they are necessary.

The answer generators work by making use of 'viewpoints' attached to the prototypical methods used by the automatic programmer. When such prototypes are instantiated, the resulting steps in the program will inherit these viewpoints, which contain information about who should receive an explanation of such a step. Explanations can therefore be customized to individual users in a manner that is more economical than the method of annotating individual steps. Issues that have already been explained in a previous context can be filtered out of the current explanation. The viewpoint attachments can be used to decide where to begin the explanation, as well as determining the level of description.

Another way of looking at this is to realize that top-down structured programming by step-wise refinement corresponds to a shift between levels of language. Given access to the control stack of the interpreter, it becomes possible to set up an explicit correspondence between levels in the refinement structure and the domain principle invoked to refine that step. If we add to this the ability of the interpreter to leave behind some trace of its activity, these computational events can be used as a basis for producing an explanation of why the program behaved as it did.

The ideas behind the XPLAIN system have since been generalized into an approach to expert systems design called the 'Explainable Expert Systems' paradigm (Neches et al., 1984). As we have seen, these ideas are compatible with the drive to differentiate and render explicit different kinds of domain knowledge, but they also include the crucial insight that many of the ultimate grounds for justification reside in the system development process. In the absence of formal machinery for recording and subsequently deploying these decisions, such information is typically lost in the implementation phase.

The USC work on explanations is still in progress, and seems set to improve upon various aspects of XPLAIN. For example, terminological knowledge is being separated out from the domain rationale embodied by domain principles. It is also envisaged that the refinement process will ultimately be an interactive one, which will allow guidance from the user.

14.3 Logic-based explanations: APES, MRS and TAG

A good deal has been written and said over the last few years about the applicability of logic to the design and construction of expert systems. What follows is a critical survey of logic-based systems from the point of view of the explanation facilities that they offer. Some kind of assessment is attempted, in terms of comparing such systems with some of the alternative approaches outlined above.

In APES (Hammond and Sergot, 1983), an explanation is simply an edited form of the proof constructed by the program. It is therefore analogous in many ways to the trace of rule activity provided by earlier systems like EMYCIN. Consequently, this facility does not answer the calls of Clancey and others for a justification of the reasoning, rather than a description of it. Since APES inherits the depth-first search strategy of PROLOG more or less whole and entire, there is no explicit representation of control decisions involving the ordering of conditions within Horn clauses or the ordering of Horn clauses in the database. This design knowledge is therefore compiled into the interpreter, and hence unavailable to any explanation facility.

The 'query-the-user' facility (Sergot, 1983) of APES makes some attempt to offer a symmetric interface between the system and the user. The user is regarded as being an extension of the system knowledge base which can be interrogated when the proof is about to fail due to incomplete knowledge. However, this facility is both too strong and too weak. It is too strong, because it assigns a rather passive role to the user by treating him or her as little more than a source of missing data (as MYCIN did). It is too weak, in that there are no mechanisms explicitly provided whereby the system can attempt to assure itself that the user's assertions are consistent with previous information supplied.

Here is an example of an APES explanation, which shows its most attractive feature: the user language at the front end.

```
To show Peter should take lomotil
I used the rule
    <person> should take <drug> if
        <person> complains-of <symptom> and
        <drug> suppresses <symptom> and
        not <drug> is-unsuitable-for <person>
You said Peter complains-of diarrhoea
I know lomotil suppresses diarrhoea
I can show not lomotil is-unsuitable-for Peter.
```

Like APES, MRS (Genesereth *et al.*, 1980) is capable of constructing a proof in order to describe how it arrived at a certain conclusion. Unless explicitly instructed to do otherwise by meta-rules, the interpreter will reason backward in response to queries and forward in response to assertions. If the 'justify' flag is on, justifications can be written into a temporary theory, which keeps track of which propositions support which, and which inference method was used to draw the inferences. Thus

$$(\text{just } P_1 \text{ bc } P_2 \ P_3 \ P_4)$$

in a theory means that MRS has succeeded in proving P_1 from premises P_2, P_3 and P_4 by means of backward chaining.

The existence of this facility, together with the possibility of writing domain-specific meta-rules and creating procedural attachments, does at least provide the tools for creating one's own explanation system. The fact that 'just' expressions of the form given above are simply propositions in a theory, which can be processed in the same way as ordinary propositions, means that one doesn't have to go outside of MRS (into LISP, say) to extend the system in this way. However, the MRS philosophy does not offer any guidelines as to how to manage explanations; this is left as an exercise for the programmer.

TAG (Jackson, 1985) is also capable of constructing a proof for any conclusions drawn. Like MRS, the interpreter treats questions and assertions rather differently, although the reasoning about control is somewhat different too. Instead of adopting a forward- or backward-chaining strategy, depending upon the nature of the input to the system, TAG adopts a minimizing or a maximizing strategy, using a game-theoretic interpretation of logic (Hintikka, 1973). Maximizing consists of looking for supporting evidence and examples, while minimizing consists of looking for refuting evidence and counter-examples. The system is critical of user assertions, and will therefore try to refute them if it can, while it attempts to respond positively to user queries, by finding variable bindings and interpretations of subexpressions that lead to a favourable outcome. There are meta-rules for recursively assigning MIN and MAX strategies to the evaluation of parts of expressions as a function of the logical operators involved. For example, in order to minimize on a conditional, such as $P_1 \& \ldots \& P_n \to Q$, the system will attempt to maximize on the premise and then minimize on the instantiated conclusion.

As a consequence of the game-theoretic approach, the system knows not merely the outcome of the game and the moves that were made (in terms of invoking rules and finding variable bindings from data), but the strategy adopted at each step. This makes it possible to go beyond a mere description of the proof and the global inference strategy in the direction of both describing and justifying the local flow of control. In response to WHY questions, the system can say something to the effect of 'I am trying to establish P_2 because I am minimizing on $P_1 \& \ldots \& P_n \to Q$'. However, it is clear that such an explanation makes more sense to a knowledge engineer, who actually understands how the interpreter works, than to a client of a consultation system written in TAG. Many of the explanation facilities provided by TAG are aimed more at the system developer and debugger than at the client.

Nevertheless, considering interactive problem solving as a language game has several things to offer in the context of justifying system behaviour.

1. The game can be considered as a metaphor for the interaction between system and user that is easy to understand.

2. User modelling can then be considered in terms of the system having some knowledge of its 'opponent', courtesy of the user's previous moves in the game.

3. Similarly, knowledge of the system can be attributed to the user on the basis of system moves that the user has seen.

None of these logic-based approaches to explanation is as thorough-going as the one proposed by the Explainable Expert Systems project. APES takes us not much further than EMYCIN; MRS provides some useful tools but no underlying rationale for constructing an explanation system; TAG provides a rationale but lacks the automatic programming methodology offered by XPLAIN. Each of these three systems has its own strengths and weaknesses in the field of explanation, and none of them has really made explanation its main priority, as the XPLAIN system has.

It seems that we are still waiting for some kind of integration between the use of logic as:

- a specification language for expert systems;
- a representation language for domain knowledge;
- a meta-language for controlling and justifying inference.

There are many theoretical and practical problems in this area which await to be addressed before we can assess the possible contributions of logic to explanation facilities. Major issues include: the representation of 'deep' knowledge in the form of causal and structural models, the use of different levels of abstraction, and the use of convenient fictions and analogies for pedagogical purposes. It is at least arguable that logic will need to be augmented by other formalisms, such as game theory and information theory, before it will become a useful tool in the construction of more transparent systems.

14.4   The future of explanations

Explanation is a complex topic and the treatment given above is not meant to be exhaustive. However, it is intended to cover the main concerns and activities of researchers who are interested in both developing a methodology for building expert systems and improving the quality of explanations they produce. The critical issues appear to be:

1. The differentiation of different kinds of knowledge.
2. The explicit rendition of strategic and structural knowledge that tends get 'compiled' into program code.
3. The modelling of individual users' knowledge or levels of skill.

Mixed knowledge representation formalisms, which combine rules and structures in such a way as to give them a clear semantics, seem to offer the best solution to the problem of differentiating between different kinds of knowledge. Logic has a role to play in the provision of such a semantics, but this need not imply that the logic programming paradigm is the best or only way to do this. Apart from considerations of efficiency in implementation, there are aspects of structural and strategic knowledge that have yet to be satisfactorily formalized in any logistic system, e.g. the problem of multiple worlds and viewpoints. Existing logic-based expert systems are no less 'compiled' in this respect than their LISP-based counterparts. Likewise, the effective modelling of user's beliefs and intentions pose similar problems to logic- and procedure-based systems alike.

It is arguable that, in addition to improving the comprehensibility of the system, from the point of view of the end user, advances under the headings of (1) and (2) will also benefit the knowledge engineer in his attempt to test, monitor and debug the system during program development. Certainly the automatic programming approach appears to point strongly in this direction. The clarity of logic as a specification language may also have something to offer here, and so it may be a mistake to regard the two approaches (logic-based versus procedure-based) as being mutually exclusive, as MRS has shown. Finally, it should be noted that many of the extant knowledge representation packages, such as LOOPS (Bobrow and Stefik, 1983), offer interesting facilities for making explanations more immediate, e.g. the use of object-based graphics and active values to implement animated sequences, gauges and the like. What is lacking from these systems, and elsewhere, is some coherent vision of what explanation is all about.

Chapter 15 Summary and Conclusions

In this, the final chapter, I would like to summarize the ground that we have covered and then consider a few outstanding problems of representation and control associated with expert systems applications. Summarization will involve trying to draw general conclusions from the strengths and weaknesses of extant knowledge representation schemes and the systems which use them. The consideration of residual problems is intended to remind the reader that many of the issues that present practitioners with design and implementation difficulties are still topics of research in AI laboratories all over the world.

Most of these problems arise because of the inherent complexity of real world domains and the way in which we reason about them. By complexity, I mean more than just the level of difficulty that human beings experience in trying to acquire and apply an intellectual skill in the solution of some non-trivial problem. I am also referring to the many and varied information processing strategies that we employ as we collect, evaluate and act upon evidence, as well as the different strategies associated with the way in which we draw inferences, using the rules and laws which attempt to describe certain regularities in the domain.

The emphasis throughout this book has been upon knowledge representation. In this chapter, some attempt is made to draw general conclusions concerning the relative effectiveness of the different schemes considered in Chapters 3 and 4, based on evidence derived from the systems considered in Chapters 5–12. Such an exercise is not without its problems, however. The implementation of an expert system is an empirical exercise, in that a running system demonstrates that a particular approach is feasible. However, it is not a controlled experiment, in that the contrast with alternative approaches is seldom systematic.

There has been some debate over the last decade as to whether or not there exists a universal representation language that is good for all problems in any domain. Claims have been made for predicate logic in this regard (e.g. Kowalski, 1980), while production rules were strongly advocated by Newell and Simon (1972). All one can say at this stage is that the case for such a language remains unsubstantiated, either in terms of an existence proof, i.e. 'Look at language L!', or a convincing argument that such a language must exist, even if we have yet to discover or invent it.

There is certainly little evidence from psychology to suggest that human beings use a single representational scheme for encoding information. Rather the evidence is in the other direction. Human beings seem to use a variety of schemes involving images derived from different sensory modalities as well as more propositional representations, and there may be many different kinds of inference at work, some of them more associationistic than strictly logical.

15.1   A critical survey of knowledge representation schemes

The principal schemes which have been used to represent what an expert knows about some topic are production rules, structured objects and various forms of predicate logic. All have been implemented as pattern-directed inference systems, consisting of independent modules which match against data structures and modify them under some control regime. Some have their origins in pure formalisms of logic and grammar, while others were intended from the outset to capture aspects of natural or common sense reasoning. In the service of expert systems, they can all be thought of as applied formalisms, with the emphasis on performance rather than purity.

Variations continue to multiply, often appearing in combination; thus a number of systems mix rules with networks, as in PROSPECTOR, or with frames, as in CENTAUR. Logic-based schemes have been more chaste to date, being generally less explored and exploited. However, experience with complex problem solving in PROLOG suggests that logic programming for expert systems will not be constrained for long by the rigours of the predicate calculus.

15.1.1   Rule-based systems

The archetypal rule-based approach depends upon a number of critical assumptions:

- rules can completely specify their own context of application;
- domain rules are functionally independent of each other;
- all rules can be applied under a single control regime.

The advantages originally cited for the rule-based approach were the following:

- individual rules represent naturally-occurring 'chunks' of knowledge;
- independence among rules keeps the rule base semantically as well as syntactically modular;
- modularity allows for incremental development of the knowledge base.

There is now some doubt regarding all three of these supposed benefits:

- there is generally an adverse trade-off between rules that are 'natural', easy to read and good for generating explanations and rules that are efficient to execute;

- since individual domain rules compete among themselves for the attention of the interpreter, they can scarcely be said to be procedurally independent, and since they are also capable of entering into logical relationships with each other, such as contradiction and subsumption, they can scarcely be said to be declaratively independent;
- given a knowledge base containing hundreds of rules, it is generally difficult to determine the effect on program behaviour of adding extra rules.

The limitations of unstructured rule sets running under uniform control regimes like backward chaining are now widely acknowledged. One alternative is to combine production rules with prototypes which define different settings or stages in the man-machine interaction where particular rules are relevant. This allows for both partition of the rule set and the local specification of control, i.e. prototypes can contain pointers to either more specialized versions of themselves, or to alternative prototypes that might be more appropriate.

A further refinement of the rule-based architecture is to have large-grained production rules which represent 'knowledge sources' running under a flexible scheduler, as in HEARSAY-III (Erman *et al.*, 1983). Each rule consists of a calling pattern, a piece of 'immediate' code, and a body. The immediate code is executed whenever the calling pattern is matched and the rule is then scheduled; the body is executed when the scheduler says so. Such a control regime allows the programmer to make the all-important distinction between entertaining a hypothesis and following it up with a view to verification or elimination.

15.1.2 Structured objects

It is generally agreed that production rules work best when knowledge lends itself to being expressed in terms of independent recognize-act pairs. They are less suitable for expressing taxonomic relations such as set membership or set inclusion. They are also less than ideal for representing such aspects of everyday reasoning as the inheritance of properties, default assumptions and exceptions.

Structured objects are especially suitable for systems which are inherently model-based rather than rule-based. One can conceive a model-space as a classification hierarchy for objects or events of the kind one is interested in, where the root node of the tree stands for the whole class of such objects, non-terminal nodes stand for important subclasses, and terminal nodes represent primitive states, a combination of which constitutes a complete description of a domain model.

Each terminal node of the tree will presumably have a distinctive set of features, while non-terminal nodes will have just those features common to their successors. Initial data invoke non-terminal nodes which constitute hypotheses; scoring these hypotheses according to how well they fit the data generates models. These serve to guide the subsequent search by suggesting avenues for acquiring new data, and setting up expectations about the outcomes of such investigations, which might, in turn, propose new models.

The INTERNIST systems have used such techniques with some success in medical diagnosis (Pople, 1977). The iteration between data- and model-driven phases is a way of sidestepping the exhaustive rule invocation of MYCIN-like systems and the exhaustive enumeration of Heuristic DENDRAL. Needless to say, such techniques have their problems, particularly with regard to the scheduling of hypotheses.

The use of structured objects like frames (Minsky, 1975) allows the knowledge engineer to accommodate aspects of common sense, everyday reasoning, like defaults and exceptions, more gracefully than is the case in the majority of rule or logic-based formalisms. Defaults can be handled by allowing slots in the frame to have default values which are adopted if no specific information is available, while exceptions can be handled by making inheritance of properties the default unless explicitly overwritten lower down in the hierarchy. Default handling by having rules which only fire if nothing else fires, or having clauses which are in some sense lower or later in the logic database than their competitors, constitutes a much more messy solution; while exception handling by adding extra clauses to the antecedent of a production rule or the conditions of a Horn clause is also somewhat messy.

However, it has been suggested that exception handling in frames renders them useless for the purposes of definition, since every concept so represented becomes primitive, in the sense that there is no true compositionality. This case can be overstated, in that a good deal depends upon how carefully you differentiate between different kinds of property and the possibly different inheritance paths through which their values are propagated. Lack of care can result in incoherent structures, but frames are not unique in this respect.

15.1.3 Logic-based systems

Systems like MYCIN, which lack the power of first-order logic, are unable to express simple rules like 'don't bother to prescribe a drug that has already been tried on a patient'. In rule interpreters like OPS5, if one wants to express such a rule, one has to include, in every rule that attempts to prescribe a drug, an extra premise which states 'don't prescribe this particular drug if it has already been tried'. Clearly, there are many meta-rules of this nature which one would like to be able to express succinctly, without making distributed alterations to the rule set.

A logic database for representing knowledge about some domain is typically a set of clauses, ordered so that: special cases occur first, e.g. particular facts and exceptions; then general cases, in the form of inference rules; and then defaults, i.e. things that can be assumed if they can't be proven. Meta-rules for controlling deduction can be expressed and ordered in exactly the same way. Many of the advantages and disadvantages cited with regard to the supposed modularity and modifiability of rule-based systems apply here; one has to be especially careful when adding new rules if the ordering of clauses is important.

Although expressions in a logic database are written in a (more or less) declarative language, this language has a procedural interpretation. In the case of PROLOG and its variants, the interpreter is essentially a linear resolution theorem prover for Horn clauses. When implementing deduction systems in LISP, one typically has procedures which set up subgoals, or decide when certain classes of inference are to be drawn. The main problem is one of control, e.g. performing conflict resolution and conjunct ordering in principled ways. Meta-rules have an invaluable role to play here in guiding the program through large and combinatorially explosive search spaces.

Logic programming techniques for expert systems are by no means as tried and tested as techniques based on rules and frames. At the present time, there are no logic-based expert systems with the stature of CENTAUR or R1. One of the few programs which give an indication of the way in which logic for expert systems might develop is MECHO.

As we saw in Chapter 11, MECHO exhibits a number of explicit departures from the syntax and semantics of first-order logic and its procedural interpretation in standard PROLOG. The architects' avowed intention was to work towards an alternative computational logic for natural reasoning which contained control primitives that would specify the way in which rules would be used. Of particular importance are 'meta-predicates', which manipulate formulae as if they were objects, and affect the way in which they are evaluated or called.

15.1.4   The changing face of knowledge representation

There is little doubt that knowledge representation for expert systems is in a state of flux, and that many of the issues which have lain dormant in recent years are seeing a renewal of interest and research. Although a number of writers would like to see a greater degree of uniformity and universality in representational schemes, there are few signs that such a standardization is taking place. Practitioners in the field have come to realize that there is no single formalism that will represent everything that one might wish to express about any topic, and that there is no *a priori* reason why such a formalism should exist.

Choice of representational scheme for a knowledge base must be based upon a number of domain-specific criteria, for example

- size and nature of the underlying search space;
- aspects of the data, e.g. redundancy, degree of noise, time-dependence;
- degree of confidence in the domain rules, consistency and completeness of the rule set.

Premature attempts to standardize upon particular representation languages or particular approaches to knowledge engineering across the entire spectrum of problem solving domains are almost certainly doomed to fail and likely to cause confusion. There are many existing tools, e.g. frame and rule interpreters, which allow one to do a reasonable job of expressing domain-specific knowledge, and it is not a major undertaking for an experienced artificial intelligence programmer to either adapt one of these to suit his ends or to build his own interpreter. Expert system shells, on the other hand, tend to cramp and confine the knowledge engineer, unless his problem corresponds in kind to the one that the original program, from which the shell was derived by abstraction, was designed to address.

15.1.5 The lessons of the last 20 years

The DENDRAL program was among the first to show that a computer could function as an intelligent assistant to a domain expert, rather than serving a more conventional data-processing function. Using a constrained form of generate-and-test, the program was able to propose plausible structural hypotheses for complex organic compounds. It was able to do this, even in the absence of a complete theory of the domain of mass spectrometry, because the language for representing chemical compounds has a simple syntax and well understood semantics, and the chemist is able to supply suitable constraints at the planning stage.

At the same time, mathematician's assistants for symbolic integration (SAINT: Slagle, 1963) and algebraic manipulation (MACSYMA: see résumé in Barr and Feigenbaum, 1982, volume 2) had shown that artificial intelligence techniques such as semantic pattern-matching and hill-climbing could be profitably applied to these domains. However, what was lacking at this stage was a demonstration that computers could play a useful role in problem-solving *outside* of the domains of mathematics and the natural sciences, where more judgemental reasoning and less symbol manipulation seemed to be required.

The MYCIN experiments reported in Buchanan and Shortliffe (1984) made a positive contribution in this regard. They demonstrated that the production rule formalism was indeed equal to the task of reasoning at an expert level in a less formal domain than mathematics or structural chemistry, provided that the domain was a restricted one, such as infectious disease diagnosis. Production rules provided a mechanism for incremental knowledge base development, with rapid feedback to guide the knowledge engineers in their task.

MYCIN is often described as a backward-chaining production system for diagnosing blood infections, but it should be remembered that this is a serious oversimplification in the following respects. The program's primary purpose is therapy recommendations, and this does not necessarily require the establishment of a categorical diagnosis. Thus a set of ranked hypotheses regarding the likely identity of offending organisms, together with information regarding patient sensitivities, is sufficient to enable this purpose. Also, there are a number of departures from the backward-chaining control regime, in the form of antecedent rules and meta-rules. These were deemed necessary when extra rules and parameters were added to the 1976 version of the system, for reasons of efficiency.

Van Melle *et al.* (1981), who worked on EMYCIN, were among the first to point out that the MYCIN approach did not constitute either a general-purpose representation language, or a general-purpose problem solving strategy. They suggested that EMYCIN was suitable for deductive problems, such as fault diagnosis, where large amounts of data are available in the form of instrument readings and test results, and where it is possible to enumerate the solution space of diagnostic categories in advance. The approach seemed less well suited to 'formation problems', i.e. the piecing together of a complex whole that must satisfy a set of constraints (as is done by R1).

A careful examination of MYCIN makes it clear that a great deal is going on behind the firing of production rules. Rules are grouped and indexed in various ways according to the medical parameters they reference, and the consultation as a whole is managed by the context tree, which structures the clinical problem under consideration and helps relate different contexts, e.g. linking cultures to the sites from which they are obtained. Extra information, such as that concerning drugs and sensitivities, is tucked away in lists and tables, and hence not directly available for inspection.

When attempts were made to use MYCIN as a basis for a tutorial system, it became apparent that this 'behind the scenes' machinery was not the only potential source of obscurity in the program's behaviour. Clancey (1983) pointed out that the inference rules contained embedded knowledge of rather different kinds, to do with the order in which tests are tried, and the order in which hypotheses are pursued. Such knowledge is really meta-knowledge, i.e. knowledge about how knowledge should be applied, and this constitutes an important aspect of expertise.

Related problems with the EMYCIN implementation of PUFF were noted by Aikins (1983). Quite different kinds of knowledge were encoded in the same production rule format and so, as a basis for generating explanations, a trace of rule activations left something to be desired. Further structuring of the rule set, achieved in a manner more explicit than the rule-indexing of EMYCIN, made it possible to exercise greater control over both the course of the consultation and the coherence of the explanation.

The imposition of structure on a large body of medical knowledge was a problem that had already been addressed by the INTERNIST project, necessitated by the sheer volume of knowledge that the programmers had to represent. Given the lack of pathognomonic associations between data from initial clinical presentations and diagnostic categories in the solution space, a complex variation on the theme of hypothesize-and-test was called for. This looseness in the coupling between data and solutions, together with the problem of patients suffering from more than one disease, seems to rule out a 'situation-action' formulation in terms of forward-chaining production rules, while a backward-chaining strategy is ruled out by the size of the underlying search space.

R1, on the other hand, succeeds with a relatively straightforward representational scheme and control structure. This is because the problem it attempts to solve is amenable to the Match method, whereby it is always possible to extend partial problem solutions towards the goal in a uni-directional fashion, that is to say, without backtracking. This system deserves attention, because it shows that in order to solve some non-trivial problem it is not always necessary to develop your own representation language from scratch; sometimes an 'off the peg' programming tool will do.

In the chapter on MECHO, we questioned another piece of conventional wisdom, namely that 'logic for expert systems' would result in clearer, cleaner, simpler and better programs possessing proven properties, such as consistency and completeness. We saw instead that researchers had been forced to import various extra-logical devices, such as schema-cueing, to make the connection between simple problems (involving pulleys and pieces of string) and the mathematical formulae that govern their behaviour. Most of the interesting features of MECHO derive from the attempt to separate object- and meta-levels in the program's reasoning, and the wide variety of devices that the researchers were compelled to employ.

Chapters 12–14 addressed more general topics, such as tools, learning and explanations, and in each case it was suggested that the knowledge representation issues involved were by no means clear cut. Future success in each of these three areas appears to place ill-understood constraints upon representational schemes to come, and anyone who really understands how those constraints can be reconciled is much cleverer than me. For example: if we are to have general-purpose learning algorithms, these are easiest to apply to uniform representation languages, such as the simple pattern language used by Mitchell (1978). Yet local flow of control and the generation of comprehensible explanations appear to demand a requisite variety from the underlying knowledge representation, as we saw in CENTAUR. There are many difficult issues here which are beyond the scope of this text; I mention them only to curb unseasonable optimism.

Researchers and practitioners in the field of knowledge representation have acquired a number of insights into the relative merits of various schemes for different purposes, and these insights are valuable for two reasons. Firstly, they can guide potential users of knowledge representation languages towards the most suitable package for the problem in hand. Secondly, they can guide the developers of hybrid systems in the development of new tools which attempt to combine the strengths of more than one basic scheme. It is with these thoughts in mind that we turn now to a critical summary of the schemes themselves. I have tried to be impartial in both my own judgements and the selection of other's people's judgements for inclusion in this critique, but the reader should bear in mind that not all of my colleagues would agree with all of the following remarks.

15.2   Choosing a knowledge representation language

The central issue for the expert systems architect is to decide what representational scheme will allow him to codify knowledge in such a way as to facilitate its subsequent application, and to choose a control regime that suits the nature of the underlying search space. Unfortunately, the decision often has to be made on pragmatic grounds, rather than on the basis of principle. That is to say, considerations such as the existing hardware configuration of the institution, the available programming skills, and the preferences of non-technical personnel often place undue constraint upon the decision that is eventually made.

This is not to say that practical considerations are not important. For example, the availability of proper documentation and the presence of in-house expertise can be determining factors in the success of an application. Nevertheless, I frequently hear of situations where decisions were made on a completely *ad hoc* basis, and then subsequently justified by spurious reasoning which was not even gone through at the time the decision was made.

Typically, people are also torn between importing a language of some kind and writing their own special-purpose language in LISP or PROLOG. There is a great temptation to assume that one's problem is beyond the state of the art, and therefore requires a radically new approach, whether or not this is in fact the case. Having decided to grow their own knowledge representation scheme, people will often agonize about whether to use LISP or PROLOG as the implementation language, and then make *that* decision on *ad hoc* grounds!

The following discussion will be conducted at the level of theory, and it assumes that hypothetical consumers have at least some degrees of freedom with regard to the hardware/software specifications of their projects. Hardware requirements for running particular representation languages are simply omitted; such information is quickly out of date and can be gleaned elsewhere. Arguments for and against different host languages, e.g. LISP versus PROLOG, are also omitted, for reasons of mental hygiene.

There are no universally agreed guidelines as to how one should go about choosing a representational scheme for a given problem. However, one can supply a few useful heuristics that will enable the implementors of knowledge-based systems to make sensible decisions and avoid the more obvious errors. The items below are based on my limited personal experience and what I have gleaned from the experiences of others, and are therefore corrigible in the light of further experience.

15.2.1   The nature of the underlying search space

If there is a basic problem solving paradigm that will work for your problem, then use it. Thus, if your problem can be solved in an acceptable fashion by the brute force and ignorance of depth-first search, then you might as well do it that way. PROLOG would give you all the pattern-matching you are likely to need, and throw in the backtracking for free. In LISP, these features would require you to write an extra page of trivial code, assuming that you don't already have things like pattern-matchers lying around in files. Answer the other questions first, though, as you may need other features which require the writing of extra code that a shell would give you for free.

For example, if the search space is small, and your data and rules are 100 per cent reliable, then an exhaustive search is quite feasible (Hayes-Roth *et al.*, 1983). If, on the other hand, you have a large search space, or an incomplete knowledge base that contains competing modules of uncertain knowledge, then some form of hypothesize-and-test is more desirable. Instead of pursuing a single line of reasoning by matching the conditions of rules against data, and then firing the 'best' rule, it becomes necessary to entertain alternative lines of reasoning and ultimately decide between them.

One can think of this as the difference between being able to specify a decision tree whose traversal is guaranteed to solve the problem, and having only a set of looser associations between initial data and hypotheses that need to be followed up by a strategy of differential reasoning that involves weighing the pros and cons and performing critical tests that will discriminate between hypotheses in an effective and efficient manner. Such reasoning may involve making use of stereotypical objects and typical states of affairs. Data will therefore relate to solution categories only indirectly, by raising expectations the fulfillment of which suggests one category over another.

Another thing to bear in mind is that although a search space is large, it may be factorable. One finds two senses of the word 'factorable' in the literature, and they are not identical. A search space is said to be factorable if there exist 'pruning rules' that will reduce the size of the space early in the computation (Stefik *et al.*, 1982, page 35). This is roughly how the constrained 'generate-and-test' of Heuristic DENDRAL works, by eliminating whole classes of candidate structures which are inconsistent with the data, and doing this as soon as possible. However, a search space is also factorable if it can be decomposed into independent components which can then be processed separately (Nilsson, 1982, page 37), perhaps by different rule sets or different partitions of the same rule set. The success of the main goal is then dependent upon the success of a conjunction of independent subgoals, and if any of these fails, then the whole computation fails without more ado.

The search space may not be factorable in either of the above senses. Many design problems are like this: partial solutions can only be evaluated in the global context of the whole design. One never knows whether one has succeeded or not until the last piece of the puzzle falls into place.

A common method for dealing with large search spaces is to consider the space at various levels of abstraction, i.e. descriptions of the space at different levels of detail. Solving problems in this way corresponds to what is sometimes called 'top-down refinement'. One achieves some high-level goal by achieving subgoals at lower (more detailed) levels of problem specification. Within each level, problems can be solved in any order, but between levels there is an ordering on tasks. The idea is to try and do away with expensive backtracking over levels, but this only works if there is no significant interaction between subproblems.

It could be that the partitioning of rules into sets needs to be augmented by meta-rules which suggest global strategies over and above those specified at the level of structures like CENTAUR prototypes. Some authors regard the chunking of rules as nothing more than an expedient: a partial solution to the problem of controlling deductive inference (Bundy, 1978). As far as I know, no-one has tried to use these two control paradigms in the same meta-level architecture, although MANDALA seems to be moving in this direction.

Regardless of people's preferences for particular techniques, there is almost universal agreement that control knowledge needs to be made more explicit. For example, Clancey (1983) and Genesereth (1983) have both argued convincingly in favour of meta-level architectures which articulate strategic information instead of burying it in the interpreter. This is seen to be essential for both incremental program development and mixing different control regimes in the same system.

15.2.2 The nature of the data

Just as rules can often be structured in a way that facilitates their application to the relevant states of the problem, so data can be organized in a fashion that will facilitate its processing by heuristic methods.

If the data has an inherent structure, then see if you can use it. For example, we saw in Chapter 8 that the taxonomic structure of diseases is an important aspect of medical knowledge. It seems unlikely that MYCIN-like systems would ever be able to cover the ground of more comprehensive systems like CADUCEUS using only a loosely structured rule set. So, if the data has a structure, make that structure explicit, rather than burying it in the formalism. That way, it can be accessed by any part of the program that needs it. Multiple uses of the structure may be possible, e.g. to guide the reasoning, to gain representational economy, and to give better explanations to the user.

Furthermore, it may be that multiple organizations are both possible and desirable. Thus, although CADUCEUS classifies disease areas according to organ location, e.g. heart disease, lung disease, and so on, it could be that alternative classifications would also be useful, e.g. infectious versus non-infectious diseases, rare versus common diseases, classification by age, sex, geographical distribution, and so on. Multiple classifications involve the construction of 'tangled hierarchies', where a given node may have more than one superordinate node from which it can inherit properties and procedures. Mechanisms must then exist for extracting those properties which are relevant to a particular perspective on a class, and for combining procedures in cases of multiple inheritance. Most LISP-based representation languages, such as FLAVORS, LOOPS and KEE, provide such mechanisms (see Chapter 4).

It is also important to determine which classes of data are static and which dynamic, i.e. which data remain unchanged during a run of the program, and which need to be updated. Static data is relatively easy to represent using some form of structured object that reflects either its position in some hierarchy of classes, or its functional connections with other objects in terms of part-whole relationships or communication channels which convey energy and information. Thus a taxonomy lends itself to being represented as a tree of frames, while a stable causal pathway might be represented by a directed graph.

If there are dynamic elements, more active data structures (such as objects with active values) may be required. A lot depends upon whether the change is simply incremental, or whether the data needs to be revised over time. A representational scheme for data that simply accumulates is generally simpler than a scheme for representing time-variant data. Data can be time-variant either because the world model is frequently changing, or because the program's perception of the world is modified in the light of experience.

There are a number of problems associated with the management of dynamic data structures which represent some state of affairs. The main one is the maintenance of consistency in the program's view of the world. This has been called 'the frame problem' by McCarthy and Hayes (1969) – and it is nothing to do with 'frames' as a representational device! The problem is not acute when changes are strictly additive, because the addition of new information does not falsify old information. This is called monotonic reasoning, and it means that 'new' theorems never invalidate 'old' theorems. Most applications of theorem-proving techniques to knowledge-based systems assume monotonicity. However, if you allow your program to make assumptions that might later turn out to be false, or jump to conclusions that may later need to be retracted, you are engaged in non-monotonic reasoning, since certain items of old information may cease to be regarded as true as new items are added to the world model.

There is an important distinction to be made here between the way in which the expert actually solves the problem, and the way in which the program might be made to work. Due to the limitations in information processing imposed by the human cognitive system, it could be that experts are sometimes forced to do non-monotonic reasoning which is not an essential aspect of the problem. In other words, since they can only effectively consider one hypothesis at a time, they may make assumptions or jump to conclusions which later turn out to be false and have to be revised, even if this is not an integral part of the way things happen in the domain. It may be possible to use the power of the computer to eliminate the non-monotonicity in certain circumstances, in which case there is nothing to be gained by following the expert's strategy.

Actions instigated by the program may also change the world model; the program may direct a robot to move both itself and other objects around. You then have to decide, for every action performed by the robot, what else has changed. Thus if the robot moves a box, b_1, from A to B, you must delete statements to the effect that the robot is at A and b_1 is at A, add statements to the effect that the robot is at B and b_1 is at B, and propagate consequences of these changes. For example, the box may have been on top of another box, b_2, in which case you might want to add a statement to the effect that b_2 no longer has anything resting on it. On the other hand, if the robot simply turns on the light in a room, this will not effect the positions of objects in the room, and you will not need to propagate such consequences.

Keeping track of such a simple world sounds trivial if you've never tried to do it; it isn't (see Kowalski, 1979, Chapter 6, for a treatment of this problem). Proving that some arbitrary set of statements is consistent is computationally intractable in any reasonably expressive logic like the predicate calculus. Thus special mechanisms are often required to maintain the world model, such as the operator tables of Fikes and Nilsson (1971). Readers interested in recent work on non-monotonic logic should consult the special issue of 'Artificial Intelligence' devoted to this topic. The papers by McDermott and Doyle (1980), McCarthy (1980) and Reiter (1980) have been particularly influential.

If the program uses a large amount of data or a large rule base, then careful thought needs to be given to the organization of data and rules. Time-dependent data may need to be structured into contexts, representing possible states of affairs, while rules could benefit from being arranged into some kind of inference network, as in PROSPECTOR (see Duda *et al.*, 1978, 1979), or divided into rule sets which constitute different knowledge sources. We saw in Chapter 9 that one can use OPS5 to partition rule sets according to task, so as to minimize the effort of constructing the conflict set. Whole sets of rules can then be invoked by matching against task tokens in working memory. On the other hand, large bodies of data can be viewed at different levels of abstraction, in which higher levels conceal and rationalize lower levels of detail. If lower levels of detail introduce deviations from generalizations at a higher level, then some form of default reasoning may be required. The whole point of such techniques is to help manage both the size of the corresponding search space and the cost of matching data against stored patterns.

Having multiple views of static data is an example of a kind of redundancy that may nevertheless be very beneficial from the program's point of view. Similarly, the creation of different contexts, representing alternative possible worlds that would follow from the application of mutually-exclusive operators at some point in time, can facilitate reasoning about change. Being able to leave such views and contexts hanging around for further processing is expensive in terms of run-time storage, but it may result in substantial savings in machine cycles. Even so, this must be done wisely, since there is an obvious space-speed trade-off here which affects the performance of even the most powerful workstations. Nevertheless, the judicious caching of intermediate results can produce exponential savings in search effort, as many chess-playing programs have demonstrated.

Another problem is that data can be unreliable for a number of reasons. Data can be 'noisy', i.e. there can be competing signals mixed in with the ones you are interested in. Data can also be incomplete (missing signal elements), or errorful (scrambled signals). Finally, it could just be that the data is inherently variable and problematic, e.g. the human speech signal, where phonemes are realized differently by different speakers, and in different articulatory contexts by the same speaker. In each of these situations, one is reasoning with imperfect information, in contrast with many games and puzzles, where the player essentially knows all there is to know about the state of play.

In order to deal with problems of this nature, it is often possible to give the program access to some internal representation of the 'ideal' signal, and have it compare incoming data with these models. The datum is then interpreted in the light of the best-fitting model, and processed accordingly. Typically, the features of the ideal signal are weighted for importance, i.e. some must be present, others might be present, others are merely consistent with the signal, and so on.

The CADUCEUS program discussed in Chapter 8 can be thought of as working in this way. Disease models are scored according to how well they fit the pattern of signs and symptoms observed in the patient. The model, once evoked, gives rise to expectations of what other indications must or might be observed. Thus data can be noisy, errorful and incomplete without paralysing the program's ability to focus upon a particular disease area and generate hypotheses. Programs written in this way will fail gracefully, in that they will always do they best they can with the data provided, and the quality of partial results will reflect the quality of that data.

15.2.3 The nature of the knowledge

Just as one can weight features of idealized representations of data, so one can weight general rules in an attempt to simulate aspects of judgemental reasoning. Such reasoning follows patterns such as 'P_1 & ... & P_n suggest Q', or 'P_1 & ... & P_n suggest $\sim Q$', with some numerical value indicating the degree of association between the conditions and the conclusion. This is in contrast with the categorical reasoning associated with standard logics, such as the predicate calculus, where propositions are either true or false.

It is also distinct from the treatment of uncertainty in probability theory. Adams (1976) has shown that the certainty factors used by MYCIN do not correspond to the probability of the hypothesis given the evidence, if you adopt a simple probability model based on Bayes Theorem. Furthermore, it is possible for two hypotheses, h_1 and h_2, to be ranked in reverse order to their respective probabilities by the use of certainty factors.

A detailed analysis of the relationship between inexact reasoning and logic, and inexact reasoning and probability theory is beyond the scope of this text. However, it is worth looking at some of the basic issues. For more thorough treatments, the reader is referred elsewhere (for example Charniak and McDermott, 1985, Chapter 8; Buchanan and Shortliffe, 1984, Chapter 11).

It is not hard to think of examples of inexact reasoning in everyday life. For example, in our dealings with other people, we often reason about their intentions, opinions, attitudes and so on, in a manner that must allow for the possibility of error on our part. However, experts also employ inexact reasoning, either because more exact methods are not known, or because such methods are inapplicable to the problem situation, due to lack of data, or problems with collecting the data, or difficulties with processing the data within the time constraints set by the problem.

Consider the use that could be made of conditional probabilities in medical diagnosis if all the necessary statistics were available. Given that a patient has a disturbing symptom, such as chest pain, one would like to know the probability of this being due to something potentially serious, such as myocardial infarction or acute pericarditis, or something less serious, such as indigestion. In other words, one would like to know the conditional probability, $P(d \mid s)$, where d is the disease in question and s the symptom.

The conditional probability of d given s is simply the probability that d occurs if s occurs, i.e. the probability that the patient really is suffering from d if he complains of s. This is given by the following formula:

$$P(d \mid s) = \frac{P(d \& s)}{P(s)}$$

However, to calculate the probability that our patient with chest pain really has had a myocardial infarction, one would need to know, at a given moment in time, how many people in the world were suffering from the disease, how many complained of the symptom, and how many were both suffering from the disease and complaining of the symptom. Such information is usually unavailable, particularly for $P(d \& s)$. Thus the definition is not much use as it stands, because the practising clinician will not have the data that this form of exact reasoning requires.

An alternative route to inexact reasoning is to work with probability estimates rather than empirically-determined ones. Doctors may not know, or be able to calculate, what proportion of chest pain patients have had heart attacks, but they will have some notion of how many heart attack patients have chest pain. Given a reasonable estimate of $P(s \mid d)$, one can use Bayes Theorem to calculate $P(d \mid s)$:

$$P(d \mid s) = \frac{P(d)P(s \mid d)}{P(s)}$$

This is not too problematic in the single symptom case, i.e. when reasoning about some set of diseases, D, and some set of symptoms, S, and limiting ourselves to calculating, for each disease d in D, the conditional probability that a patient is suffering from d given that he complains of a single symptom in S. Given m diseases in D and n symptoms in S, we require $mn + m + n$ probabilities. This will not be a small number for a reasonable set of diagnostic categories, such as the 2000 or more that clinicians actually use, and the wide range of signs and symptoms that people exhibit. Even if we exclude redundant information to the effect that the probability of a heart attack patient exhibiting such and such a symptom is quite small, life gets considerably more complicated if one attempts to take more than one symptom into account when performing the diagnosis.

The more general form of Bayes rule,

$$P(d \mid s_1, ..., s_k) = \frac{P(d)P(s_1 \& ... \& s_k \mid d)}{P(s_1 \& ... \& s_k)}$$

requires $(mn)^k + m + n^k$ probabilities, which is a very large number for even modest values of k. Life gets easier again if you can assume that the symptoms are conditionally independent of each other, i.c. if for any pair of symptoms, s_1 and s_2, it is the case that

$$P(s_1) = P(s_1 \mid s_2)$$

because then it follows that

$$P(s_1 \& s_2) = P(s_1)P(s_2)$$

which requires no more probabilities than the single symptom scenario.

Thus, for signs and symptoms that really are independent, their joint probability is simple to calculate. Where independence cannot be assumed, the conditional probabilities must be known, since in the case where s_2 depends on s_1:

$$P(s_1 \& s_2) = P(s_1)P(s_2 \mid s_1).$$

Alternatively, one can use an approximation technique, whereby non-independent symptoms are combined into one 'super-symptom', whose probability is estimated. This is not very satisfactory in some respects, but it is perhaps not significantly less reliable than the figures for single independent symptoms, which are estimates anyway, and extremely dependent on locality.

If we return to MYCIN's use of certainty factors, we are now in a position to see how this deviates from probability theory.

In a perfect world, one would like to be able to calculate $P(d_i \mid e)$, where d_i is the ith diagnostic category and e is all the evidence you need, using only the $P(d \mid s_j)$, where s_j is the jth clinical observation. Bayes Theorem will allow you to do this only if all the $P(s_j \mid d_i)$ are available, and then only under the (unrealistically) favourable circumstance in which the s_j are all conditionally independent. The situation quickly becomes unworkable, even if estimates are used, once the number of diagnostic categories and the number of symptoms considered grows at all large.

The alternative explored by MYCIN was to use a rule-based approach, in which statements of conditional probability are expressed as decision criteria, along the lines of

IF   the patients has signs and symptoms s_1 & ... & s_k
THEN   conclude that he has disease d_i, with certainty x.

The idea was to use rules of this kind in an attempt to approximate the calculation of $P(d \mid e)$ from the signs and symptoms composing e. Buchanan and Shortliffe (1984, Chapter 11) argue that a rigorous application of Bayes Theorem would not have produced accurate probabilities in any case, since the conditional probabilities used would have been subjective. The goal was to encode decision rules as pattern-directed modules and provide a scheme for accumulating evidence that reflected the reasoning process used by an expert.

It was mentioned in Chapter 6 that MYCIN uses certainty factors (CFs) instead of probabilities in an attempt to quantify the degree of confidence associated with a hypothesis, and that the certainty factor associated with a hypothesis, h, given the evidence accumulated so far, e, was a combination of the measure of belief (MB) in the hypothesis and the measure of disbelief (MD), as follows:

$$CF(h,e) = MB(h,e) - MD(h,e)$$

It is therefore a matter of some interest as to how these two measures of belief and disbelief are updated in the face of fresh evidence. Let the expert's subjective probability that hypothesis h is correct be $P(h)$. This can be taken to reflect the expert's degree of belief in h at any given moment in time.

If we now complicate matters, by adding fresh supporting evidence e, such that $P(h \mid e)$, the posterior probability, is greater than $P(h)$, the prior probability, then the increase in the expert's degree of belief in h is given by:

$$\frac{P(h \mid e) - P(h)}{1 - P(h)}$$

If, on the other hand, e constitutes evidence against h, such that $P(h \mid e) < P(h)$, then the increase in the expert's degree of disbelief is given by:

$$\frac{P(h) - P(h \mid e)}{P(h)}$$

Buchanan and Shortliffe (1984, page 249) describe the certainty factor that results from applying the formula for calculating $CF(h,e)$ as 'an artifact for combining degrees of belief and disbelief into a single number'. Thus, although both $MB(h,e)$ and $MD(h,e)$ can be related to the underlying subjective probabilities in a fairly direct way, $CF(h,e)$ is a composite number which is needed to guide the program in its reasoning.

Nevertheless, these numbers behave sensibly enough:

if $P(h \mid e) = 1$, i.e. if h is certainly true,
then $MB(h,e) = 1$, $MD(h,e) = 0$ and $CF(h,e) = 1$;
if $P(\sim h \mid e) = 1$, i.e. if h is certainly false,
then $MB(h,e) = 0$, $MD(h,e) = 1$ and $CF(h,e) = -1$;

if $P(h \mid e) = P(h)$, i.e. if h and e are independent,
then $MB(h,e) = 0$, $MD(h,e) = 0$ and $CF(h,e) = 0$.

However, as Adams (1976) points out, values for MB and MD for different pieces of evidence cannot be chosen independently. If some piece of evidence is an absolute diagnostic indicator for a particular illness, i.e. if all patients with symptom s have disease d, then no other piece of evidence has any diagnostic value. In other words, if there are two pieces of evidence, e_1 and e_2, to be considered, and $P(h \mid e_1) = P(h \mid e_1 \ \& \ e_2)$, then $P(h \mid e_2) = P(h)$, which places an absolute restriction on the value that $P(h \mid e_2)$ can take, once $P(h \mid e_1)$ has been determined.

Adams also criticizes the treatment of conjoined hypotheses. The MYCIN model assumes that

$$MB(h_1 \ \& \ h_2,e) = \min(MB(h_1,e),MB(h_2,e))$$
$$MD(h_1 \ \& \ h_2,e) = \max(MD(h_1,e),MD(h_2,e)).$$

This is not to be confused with the use of min and max to derive the certainty factor for the antecedent of a production rule, described in Chapter 6. Rather, it relates to the degree of belief in a joint hypothesis, given that degrees of belief are available for the component hypotheses considered alone. The rules state that our degree of belief in $h_1 \ \& \ h_2$ should be only as great as our belief in the weakest hypothesis while our degree of disbelief should be as great as that associated with the strongest hypothesis.

As Adams points out, this treatment makes strong assumptions regarding the independence of h_1 and h_2. If h_1 and h_2 are not independent, but mutually exclusive alternatives, then $P(h_1 \ \& \ h_2 \mid e) = 0$, for any e, i.e. regardless of the evidence. There is a similar criticism of the treatment of disjoined hypotheses.

MYCIN collects evidence for and against a hypothesis separately, i.e. it calculates $MB(h,e_f)$, where e_f is the combined evidence for h, and $MD(h,e_a)$, where e_a is the evidence against. These constitute approximations to the $P(h \mid e_f)/P(h)$ and $P(h \mid e_a)/P(h)$ of Bayes Theorem, and could be combined to give $P(h \mid e_f \ \& \ e_a)/P(h)$, using standard probability theory. This expression would be an estimate of the change in the probability associated with h, given the evidence for and against. The real point of departure between MYCIN and probability theory occurs in the choice of the alternative combinatory function

$$CF(h,e_f \ \& \ e_a) = MB(h,e_f) - MD(h,e_a).$$

One of the main uses of CFs in MYCIN is to rank hypotheses, and Adams shows that in some circumstances this ranking will depart from that produced by the application of probability theory. The example he gives is the following.

Let h_1 and h_2 be two hypotheses, and e be a body of evidence that tends to confirm both of them. Let the prior probabilities be such that $P(h_1) \geqslant P(h_2)$ and $P(h_1 \mid e) > P(h_2 \mid e)$. In other words, h_1 has a higher subjective probability than h_2 to begin with, and this superiority remains after the consideration of the evidence. Under these circumstances, it is possible that $CF(h,e_1) < CF(h,e_2)$.

Suppose that

$$P(h_1) \quad = 0.8$$
$$P(h_2) \quad = 0.2$$
$$P(h_1 \mid e) = 0.9$$
$$P(h_2 \mid e) = 0.8$$

then the increase in belief in h_1 is given by

$$\frac{0.9 - 0.8}{0.2} = 0.5$$

while the increase in belief in h_2 is given by

$$\frac{0.8 - 0.2}{0.8} = 0.75$$

Since $MD(h_1,e) = MD(h_2,e) = 0$, the respective certainty factors are

$$CF(h_1,e) = 0.5$$
$$CF(h_2,e) = 0.75$$

so that $CF(h_1,e) < CF(h_2,e)$ even though $P(h_1 \mid e) > P(h_2 \mid e)$.

Adams describes this as an 'undesirable feature' of certainty factors. To avoid it, all prior probabilities would have to be equal; one can easily see that the effect in the above example is due to the fact that the evidence favoured h_2, even though h_1 triumphed in the end, due to a superior prior probability. However, such an equality would be at variance with the way in which diagnosticians reason, given the widely differing frequencies of occurrence associated with different diseases.

One might ask why hypotheses are ranked according to certainty factors in the first place. Adams suggests that it is guided by the intuition that if some evidence, e, implies an intermediate hypothesis, i, with probability $P(i \mid e)$, and i implies a final hypothesis, h, with probability $P(h \mid i)$, then

$$P(h \mid e) = P(h \mid i)P(i \mid e)$$

This transitive relation across chains of reasoning seems acceptable at first sight, but it is not true in general, as Adams points out. Let the subsets of the population associated with properties h, i and e be H, I and E respectively. The underlying assumption is that H is a subset of I is a subset of E, which need not be the case.

Thus the twin proposals in MYCIN to the effect that

$$MB(h,e) = MB(h,i)\max(0,CF(i,e))$$
$$MD(h,e) = MD(h,i)\max(0,CF(i,e))$$

are not true in general for the chains of reasoning that the program performs.

Adams concludes that the empirical success of MYCIN may be due to the fact that the chains of reasoning are short and the hypotheses involved are simple. He argues that these shortcomings in MYCIN illustrate the difficulty of creating a useful and internally consistent system of inexact reasoning that is not simply a subset of probability theory. Thus the careful comparison of such systems with the standard theory can be beneficial in showing exactly where the differences and possible difficulties lie.

A number of alternatives to the use of certainty factors in expert systems have been identified in the literature, e.g. fuzzy set theory (Zadeh, 1965, 1975) and the Dempster-Shafer theory of evidence (Shafer, 1976). A discussion of these topics is beyond the scope of an introductory text, other than to note that neither has yet been universally adopted by theoreticians or practitioners, and that neither approach was developed specifically with expert systems in mind. A critique of fuzzy set theory can be found in Haack (1978), while a discussion of Shafer's theory in the context of MYCIN can be found in Buchanan and Shortliffe (1984, Chapter 13).

15.3 Final remarks

By now, it will be obvious to the reader that expert systems research is a varied field with many facets. Different researchers have tackled different problems in rather different ways; it is the nature of pioneers to 'do it their way', particularly when faced with difficult and ill-structured problems. Nevertheless, a number of lines of development are visible at the present time and look set to continue into the future.

- Making knowledge explicit. What distinguishes knowledge-based programs from more conventional problem-solving programs is the fact that real-world knowledge is explicitly represented in modular pieces of code which can be invoked in a pattern-directed fashion. However, in addition to rendering domain or object-level knowledge in this way, there is a move towards making meta-knowledge explicit too, by encoding knowledge about problem structure and problem-solving strategy in the same kinds of module.

- Developing high-level tools. The design, construction and testing of such programs calls for a quite different conception of software engineering than that currently entertained in computer science. Just as the advent of interpreted list-processing languages for artificial intelligence applications gave rise to an entirely new range of interactive debugging tools, so the advent of knowledge-based systems is already giving rise to a new generation of sophisticated programming environments.

- A new eclecticism. The architects of knowledge-based systems have already exhibited a considerable versatility and flexibility in terms of exploiting ideas developed in the context of other disciplines. For the moment, I think it is true to say that practice still dominates theory, in that practitioners tend to go out and do things, armed with certain intuitions, and then ponder the significance of what they've done afterwards. People are more interested in whether or not ideas work in practice than whether or not they accord with conventional wisdom, or some organized body of knowledge lying on a bookshelf. This doesn't worry me nearly as much as it worries some of my contemporaries, because I feel that the instincts of people working in this area are basically correct, even if they are not always capable of formally describing what they are doing and relating it to some well-articulated theory.

This chapter hardly scratches the surface of the many and multifarious problems associated with trying to write programs which perform at an expert level. Nevertheless, it is true to say that a set of principles is emerging which ultimately will help expert system architects with some of the design difficulties that they face. The whole area of expert systems has awakened considerable commercial interest, both in the US and in Europe, and most people are coming to realize that real progress in the field is only possible if there is a concerted research effort which combines both academic and industrial expertise.

However, for a number of reasons, it would be unfortunate if expert system technology were to develop in such a way as to lose its roots in the theory and practice of artificial intelligence. Firstly, progress in core areas such as knowledge representation and control of inference is unlikely to be achieved in the absence of input from the parent discipline. Secondly, results from related areas of research, such as belief systems, man-machine dialogue and planning, will undoubtedly be decisive in shaping the expert systems of the future. Finally, there are many issues to do with the rights of people affected by such technology which need to be addressed in an arena detached from financial and political considerations. Such issues are beyond the scope of this book, but they are none the less real, and need to be subject to debate in a manner that is accessible to all. The parent discipline has an educative role to play in this respect, with regard to promoting public awareness of the issues with a view to encouraging informed debate.

Bibliography

Adams, J. B. (1976). 'A probability model of medical reasoning and the MYCIN model' *Mathematical Biosciences*, **32**, 177–186. See also Chapter 12 of Buchanan and Shortliffe; Eds. (1984)

Aikins, J. (1983). 'Prototypical knowledge for expert systems' *Artificial Intelligence*, **20**, 163–210

Alvey, P. (1983). 'Problems of designing a medical expert system' *Proceedings of Expert Systems*, **83**, 20–42

Amarel, S. (1968). 'On representations of problems of reasoning about actions' In Michie, D; Ed. *Machine Intelligence 3*. Elsevier, 131–171

Barr, A. and Feigenbaum, E. A.; Eds. (1981). *The Handbook of Artificial Intelligence*, Vol. 1. Los Altos, Calif.: Morgan Kaufmann

Barr, A. and Feigenbaum, E. A.; Eds. (1982). *The Handbook of Artificial Intelligence*, Vol. 2. Los Altos, Calif.: Morgan Kaufmann

Bobrow, D. G. (1984). 'If Prolog is the answer, what is the question?' *Proceedings of the International Conference on Fifth Generation Computer Systems*, 138–145

Bobrow, D. G. and Collins, A.; Eds. (1975). *Representation and understanding*. New York: Academic Press

Bobrow, D. G. and Stefik, M. (1983). *The LOOPS Manual*. Xerox Corporation

Bobrow, D. G. and Winograd, T. (1977). 'An overview of KRL, a knowledge representation language' *Cognitive Science*, **1**, (1)

Bobrow, D. G. and Winograd, T. (1979). 'KRL: another perspective' *Cognitive Science*, **3**, (1)

Boden, M. (1977). *Artificial intelligence and natural man*. New York: Basic Books

Boolos, G. S. and Jeffrey, R. C. (1980). *Computability and logic*. Cambridge: Cambridge University Press, 2nd edn.

Brachman, R. J. (1985). 'I lied about the trees' *AI Magazine*, **6**, (3)

Brachman, R. J. and Levesque, H. J. (1985). *Readings in knowledge representation*. Los Altos, Calif.: Morgan Kaufmann

Brachman, R. J. and Smith, B. C.; Eds. (1980). Special issue on knowledge representation. *SIGART Newsletter*, No. 70, February 1980

Bramer, M. A.; Ed. (1985). *Research and development in expert systems*. Cambridge: Cambridge University Press

Brodie, M. L., Mylopoulos, J. and Schmidt, J.W. (1984). *On conceptual modelling*. Berlin: Springer-Verlag

Bronowski, J. (1965). *The identity of man*. Harmondsworth: Penguin Books

Brownston, L., Farrell, R., Kant, E. and Martin, N. (1985). *Programming expert systems in OPS5*. Reading, Mass.: Addison-Wesley

Bruynooghe, M. (1982). *The memory management of PROLOG implementations*. (Eds. Clark and Tarnlund), 83–98.

Buchanan, B. G. (1982). *New research on expert systems.* (Eds. Hayes, Michie and Pao)

Buchanan, B. G., Barstow, D., Bechtel, R., Bennet, J., Clancey, W., Kulikowski, C., Mitchell, T. M. and Waterman, D.A. (1983). *Constructing an expert system.* (Eds. Hayes-Roth, Waterman and Lenat), Chapter 5

Buchanan, B. G. and Feigenbaum, E. A. (1978). 'DENDRAL and Meta-DENDRAL: Their applications dimension' *Artificial Intelligence,* **11,** 5–24

Buchanan, B. G. and Mitchell, T. M. (1978). *Model-directed learning of production rules.* (Eds. Waterman and Hayes-Roth), 297–312

Buchanan, B. G. and Shortliffe, E. H.; Eds. (1984). *Rule-based expert systems.* Reading, Mass.: Addison-Wesley

Buchanan, B. G., Sutherland, G. L. and Feigenbaum, E. A. (1970). *Rediscovering some problems of artificial intelligence in the context of organic chemistry.* (Eds. Meltzer and Michie) 209–254

Bundy, A. (1977). 'Exploiting the properties of functions to control search' *DAI Research Report 45,* Department of Artificial Intelligence, University of Edinburgh

Bundy, A. (1978). 'Will it reach the top? Prediction in the mechanics world.' *Artificial Intelligence,* **10,** 129–146

Bundy, A. (1983). *The computer modelling of mathematical reasoning.* London: Academic Press

Bundy, A., Byrd, L., Luger, G., Mellish, C. and Palmer, M. (1979). *Solving mechanics problems using metalevel inference.* (Ed. Michie), 50–64

Bundy, A., Silver, B. and Plummer, D. (1985). 'An analytic comparison of some rule-learning programs' *Artificial Intelligence,* **27,** 137–181

Campbell, J. A.; Ed. (1984). *Implementations of PROLOG.* Chichester: Ellis Horwood

Cannon, H. I. (1982). 'Flavors: a non-hierarchical approach to object-oriented programming' Unpublished paper

Carhart, R. E. (1979). *CONGEN: An expert system aiding the structural chemist.* (Ed. Michie), 65–82

Charniak, E. and McDermott, D. (1985). *Introduction to artificial intelligence.* Reading, Mass.: Addison-Wesley

Chomsky, N. (1965). *Aspects of the theory of syntax.* Cambridge, Mass: MIT Press

Clancey, W. J. (1982). *Tutoring rules for guiding a case method dialogue.* In Sleeman and Brown, 201–225

Clancey, W. J. (1983). 'The epistemology of a rule-based expert system: A framework for explanation' *Artificial Intelligence,* **20,** 215–251. See also Chapter 29 of Buchanan and Shortliffe, Eds. (1984)

Clancey, W. J. and Letsinger, R. (1981). 'NEOMYCIN: Reconfiguring a rule-based expert system for application to teaching' *Proceedings of the 7th International Joint Conference on Artificial Intelligence,* 829–836

Clark, K. L. and Tarnlund, S-A. (1982). *Logic Programming.* London: Academic Press

Clocksin, W. F. and Mellish, C. S. (1981). *Programming in Prolog.* Berlin: Springer-Verlag

Collins, A. M. and Quillian, M. R. (1969). 'Retrieval time from semantic memory' *Journal of Verbal Learning and Verbal Behavior,* **8,** 240–247

Coombs, M. J.; Ed. (1984). *Developments in expert systems.* London: Academic Press

Davis, R. (1976). *Applications of meta-level knowledge to the construction, maintenance and use of large knowledge bases.* In Davis and Lenat, (1980), 229–490

Davis, R. (1977). 'Interactive transfer of expertise: Acquisition of new inference rules' *Proceedings of the 5th International Joint Conference on Artificial Intelligence*, 321–328

Davis, R. (1980). 'Meta-rules: Reasoning about control' *Artificial Intelligence*, **15**, 179–222

Davis, R. (1982). 'Expert systems: Where are we? And where do we go from here?' *AI Magazine*, **3**, (2)

Davis, R. and King, J. (1977). *An overview of production systems*.(Eds. Elcock and Michie), 300–332

Davis, R. and Lenat, D. (1980). *Knowledge-based systems in artificial intelligence*. New York: McGraw-Hill

Degano, P. and Sandewall, E.; Eds. (1983). *Integrated interactive computing systems*. New York: North-Holland

De Kleer, J. (1979). *Qualitative and quantitative reasoning in classical mechanics*. (Eds. Winston and Brown), **1**, Cambridge, Mass.: MIT Press

Dreyfus, H. L. (1972). *What computers can't do*. New York: Harper and Row

Duda, R. O., Gaschnig, J. G. and Hart, P. E. (1979). *Model design in the PROSPECTOR consultant system for mineral exploration*. (Ed. Michie), 153–167

Duda, R. O., Hart, P. E., Nilsson, N. J. and Sutherland, G. (1978). *Semantic network representations in rule-based inference systems*. (Eds. Waterman and Hayes-Roth), 203–221

Erman, L. D., London, P. E. and Fickes, S. F. (1983). 'The design and an example use of Hearsay-III' *Proceedings of AAAI-83*, 409–415

Feigenbaum, E. A. (1977). 'The art of artificial intelligence: Themes and case studies of knowledge engineering' *Proceedings of the 5th International Joint Conference on Artificial Intelligence*, 1014–1029

Feigenbaum, E. A. and Feldman, J.; Eds. (1963). *Computers and thought*. New York: McGraw-Hill

Fikes, R. E. and Nilsson, N. J. (1971). 'STRIPS: a new approach to the application of theorem-proving to problem solving' *Artificial Intelligence*, **2**, 189–208

Findler, N. V.; Ed. (1979). *Associative networks*. New York: Academic Press

Forgy, C. L. (1979). *On the efficient implementation of production systems*. Department of Computer Science, Carnegie-Mellon University

Forgy, C. L. (1981). *OPS5 User's Manual. Technical Report CMU-CS-81-135*, Department of Computer Science, Carnegie-Mellon University

Forgy, C. L. (1982). 'Rete: A fast algorithm for the many pattern/many object pattern match problem' *Artificial Intelligence*, **19**, 17–37

Furukawa, K., Takeuchi, A., Kunifuji, S., Yasukawa, H., Ohki, M. and Ueda, K. (1984). 'MANDALA: A logic based knowledge programming system' *Proceedings of the International Conference on Fifth Generation Computer Systems*, 613–622

Genesereth, M. R. (1983). 'An overview of meta-level architecture' *Proceedings of AAAI-83*, 119–124

Genesereth, M. R., Greiner, R. and Smith, D. (1980). *MRS Manual. Stanford Heuristic Programming Project Memo HPP-80-24*, Stanford University

Goldberg, A. (1981). 'Introducing the Smalltalk-80 system' *BYTE*, **6**, (8)

Goldberg, A. and Robson, D. (1983). *Smalltalk-80: The language and its implementation*. Reading, Mass.: Addison-Wesley

Green, C. C. (1969). 'The application of theorem-proving to question-answering systems' *Proceedings of the 1st International Joint Conference on Artificial Intelligence*, 219–237

Haack, S. (1978). *Philosophy of Logics*. Cambridge: Cambridge University Press

Hammond, P. and Sergot, M. (1983). 'A PROLOG shell for logic based expert systems' *Proceedings of Expert Systems 83*, 95–104

Hasling, D. W., Clancey, W. J. and Rennels, G. (1984). *Strategic explanations for a diagnostic consultation system*. (Ed. Coombs, M.J.), (1984)

Haugeland, J.; Ed. (1981). *Mind design*. Cambridge, Mass.: MIT Press

Hayes, J. E., Michie, D. and Pao, Y. H. (1982). *Machine Intelligence 10*. Chichester: Wiley and Sons

Hayes-Roth, F., Waterman, D. A. and Lenat, D. (1983). *Building expert systems*. Reading, Mass.: Addison-Wesley

Hewitt, C. (1972). 'Description and theoretical analysis (using schemata) of PLANNER, a language for proving theorems and manipulating models in a robot' *Rep No. TR-258*, AI Laboratory, Massachusetts Institute of Technology

Hewitt, C. (1977). 'Viewing control structures as patterns of passing messages' *Artificial Intelligence*, **8**, 323–364

Hintikka, J. (1973). *Logic, language games and information*. Oxford: Oxford University Press

Jackson, P. (1985). *Reasoning about belief in the context of advice-giving systems*. (Ed. Bramer), 73–83

Jones, N. (1984). 'An expert system for first aid' *MSc Thesis*, Department of Artificial Intelligence, University of Edinburgh

Klahr, P., McArthur, D. and Narain, S. (1982). 'SWIRL: An object-oriented air battle simulator' *Proceedings of AAAI-82*, 331–334

Kluzniak, F. and Szpakowicz, S. (1984). *Prolog – a panacea?* (Ed. Campbell), 71–84

Kowalski, R. (1979). *Logic for Problem Solving*. Amsterdam: North Holland

Kunz, J. C., Fallat, R. J., McClung, D. H., Osborn J. J., Votteri R. A., Nii, H. P., Aikins, J. S., Fagan, L. M. and Feigenbaum, E. A. (1978). 'A physiological rule-based system for interpreting pulmonary function test results' *Report No. HPP-78-19*, Heuristic Programming Project, Computer Science Department, Stanford University

Lehnert, W. and Wilks, Y. (1979). 'A critical perspective on KRL' *Cognitive Science*, **3**, 1–28

Lenat, D. B. (1982). 'The nature of heuristics' *Artificial Intelligence*, **19**, 189–249

Lemmon, E. J. (1965). *Beginning Logic*. Walton-on-Thames: Thomas Nelson

Levesque, H. (1984). *The logic of incomplete knowledge bases*. (Eds. Brodie, Mylopoulos and Schmidt)

McCarthy, J. (1980). 'Circumspection – A form of non-monotonic reasoning, *Artificial Intelligence*, **13**, 27–39

McCarthy, J. and Hayes, P. (1969). *Some philosophical problems from the standpoint of artificial intelligence*. (Eds. Meltzer and Michie), 463–502.

McDermott, D. and Doyle, J. (1980). 'Non-monotonic logic I' *Artificial Intelligence*, **13**, 41–72

McDermott, J. (1980). 'R1: An expert in the computer system domain' *Proceedings of AAAI-80*, 269–271

McDermott, J. (1981). 'R1's formative years' *AI Magazine*, **2**, (2)

McDermott, J. (1982). 'R1: A rule-based configurer of computer systems' *Artificial Intelligence*, **19**, 39–88

McDermott, J. (1984). 'R1 revisited: Four years in the trenches' *AI Magazine*, Fall 1984, 21–32

McDermott, J. and Forgy, C. L. (1978). *Production system conflict resolution strategies*. (Eds. Waterman and Hayes-Roth), 177–199

Meltzer, B. and Michie, D.; Eds. (1969). *Machine Intelligence 4*. Edinburgh: Edinburgh University Press

Meltzer, B. and Michie, D.; Eds. (1970). *Machine Intelligence 5*. Edinburgh: Edinburgh University Press

Michalski, R. S., Carbonell, J. G. Jr. and Mitchell, T. M. (1983). *Machine learning*. Los Altos, Calif: Morgan Kaufmann

Michalski, R. S. and Chilausky, R. L. (1980). 'Learning by being told and learning from examples' *International Journal of Policy Analysis and Information Systems*, 4, 125–161

Michalski, R. S. and Larson, J. B. (1978). 'Selection of most representative training examples and incremental generation of VL1 hypotheses' *Report No. 867*, Computer Science Department, University of Illinois

Michie, D.; Ed. (1979). *Expert systems in the micro electronic age*. Edinburgh: Edinburgh University Press

Miller, G. A. and Chomsky, N. (1963). *Finitary models of language users*. In Luce, R. D., Bush, R. and Galanter, E.; Eds. *Handbook of Mathematical Psychology*, Vol. II, Ch. 13, 419–492. New York: Wiley and Sons

Minsky, M.; Ed. (1968). *Semantic information processing*. Cambridge, Mass.: MIT Press

Minsky, M. (1975). *A framework for representing knowledge*. (Ed. Winston)

Mitchell, T. M. (1978). 'Version spaces: An approach to concept learning' *Report No. STAN-CS-78-711*. Computer Science Department, Stanford University

Mitchell, T. M. (1982). 'Generalization as search' *Artificial Intelligence*, 18, 203–226

Mizoguchi, F., Ohwada, H. and Katayama, Y. (1984). 'LOOKS: Knowledge representation system for designing expert systems in a logic programming framework' *Proceedings of the International Conference on Fifth Generation Computer Systems*, 606–612

Moon, D., Stallman, R. M. and Weinreb, D. (1983). *Lisp machine manual*. Artificial Intelligence Laboratory, Massachussets Institute of Technology

Moore, R. C. (1975). 'Reasoning from incomplete knowledge in a procedural deduction system' *AI-TR-347*, Artificial Intelligence Laboratory, Massachusetts Institute of Technology

Myers, C. D., Fox, J., Pegram, S. M. and Greaves, M. F. (1983). 'Knowledge acquisition for expert systems: Experience using EMYCIN for leukaemia diagnosis' *Proceedings of Expert Systems 83*, 277–283

Neches, R., Swartout, W. R., and Moore, J. (1984). 'Enhanced maintainance and explanation of expert systems through explicit models of their development' *Proceedings of IEEE Workshop on Principles of Knowledge-Based Systems*, 173–183

Neisser, U. (1976). *Cognition and reality*. New York: Freeman

Newell, A. and Simon, H. A. (1972). *Human problem solving*. Engelwood Cliffs, N. J.: Prentice–Hall

Nilsson, N. J. (1982). *Principles of artificial intelligence*. Heidelberg: Springer-Verlag

Pople, H. E. Jr. (1973). 'On the mechanization of abductive logic' *Proceedings of the 3rd International Joint Conference on Artificial Intelligence*, 147–152

Pople, H. E. Jr. (1977). 'The formation of composite hypotheses in diagnostic problem solving: An exercise in synthetic reasoning' *Proceedings of the 5th International Joint Conference on Artificial Intelligence*, 1030–1037

Pople, H. E. Jr., Myers, J. D. and Miller, R. A. (1975). 'DIALOG: A model of diagnostic logic for internal medicine' *Proceedings of the 4th International Joint Conference on Artificial Intelligence*, 848–855

Quillian, M. R. (1968). *Semantic memory*. (Ed. Minsky), 227–270

Rawlings, C. and Fox, J. (1983). 'The UNITS package – A critical appraisal of a frame-based knowledge representation system' *Proceedings of Expert Systems 83*, 15–29

Reiter, R. (1980). 'A logic for default reasoning' *Artificial Intelligence*, **13**, 81–132

Rich, E. (1983). *Artificial Intelligence*. New York: McGraw-Hill

Robinson, J. A. (1965). 'A machine-oriented logic based on the resolution principle' *Journal of the ACM*, **12**, 23–41

Robinson, J. A. (1979). *Logic: Form and Function*. Edinburgh: Edinburgh University Press

Rosch, E. (1973). 'Natural categories' *Cognitive Psychology*, **4**, 328–350

Rosch, E. (1975). 'Cognitive representations of semantic categories' *Journal of Experimental Psychology: General*, **104**, 192–233

Searle, J. R. (1981). *Minds, brains and programs*. (Ed. Haugeland)

Sergot, M. (1983). *A query-the-user facility for logic programming*. (Eds. Degano and Sandewall), 27–41

Shafer, G. (1976). *A mathematical theory of evidence*. Princeton: Princeton University Press

Shannon, C. E. (1950). 'Automatic chess player' *Scientific American*, **182**, (48)

Shapiro, E. and Takeuchi, A. (1983). 'Object Oriented Programming in Concurrent Prolog' *New Generation Computing*, **1**, (1)

Shepherdson, J. C. (1984). 'Negation as failure' *First IKBS Workshop on Inference*, Imperial College London, 19–20 September

Shortliffe, E. H. (1976). *Computer-Based Medical Consultations: MYCIN*. New York: Elsevier

Simon, H. A. (1976). *The sciences of the artificial*. Cambridge, Mass.: MIT Press

Slagle, J. R. (1963). *A heuristic program that solves symbolic integration problems in freshman calculus*. (Eds. Feigenbaum and Feldman), 191–203

Sleeman, D. and Brown, J. S. Eds. (1982). *Intelligent tutoring systems*. New York: Academic Press

Sridharan, N. S. (1978). Guest editorial. *Artificial Intelligence*, **11**, 1–4

Stefik, M. (1979). 'An examination of a frame-structured representation system' *Proceedings of the 6th International Joint Conference on Artificial Intelligence*, 845–852

Stefik, M., Aikins, J., Balzer, R., Benoit, J., Birnbaum, L., Hayes-Roth, F. and Sacerdoti, E. (1982). *Basic concepts for building expert systems*. (Eds. Hayes-Roth, Waterman and Lenat) Chapter 3

Stefik, M., Bobrow, D. G., Mittal, S. and Conway, L. (1983). 'Knowledge programming in LOOPS: Report on an experimental course' *AI Magazine*, Fall 1983, 3–13

Swartout, W. R. (1983). 'XPLAIN: a system for creating and explaining expert consulting programs' *Artificial Intelligence*, **21**, 285–325

Van Melle, W., Scott, A. C., Bennett, J. S. and Pears, M. A. S. (1981). 'The EMYCIN manual' *Report No. HPP-81-16*, Heuristic Programming Project, Computer Science Department, Stanford University

Warren, D. H. D. and Pereira, F. C. N. (1981). 'An efficient easy adaptable system for interpreting natural language queries' *DAI Research Report 155*. Department of Artificial Intelligence, University of Edinburgh

Waterman, D. A. (1985). *A guide to expert systems*. Reading, Mass.: Addison-Wesley

Waterman, D. A. and Hayes-Roth, F. (1978). *Pattern directed inference systems*. New York: Academic Press

Wielinga, B. J. and Breuker, J. A. (1984). 'Interpretation of verbal data for knowledge acquisition' *ECAI '84: Advances in Artificial Intelligence*. (Ed. O'Shea). Amsterdam: Elsevier Science Publishers

Winograd, T. (1972). 'Understanding natural language' *Cognitive Psychology*, **1**, 1–191

Winston, P. H. (1984). *Artificial Intelligence*. 2nd edn. Reading, Mass.: Addison-Wesley

Winston, P. H.; Ed. (1975). *The psychology of computer vision*. New York: McGraw-Hill

Winston, P. H. and Brown, R. H. (1979). *Artificial intelligence: an MIT perspective*. Vols 1 and 2. Cambridge, Mass.: MIT Press

Winston, P. H. and Horn, K. P. (1981). *Lisp*. Reading, Mass.: Addison-Wesley

Winston, P. H. & Horn, K. P. (1984). *Lisp*. 2nd edn. Reading, Mass.: Addison–Wesley.

Woods, W. (1975). *What's in a link: foundations for semantic networks*. (Eds. Bobrow and Collins)

Young, R. M. and O'Shea, T. (1981). 'Errors in children's subtraction' *Cognitive Science*, **5**, 153–177.

Zadeh, L. A. (1965). 'Fuzzy sets' *Information and Control*, **8**, 338–353.

Zadeh, L. A. (1975). 'Fuzzy logic and approximate reasoning' *Synthese*, **30**, 407–428.

Index